National Health Insurance and Income Distribution

National Health Insurance and Income Distribution

Rita M. Keintz

Lexington Books
D.C. Heath and Company
Lexington, Massachusetts
Toronto

Grateful acknowledgement is made for use of material reprinted herein: three tables and quoted material from *Setting National Priorities: The 1974 Budget,* by Edward R. Fried, Alice M. Rivlin, Charles L. Schultze, and Nancy H. Teeters, © 1974 by The Brookings Institution, Washington, D.C.; five figures and two tables from *The Payroll Tax for Social Security,* by John A. Brittain, © 1972 by The Brookings Institution, Washington, D.C.; quoted material from "Effect of Public Expenditures on the Distribution of Income," by W. Irwin Gillespie, from *Essays on Fiscal Federalism,* edited by Richard A. Musgrave, © 1965 by The Brookings Institution, Washington, D.C.; Mark Pauly, *Medical Care at Public Expense: A Study of Applied Welfare Economics,* © 1971 by Praeger Publishers, Inc.; and Gabriel Kolko, *Wealth and Power in America,* © 1962 by Frederick A. Praeger, Inc.

Library of Congress Cataloging in Publication Data

Keintz, Rita M.
National health insurance and income distribution.

Bibliography: p.
1. Insurance, Health–United States. 2. Income distribution–United States. I. Title.
HD7102.U4K43 368.4'2'00973 73-21111
ISBN 0-669-92916-6

Published simultaneously in Canada

Printed in the United States of America

International Standard Book Number: 0-669-92916-6

Library of Congress Catalog Card Number: 73-21111

Table of Contents

List of Figures

List of Tables

Preface

This study originated several years ago during my postdoctoral work at Johns Hopkins School of Hygiene and Public Health at the suggestion of Dr. Vicente Navarro. In the interim period, the topic of national health insurance has been addressed from a range of perspectives—discussion of proposed legislation, research of certain technical aspects, and plotting of political strategies. The intention here is to present one major focus on the issue of national health insurance, i.e., the possible effects of national health insurance for people at the various income levels. The approach of the book is meant to provide an understanding of the details of the relevant technical literature. The findings presented are important to political decisions regarding the distribution of the costs and benefits of a national health insurance plan.

Because this study was undertaken without the support of public or private funding, perhaps a larger than usual number of people made contributions of their time, effort, and commitment to its completion. Some merit particular mention—Carol Van Why, in Minneapolis, whose skills as a librarian produced most of the research and reference materials in the fastest possible time, Sandra Sheldon, who typed much of the manuscript at that horrible draft stage, and Gordon Snyder and Jane Wentzell, who did the art work.

Louis Esposito and Bruce Stuart read the complete manuscript and gave helpful comments. Martin Roysher read parts of the manuscript and was particularly helpful with the rewriting of Chapters 6 and 7. I sincerely appreciate their assistance and I alone remain responsible for any errors in fact or judgment. A special thanks to the many friends who gave their support in a hundred different ways and to my parents who have done the same for as long as I can remember.

1 Introduction

Our nation has rarely experienced the kind of public debate that is currently directed at all aspects of the issue of health care in the United States. Much of this debate, in fact, has occurred over a long period of time, and—while the nature of the forum and the content has altered—the culmination to its present status merely reflects the critical concerns in terms of political and economic goals and consequences.[1] Among the major unresolved issues that confront us is national health insurance. The passing of a national health insurance bill by the Congress of the United States will have significant impact on the lives of all members of our society. The number of interest groups—including labor, health care providers, and the private health insurance industry—and the diversity of interests and backgrounds of the legislative sponsors of the various proposed bills suggest the complexity of the national health insurance debate.

Recent reports on national health insurance proposals have attempted primarily to highlight the particular provisions of the proposals, e.g., benefit packages, population covered, the role of Medicare, etc. At times, reports will also set forth the estimated costs of the initial implementation stage of specific plans and the proportion of these costs to be assumed by the public and private sectors. The citizen or even a public representative is infrequently, if ever, presented with an analysis of what the "benefits" and the "costs" of a national health insurance plan will be for individuals and families in particular income groups.

The importance of the distributional effects of a national health insurance program is perhaps initially best set forth in the context of the federal budget process and the policy choices involved in such a process. In Figure 1-1, the federal budget dollar is presented in terms of "where it comes from" and "where it goes." This basic approach to distinguishing the various sources of budget funds and the allocation of budget expeditures is commonly employed for other sectors of the economy also, e.g., education, transportation, etc.

For fiscal year 1975, taxes from various sources almost completely account for the estimated funding of the federal budget, with borrowing and all other sources estimated at only 8 percent. Personal income taxes are the largest source, followed by payroll taxes, with corporate income taxes being the third largest source and excise taxes contributing only 6 percent. The largest use of the federal revenues is benefit payments to individuals, followed closely by national defense expenditures. Grants to state and local governments, other federal operations (largely administrative costs), and net interest (payments on the accumulated

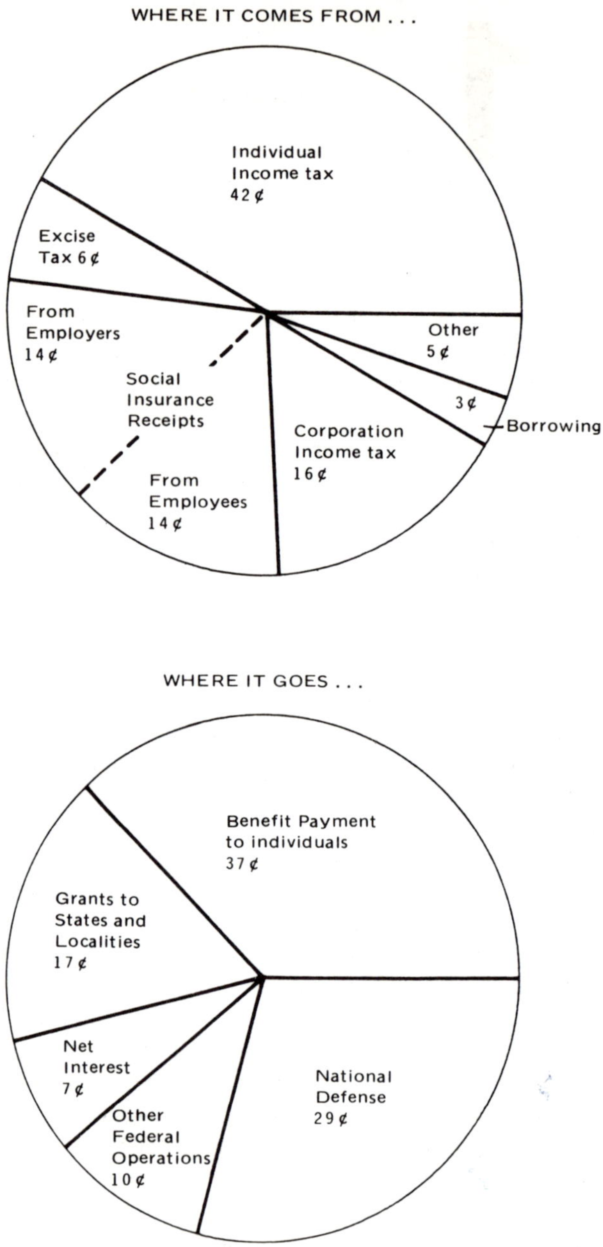

Source: *The Nation's Health,* American Public Health Association, Vol. 4, No. 3 (March, 1974), p. 1.

Figure 1-1. The Federal Budget Dollar—Fiscal Year 1975 Estimates

federal debt) are the remaining categories of expenditures by the federal government.

The federal budget reflects at least four kinds of policy choices:

1. Choices among *objectives*—what are the priorities among the various goals which the federal government is attempting to achieve?
2. Choices concerning the major *roles* or *strategies*—how should the federal government pursue its objectives?
3. Choices regarding *distribution*—who should benefit from federal programs and who should pay for these benefits?
4. Choices about the overall *size* of the budget—how large a share of national output should be devoted to the activities of the federal government?[2]

These choices interact with each other in the determination of alternative policy decisions with respect to the final budget allocation. In the case of national health insurance, debate has centered on (1) its relative priority, (2) the best strategy in terms of federal financing and administration of any national health insurance plan, and (3) the potential impact of the plan on the size of the federal budget. The distribution of benefits and costs for individuals and groups appears to be of little or no importance. In fact, one might argue that the income distribution effects inherent in the present national health insurance proposals are outcomes specified by the other policy choices.[3]

Given the federal government has set national health insurance as one of its policy goals or objectives, the choice of role or strategy largely involves whether national health insurance should be financed solely by public or private sources or some combination of public and private sources, and who should administer the plan. The choice of the dollar amount of the federal budget that might be committed to financing national health insurance is, therefore, by necessity integrated with the decisionmaking process regarding the choice of role or strategy. Estimates of the total costs of alternative national health insurance plans show only marginal differences and thus the overall cost of national health insurance allows for very little argument about the alternative choices. Discussions concerned with these particular aspects of national health insurance policy are adequately presented elsewhere—the perspective of this book is consistently on choices regarding the distribution of income.[4]

The primary purpose of this book is to refine the definition and understanding of the alternative choices regarding the financing of health care and the "tradeoffs" in terms of the costs and benefits that are inherent in the choice of any one national health insurance plan. A secondary concern is the analysis of various national health insurance proposals presently before the Congress in terms of the redistributive effects across income groups. This type of discussion is necessary in order to prevent having distributional effects determined incidentally or accidentally external to the decisionmaking process and to bring focus directly on alternative policy choices regarding the structure of benefits and costs under national health insurance. Further information regarding the incidence and the magnitude of these distributional effects is essential to the decisionmaking process, whereby federal policymakers and their constituencies select a national health insurance plan.

National health insurance plans are primarily programs directed at the removal of the financial barriers to health care that currently exist and are reflected in the patterns of utilization of and expenditures for health care services across income groups. Although several components of the various proposals for national health insurance also address current problems in the health care delivery system, in the planning and organization of health resources, and in the costs and quality of health care services, additional programs for resolving these health care problems are necessary in order to provide for a complete complement of national actions. The sponsorship of these further changes in the system, therefore, must be given strong and simultaneous consideration in building an overall effective national program for health care. Those provisions in national health insurance proposals that specifically attempt to address these health care problems are not discussed in the book, except in those few instances when more general descriptive information about proposals is given.

The study focuses on an objective analysis of the provisions set forth by national health insurance proposals with respect to the distribution of cost burdens and expenditure benefits across the different income groups. A conceptual framework of this kind of study is presented in Figure 1-2. The diagram illustrates the role of the two sources of distributional effects. Income can be redistributed by a national health insurance plan through its "inputs" or the cost structure plan *and* through its "outputs" or the benefit structure plan. By this process, national health insurance plans can be classified according to the regressive or progressive nature of their cost and benefit structures; that is, does the proportion of the total costs incurred decline or increase as income rises, and does the proportion of total benefits received decline or increase as income rises. The analysis relies on: (1) our knowledge regarding the current patterns of utilization of and expenditures for personal health services by family income groups (given the costs of these services), and (2) the evidence regarding the distribution of the burdens of program costs in the form of premiums, coinsurance and deductibles, and the incidence of certain types of taxes, and federal subsidies for these same income groups.

Gillespie in arguing for this need to analyze the distributional impact of various public expenditure policies writes:

> It may well be argued that it is this redistributional result which matters in the end, and which must be considered in appraising the "progressive" or "regressive" value of fiscal operations at various levels of government . . . when a public sector is introduced into a private economy, each family finds that its income

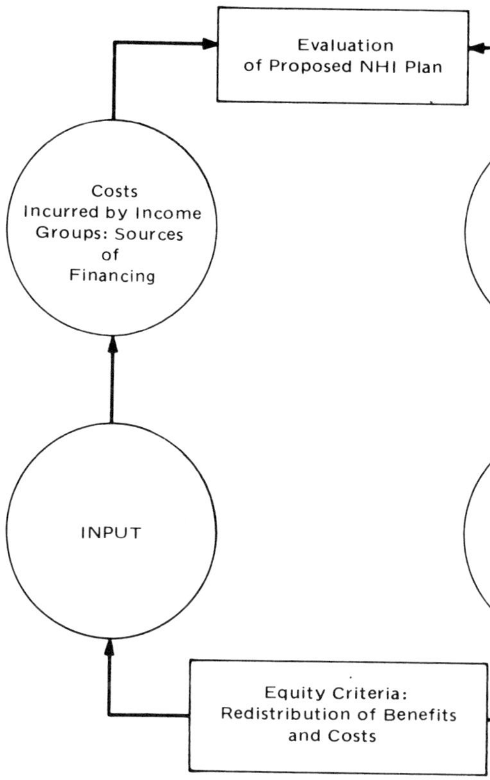

Figure 1-2. Conceptual Framework of Analysis

position relative to others is altered both by the tax payments it makes and by the value of the benefits that it receives from government expenditures. It is in this sense that fiscal incidence can be defined as the changes in the relative income positions of families due to the tax and expenditure policies of the public sector.[5]

The evidence available for analyzing the incidence of the various sources of financing national health insurance offers considerable depth and breadth. However, studies of the actual incidence of benefits under national health insurance require estimates of the demand for health services (covered *and* uncovered), price elasticities and income elasticities, and also analysis that considers the indirect impact on the demand for health services of the various cost burdens incurred by consumers. This latter type of research and evidence is not available and thus the analysis of the distributional effects associated with benefit structures actually deals with the relative increases or declines in benefit availability and not benefit incidence.

In Figure 1-3, a simple diagram is given to indicate the kinds of interrelationships among the factors that affect health insurance coverage. As is shown by the directional arrows, the extent of health insurance coverage is affected by health services utilization and expenditures, sociodemographic characteristics of the population, and illness patterns. Health services utilization and expenditures, in turn, are affected by each of the other three factors, i.e.. health insurance coverage, sociodemographic characteristics, and illness patterns. In addition, illness patterns or health status is interrelated with a number of sociodemographic characteristics (including income) in a two-way relationship.

The analysis of the benefits of national health insurance places particular importance on family income and its multiple impacts on health insurance coverage and health services utilization and expenditures. This analysis places relatively little emphasis on the effects that specific illness patterns might have on the other three factors because of the many direct influences on health status, which merit consideration also. In addition to income, these influences include: age, occupation, race, environment, and social behavior.

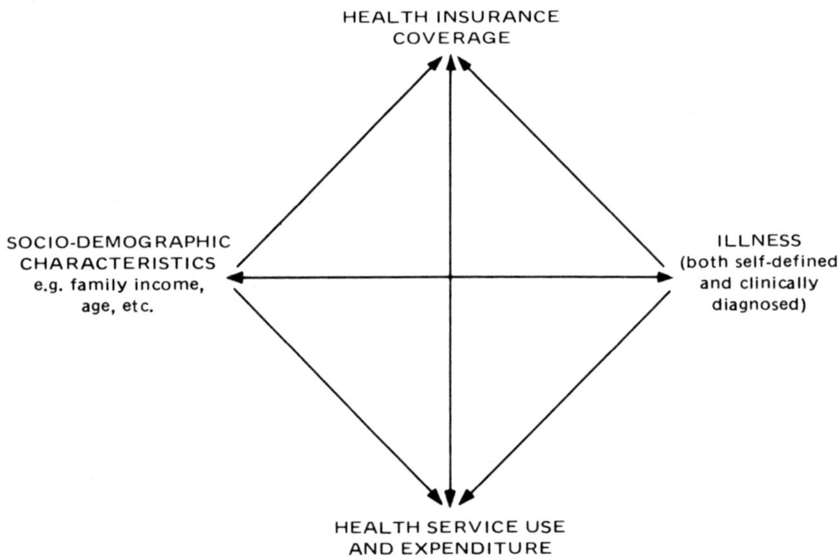

Source: Ronald Anderson and Donald C. Riedel, *People and Their Hospital Insurance,* Center for Health Administration Studies, University of Chicago (1967), Research Series 23, p. 29.

Figure 1-3. Interrelationship of Factors Affecting Health Insurance Coverage

The evaluation of national health insurance proposals employs an equity criterion to judge whether a particular proposal would result in a more equitable distribution of income, i.e., a redistribution of income that permits relative gains for the lower income groups, given the inequalities that currently exist in the distribution of health care.[a] Using this approach to evaluating the various provisions of proposed legislation, a ranking of the national health insurance proposals can also be formulated, whereby the plan that would perform better than another in meeting the criterion of equity is given a higher ranking.

Pauly discusses the "appropriateness of the distribution of income" in his normative analysis of the overall economic efficiency of public medical expenditures.

> The argument properly based on income distribution must be that even if the individual bought or were compelled to buy "enough" medical care, the observer would feel that the individual could not "afford" it if the individual's income remained the same. To provide him with free or subsidized care would improve matters, one would say, because it would allow him to have more medical care and more of everything else.
>
> The standard reply to this line of reasoning is that if indeed the distribution of income is at fault, the proper procedure would be for that distribution to be corrected through appropriate taxes and transfers of money, not through redistribution of particular goods or services. If this redistribution were effected through a subsidy for medical care only, an efficiency loss might be imposed if the amount of care transferred is worth less than its cost to donor taxpayers. This orthodox solution calling for lump-sum subsidies has been rejected on the grounds that, in fact, voters in the political process *choose* to redistribute income through differential provision of medical services, or other goods or services, rather than through direct redistribution of money income.[6]

The criterion of equity is more generally employed in the process of formulating a judgment as to whether a tax system is "fair" or "unfair".[b] The fairness of a tax structure, however, is totally dependent on the principle or philosophy (usually chosen within the political process) of which income groups or other defined groups should bear the ultimate burden of the tax. One such philosophy is the benefit principle, i.e.. the distribution of the ultimate bearers of the tax burdens is in accordance with the distribution of the recipients of the benefits from the spending of the tax. An alternative criterion of equity or fairness is the ability-to-pay principle, which provides for the concepts of

[a]The size of the relative gains depends on the extent to which higher-income groups incur larger program costs than the lower-income groups and/or receive relatively smaller program benefits.

[b]The criterion of equity requires a value judgment of some degree, since there is always the possibility that what is "equitable" for one person need not be so in the opinion of another person.

horizontal equity or "equal treatment of equals" and *vertical equity* or "unequal treatment of unequals." This latter principle of vertical equity which asks for some "proper" distribution of tax burdens among the members of the different income groups is employed in the evaluation of national health insurance proposals in this book. Thus, the proper distribution of the costs and benefits of national health insurance is one which eliminates the inequalities in the current distribution of income as a result of the gross redistributional effects of the specified cost and benefit structures.[c]

The approach of the analysis is a partial and limited one. For example, the analysis assumes that the income distribution does not alter substantially due to certain exogenous factors; that is, the present distribution of income will remain generally at current levels when a national health insurance plan is implemented. Also, no direct measures of the impact of the plans on the supply of health services is incorporated into the analysis. The number and kinds of *induced* program costs and benefits that might occur in both the public and private sectors as adjustments to the implementation of a plan need also to be identified and measured. However, as an initial effort, this study attempts only to assess the direct impacts of the different national health insurance plans on the distribution of income. In this regard, the method of analysis employs a "gross" incidence approach, rather than a "marginal" approach.

With this chapter as an introduction to the analysis which follows, Chapters 2 to 5 present further background information on national health insurance and income distribution. Chapter 2 outlines briefly the various approaches to national heath insurance and summarizes selected bills presently under consideration. These are reviewed in detail in the later analysis of the impact of cost and benefit structures on the distribution of income. Chapter 3 discusses the distribution of personal income in the United States for families and unrelated individuals and various measures of inequality in the distribution of income. Chapter 4 offers a summary of the current levels and trends in both national and personal health care expenditures by source of funds and by type of service. Chapter 5 presents a discussion of enrollment in private health insurance plans, benefits received, and costs incurred.

In Chapter 6, recent data on the utilization of health services by persons in different income groups are analyzed in order to define the current inequalities in the distribution of health care services. Chapter 7 follows with an investigation of the distribution of personal health care expenditures across income groups within the present patterns of financing health care. Chapter 8 analyzes the particular benefit structures of the selected national health insurance proposals in terms of eligibility criteria, covered services, consumer cost sharing,

[c]This evaluation, of course, is based on only one criterion; other criteria may also be considered important in evaluating the national health insurance proposals, but they are beyond the scope of this study.

and coverage for catastrophic expenses. Cost sharing provisions are usually analyzed in terms of the cost structures. However, the review of the role of cost sharing is included in Chapter 8 in order to emphasis its direct link to covered services and benefit availability, as opposed to cost incidence. Chapter 9 initially offers a detailed discussion of the available evidence regarding the burdens of the alternative sources of financing for different income groups. The cost structures of the various national health insurance plans are then analyzed in terms of this evidence on cost incidence.

Chapter 10 discusses the distribution of the benefits and costs under the Medicare and Medicaid programs and the lessons for national health insurance based on the experience of Medicare and Medicaid. Chapter 11 presents the overall findings and conclusions regarding the benefit and cost structures of national health insurance. Evaluations of the selected national health insurance proposals based on the criterion of provision of a more equitable distribution of the health care services and their costs, are made by establishing rankings of the proposals according to their distributional effects. Recommendations concerning the alternative choices among the various approaches to national health insurance proposals are also given in Chapter 11.

Notes

1. For a brief history of the issues regarding national health insurance, see Theodore R. Marmor, *The Politics of Medicare* (Chicago: Aldine Publishing Company, 1964), especially Chapter 1. For a general history of the health care sector, see Herman Somers and Anne Somers, *Doctors, Patients, and Health Insurance* (Washington, D.C.: The Brookings Institution, 1961) and Barbara Ehrenreich and John Ehrenreich, *The American Health Empire: Power, Profits, and Politics* (New York: Random House, Inc. 1970). Detailed information on the Medicare program is given in H.M. Somers and A.R. Somers, *Medicare and the Hospitals: Issues and Prospects* (Washington, D.C.: The Brookings Institution, 1967). For a complete discussion of the private health insurance industry, see John Krizay and Andrew Wilson, *The Patient as Consumer: Health Care Financing in the United States* (Lexington, Mass.: Lexington Books, 1974). A comparison of health financing in selected foreign countries is given in *National Health Insurance Resource Book*, prepared by the Staff of the Committee on Ways and Means for the Use of the Committee (Washington, D.C.: U.S. Government Printing Office, 1974).

2. Edward R. Fried et al., *Setting National Priorities: The 1974 Budget* (Washington, D.C.: The Brookings Institution, 1973), pp. 3-4.

3. In discussion of the federal budget and the interactions among these choices, see ibid., p. 4:

These choices interact and influence each other. How much is devoted to any governmental program is influenced by judgments about how large total government expenditures should be, which in turn are influenced by the urgency of the problems with which governmental programs deal. Questions of distribution affect the allocation of budget resources among roles or strategies, and vice versa. And none of these four kinds of choices is debated or made in the abstract. No one explicitly decides on the relative weights to be given to health and pollution control or on the proportion of the budget to be devoted to old people and children. Nevertheless, decisions do get made and they often involve choices in several dimensions at once.

4. See Karen Davis, *National Health Insurance–Benefits, Costs, and Consequences* (Washington, D.C.: The Brookings Institution, 1975), Chapter 6 and Committee on Ways and Means, *National Health Insurance Hearings,* Vol. 2, 93rd Congress, "Estimated Health Expenditures under Selected National Health Insurance Proposals, A Report to the Congress".

5. W. Irwin Gillespie, "Effect of Public Expenditures on the Distribution of Income," in *Essays on Fiscal Federalism,* Richard A. Musgrave, ed. (Washington, D.C.: The Brookings Institution, 1965), pp. 122-123.

6. See Mark V. Pauly, *Medical Care at Public Expense: A Study of Applied Welfare Economics* (New York: Praeger Publishers, 1972), p. 13.

2 National Health Insurance Proposals

Any discussion of the issues involved in national health insurance is complex even at the initial stages. As many as nineteen national health insurance bills were introduced into the 93rd Congress, with the prominent addition of the Administration's bill and the Kennedy-Mills compromise bill in April, 1974. While many of these bills were not given very strong consideration, a broad overview of their alternative approaches assists in highlighting the basic similarities and differences that surround several of the more specific issues within the national health insurance debate, which admittedly represent a variety of constituencies, priorities, and political biases. The following discussion briefly outlines the provisions related to the structure of costs and of benefits for fifteen of these bills.[a]

Several changes have occurred in the mix of bills before the 94th Congress. Notably, the Administration's bill and the Kennedy-Mills bill have not been reintroduced. Instead, the revised Fulton bill, supported by the American Medical Association (AMA), has adopted a number of the provisions found in the earlier Administration's bill in conjunction with the general approach of tax credits in the previous version of the AMA bill. And, the new Young bill, endorsed by the Friends Committee on National Legislation, has been introduced that provides for a benefit structure similar to the Corman-Kennedy bill (Health Security Act).

Six major bills, as introduced into the 94th Congress, have been selected for a more complete analysis in the later chapters. These six bills, identified by their respective sponsors are: Burleson-McIntyre, Corman-Kennedy, Fulton-Duncan, Long-Ribicoff, Ullman, and Young. This selection is based primarily on the fact that these bills have strong public and private support and will most probably be given further consideration by Congress, either because of the individual merits of their presently proposed plans or by virtue of having a role in any movement for a compromise bill. Brief summaries of the overall approach of these bills and the cost and benefit structures in their proposed national health insurance plans are included in this chapter.

---

[a]Of the 19 bills introduced in the 93rd Congress as of May, 1974, four national health insurance proposals are omitted from the general discussion here. Each of these bills was first introduced in the 92nd Congress and in all but one case a modified version of the proposal was introduced in the later congress by its original sponsor or sponsors, although the same or similar bills were also introduced by other sponsors.

Overall Comparison of Particular Provisions

A common method of narrowing the scope of discussion of the many different proposals is to categorize the various kinds of plans according to the specific principles and provisions set forth by the national health insurance bills. For example, the plans are frequently grouped according to their primary approach to the financing of health care—mainly public plans, mixed public and private plans, tax credit plans, and catastrophic protection plans. This kind of classification is of some value, since it permits comparisons within each of these groups, although there is an abitrariness in classifying public versus private plans. More importantly, discussion of the alternative choices regarding the cost and benefit structures of the plans appear also then to be limited to *within* each group or class and based only on the primary approach to financing indicative of any one group of proposals. There is also merit in the many summary discussions that present the specific provisions of the various bills by listing annotative information on such classifications as: coverage of the population, benefit structure, administration, financing mechanisms, etc.[1] However, this kind of information aids little in directly assessing the potential impacts of certain program characteristics, such as income distribution, and, therefore, is little help in formulating policy alternatives prior to an enactment of national health insurance legislation. The main purpose of this chapter is to briefly outline national health insurance proposals in terms of the factors or characteristics of the cost and benefit structures of the various programs that they would establish.

Of initial importance are the differences in the general approach of the proposals as reflected in the need to treat subgroups of the population under separate programs or components within national health insurance plans. Often these broad distinctions are quickly forgotten in the details and specific provisions of the programs. In this regard, the initial questions are:

1. Does the plan provide for universal coverage?
2. Does the plan identify subgroups of the population, i.e., employee-employer and "low-income" groups?
3. Does the plan modify or eliminate the Medicare and Medicaid programs?

A summary comparison of these characteristics for the national health insurance bills introduced into the 93rd Congress is given in Table 2–1.

The complexity of analyzing the differences in cost and benefit structures for all programs established by such a large number of proposals necessitates further classification, particularly for those factors or characteristics of the plans that might directly affect the distribution of income.[2] Further questions regarding these characteristics of the proposals are:

1. What are the primary sources of financing for the plan?
2. Is some form of consumer cost sharing present in the structure of costs and benefits?

Table 2-1
Comparison of National Health Insurance Bills in the 93rd Congress by General Approach to Selected Subgroups of the Population

Proposal	*Universal Coverage*	*Employee/ Employer*	*Low-income Groups*	*Medicare Program*	*Medicaid Program*
Administration		X	X	Expanded	Replaced
Burleson-McIntyre		X	X	Remains	Phased out and replaced
Dingell	X	X		Remains	Remains[a]
Fannin		X	X	Remains	Replaced
Fulton-Broyhill-Hartke	X[b]			Remains	Remains[a]
Griffiths-Kennedy	X			Abolished	Remains[a]
Javits	X			Expanded	Remains[a]
Kennedy-Mills	X[b]			Remains	Replaced
Long-Ribicoff			X	Remains	Abolished
Pell-Mondale		X		Remains	Remains
Railsback		X	X	Remains	Altered
Saylor			X	Remains[a]	Replaced
Scott-Percy	X[c]	X		Abolished	Remains[a]
Staggers		X	X	Remains[a]	Remains[a]
Ullman		X	X	Abolished	Remains[a]

[a]The program continues, but would not pay for services covered by other provisions and programs established by the proposal.
[b]Universal coverage, but on a voluntary basis.
[c]Universal coverage for supplementary medical care insurance, but on a voluntary basis.

3. Does the plan provide for benefits under a catastrophic coverage program?

The summary findings of this second type of comparison of these proposals is given in Table 2–2.

Summary of Selected Bills

Burleson-McIntyre Bill

The National Health Care Act of 1975 (H.R. 5990/S. 1438) is supported by the Health Insurance Association of America (HIAA). This proposal includes three different voluntary private health insurance programs: (1) an employee-employer plan; (2) a plan for individuals; and (3) a State plan for the poor and medically indigent. The proposal sets the same minimum standards for the type of benefits and coverage under all three programs and provides incentives for compliance with these standards. In addition, the Medicare program would remain unchanged, while the Medicaid program would be "phased out" by July 1977. All public assistance recipients would be covered under the State plan.

The employee-employer plan includes all employees and their families who voluntarily elect coverage under a qualified plan, with the premium cost shared by both the employee and the employer according to the arrangements which they negotiate. While the proposal does not stipulate a given percentage of the premium to be paid by the employer, the premium contribution of all workers would vary according to their wage level up to a limit of 10 percent of monthly wages after certain minimal wage levels, with the employer paying the remainder of the premium cost. Persons who do not qualify for the employee plan or the State plan, largely the self-employed, must pay the entire premium under the proposed voluntary program for qualified private health insurance coverage for individuals.

The State plan would cover those persons who are the recipients of public assistance, the medically indigent, and the uninsurables. No premium is required of the lowest-income group; for other enrollees in the State plan, the amount of the premium they would pay varies according to their income. Any costs of the State plan not covered by premium revenues would be financed by federal and state general revenues, with the federal government reimbursing states with qualified plans for 70 to 90 percent of its costs according to the per capita income level in the state.

The benefits provided by this proposal would be phased in over an eight-year period in two stages with the same benefits offered through all three types

Table 2-2
Comparison of National Health Insurance Bills in the 93rd Congress by Selected Characteristics of Their Cost and Benefit Structures

Proposal	*Premiums*	*Federal General Revenues (Personal Income Tax)*	*Payroll Tax*	*Cost Sharing*	*Catastrophic Coverage*
Administration	X	X	X	X	X
Burleson-McIntyre	X	X	a	X	X
Dingell		X	X		
Fannin	X	X	a	X	
Fulton-Broyhill-Hartke	X[b]	X	a	X	X
Griffiths-Kennedy		X	X		X
Javits		X	X	X	
Kennedy-Mills		X	X	X	X
Long-Ribicoff		X	X	X	X
Pell-Mondale	c	d	a		X
Railsback	X	X	a	X	
Saylor	X	X	X	X	X
Scott-Percy	X	X	X[a]	X	X
Staggers	X	X	a	X	X
Ullman	X	X	X	X	X

[a]The financing of these plans will *not* increase the rate of the payroll tax, but since the Medicare program is retained within the overall plans for financing health care, the effects of the present payroll tax on the cost structure must be considered. The Scott-Percy bill would abolish the Medicare program but would divert the present Medicare payroll taxes to assist in financing its catastrophic inpatient care plan.

[b]The Medicredit bill, of course, employs the tax credit on the personal income tax return to "offset" the premium payment.

[c]The employee-employer plan in the Pell-Mondale bill would be financed by premiums, but the requirement is made that the employer pay the total cost of the premiums.

[d]The Pell-Mondale proposal would not employ general revenues to finance new programs, but the Medicaid program continues and thus general revenues must be considered a part of the overall cost structure.

of plans. Most of the covered services have a 20 percent coinsurance factor attached to them; some services have coinsurance rates at the 50 percent level. The maximum deductible allowed in a qualified policy is $100. Families and individuals in the lowest-income groups enrolled in the State plan would not pay any deductible or coinsurance, but other enrollees in the State plan would face cost sharing amounts according to their income level. There would be an annual limit on cost sharing of $1,000 per family under all plans after which catastrophic benefits would become effective with no additional out-of-pocket expenses necessary for the consumer.

The proposal has further provisions for (1) the training of personnel needed in comprehensive ambulatory care centers, (2) the encouragement of the development of comprehensive ambulatory care centers through grants for construction and modernization, and (3) health planning.

Corman-Kennedy Bill

The Health Security Act of 1975 (H.R. 21/S. 3) would establish a national health insurance program to cover the entire population for a broad range of health services. This proposal is supported by the Committee for National Health Insurance (CNHI) and the AFL-CIO.

This plan would be financed by a payroll tax, a tax on self-employment income and unearned income, and also federal general revenues. All workers under the social security program are subject to the payroll tax, as are government employees at all levels. State and local governments, however, do not pay the employer's portion of this tax. The specified tax rates are: (1) 1.0 percent on employee wages; (2) 3.5 percent for employers on total payroll; and (3) 2.5 percent on earnings from self-employment and unearned income. For families and individuals, only the first $21,150 of annual income (whether from wages or from other sources) is subject to the taxes. Employers are taxed on their total payroll. Financing from federal general revenues would be equal to the same amount as the total receipts from the payroll tax revenues.

The benfits of this plan are comprehensive and almost completely free of any limitations—the major exceptions are placed on the benefits for adult dental care, psychiatric care, long-term nursing-home care, and drugs. The plan does not require consumer cost sharing of any form. The covered benefits include regular physical checkups and a number of health-related social services, if provided by an institution or agency contracting with the federalized system. The Medicare program would be abolished by the provisions of this proposal, and the federal government would no longer participate financially in the cost of the Medicaid program, except where certain services are not covered by the universal plan.

The plan would be administered by the Department of Health, Education and Welfare and a five-member appointed full-time board with advisory councils at the regional and subregional levels. Further provisions provide for cost and quality control and to some extent the reorganization of the health care system and the development of health resources.

Fulton-Duncan Bill

The Comprehensive Health Care Insurance Act of 1975 (H.R. 6222), supported by the AMA, is a revised version of earlier proposed legislation which incorporates many of the provisions found in the Administration's bill introduced into the 93rd Congress.

This proposal requires all employers to offer qualified private health insurance coverage to employees and their families. At least 65 percent of the premium cost must be paid by the employer, with the employee paying the remaining cost. Small employers would receive cash subsidies from the federal government—or apply for tax credits—if the insurance program would increase their total payroll by 3 percent or more. This program does not include unemployed and self-employed persons, who instead would also apply for federal tax credits against income tax, as proposed in the earlier AMA Medicredit bill. These tax credits or "certificates of enrollment" (acceptable to third party insurers toward the payment of premiums) are based on income tax liability, and in this way the Federal government assists by incurring some of or all the premium cost. Employed persons are *not* eligible for participation in this latter program, but the proposal assumes that the needs of the poor, the medically indigent, and the aged will be met by this tax credit plan.

The range of covered benefits are broad and relatively comprehensive, but some limitations are placed on certain types of services. The benefits would be subject to consumer cost sharing with a coinsurance rate of 20 percent. Limits are fixed for the total amount of coinsurance each family or individual would pay according to income levels; certain low-income groups would not pay coinsurance. This proposal provides for catastrophic coverage by removing the annual coinsurance payments beyond $1,500 for an individual and $2,000 for a family.

The Medicare program would be expanded so that the benefits are the same as offered to the general population; the Medicaid program would be abolished. This proposal offers no major changes to the present mechanisms for cost and quality control of services. A Health Insurance Advisory Board at the national level would set standards and regulations for state insurance departments to employ in their review of the various insurance policies and programs.

Long-Ribicoff Bill

The Catastrophic Health Insurance and Medical Assistance Reform Act (S. 2513) would provide: (1) benefits for all persons who have incurred extraordinary health care expenditures by establishing a catastrophic illness insurance program; (2) basic and catastrophic benefits for poor and medically indigent persons; and (3) certification of private insurance policies that cover basic benefits through a voluntary program.

All persons of all ages who are insured or receiving benefits under Social Security would be eligible for the catastrophic plan. This plan would be financed by a special payroll tax on selfemployment income and on employers' payrolls, which are currently also subject to the social security tax. There would be no additional payroll tax on employees' earnings or contributions from federal or state general revenues to finance this catastrophic coverage. The benefits under the catastrophic plan would be payable after \$2,000 of out-of-pocket expenses have been incurred by a family or individual for medical services *or* after sixty days in the hospital for hospital expenses. There are certain provisions regarding how much of a family member's expenses can be included in determining the catastrophic limit for expenses and similarly for expenses incurred for mental health services.

The Long-Ribicoff proposal would replace the present Medicaid program with its medical assistance plan. Uniform national benefits—somewhat broader than those offered under the current Medicare program—would be available to low-income persons whose family income is below specified amounts closely aligned with the poverty level. There are no provisions for including the medically indigent groups as eligibles for this medical assistance plan. Benefits for covered services do not have restrictions or limits, except for hospital inpatient services which are limited to sixty covered days. For the medical assistance plan, cost sharing is present only in the form of a copayment of \$3 for the first ten physician visits per family.

The medical assistance program would be financed by both federal and state general revenues. The state contribution is based on its share of the costs of the present Medicaid program, with some additional costs possible for any new covered services. Federal general revenues would assume any balance in the total cost of this plan.

The third plan proposed is a voluntary program for qualified basic private health insurance coverage. A qualified policy would (1) offer at least those covered services that are benefits under the Medicare program, (2) limit the deductible for hospital services to \$100 and for medical services to \$50, and (3) allow for cost sharing of up to 20 percent coinsurance. The Long-Ribicoff would also maintain the current Medicare program for the elderly.

This proposal would have the catastrophic plan, the medical assistance program, and the Medicare program administered by the Social Security Administration. The Secretary of Health, Education and Welfare would certify private plans under the voluntary program. Only those private insurers offering certified policies would serve as intermediaries for the Medicare program. Cost and quality control would rely on present mechanisms under this proposal, and no provisions were made for affecting the health care delivery system.

Ullman Bill

The National Health Care Services, Financing and Reorganization Act (H.R.1), supported by the American Hospital Association (AHA), would establish a three-part plan also for national health insurance: (1) a program requiring all employers to provide specified private health insurance coverage for employees and their families; (2) a program of providing group coverage for the selfemployed and other individuals; and (3) a program for the aged, low-income, and medically indigent persons whereby the Federal government contracts with private health insurance carriers.

Included in the private employee-employer plan are those employees and their families who elect coverage. The employer must pay at least 75 percent of the premium, with the employee paying the remaining 25 percent or any other balance of the premium cost. Federal subsidies are available in the form of tax credits for the low-income worker and the qualified small group employers. The second plan that this proposal would establish would enroll low-income and medically indigent families and the aged. The lowest-income group would not pay a premium, while the medically indigent would pay a portion of the premium according to income level and family size. For example, a family of four or more with an annual income of $6,001-$7,500 would pay $125 per year as a premium contribution. The remaining costs of the plan for the low-income, medically indigent, and aged are financed by federal general revenues and payroll taxes at the rate required by the present Medicare program. Parts A and B of Medicare are merged under this proposal.

The benefits provided by this proposal would be phased in over a five-year period and their structure would, in the final stage, apply to enrollees of the three plans. The final scope of services have copayments and coinsurance attached to all benefits. The proposal does include a provision for catastrophic coverage; the sepcified limit on the amount of expenditures paid by the enrollee for certain noncovered services varies with family income and age. Only when costs have reached this catastrophic level is the cost sharing on all benefits and the limitation on the number of hospital days and physician visits removed.

This plan relies on the private health insurance industry, whereby the federal government would contract with private carriers for the subsidized program that replaced Medicaid. Standards and guidelines for cost and quality control would be set at the national level, with state level implementation and approval. Other provisions emphasize the development of state health care corporations and nonprofit health care corporations.

Young Bill

The Comprehensive National Health Care Act of 1975 (H.R. 6283) is a new proposal made in the 94th Congress, rather than being the reintroduction of some revised version of earlier proposed legislation. The bill is supported by the Friends Committee on National Legislation.

The proposal relies on a system of national health care benefits for all U.S. residents provided through a proposed independent Social Security Administration. The role of private health insurance organizations would be phased out over the first ten years of the implementation of this system. Both the Medicare and the Medicaid programs would be abolished.

Under this proposal, no income or age requirements are necessary for eligibility. The covered services provided by this bill are comprehensive in scope, with *no* deductibles or coinsurance payments or any other form of cost sharing for the consumer. The Social Security Administration (SSA) would continue to use fiscal intermediaries as it does now under the Medicare program for institutional services. For other types of services, including physicians' services, third-party insurers approved by SSA would be selected by employers to administer plans with 1,000 or more employees.

The financing of the proposed plan relies *solely* on a payroll tax: (1) 2.0 percent tax on employees' wages and salaries; (2) 6.0 percent tax on employers' total payroll; and (3) 5.0 percent on unearned income and self-employment earnings. Federal income tax credits would also be available, with limits, for both employee and employer contributors.

This bill would structure Area Health Services Boards for local review of policy that would also be responsible for improvement in the health delivery system, and there would be an advisory council at the national level. Management incentive payments are provided for the maintainence of high standards of service. The bill would also automatically fund new programs and make available manpower incentives under the Health Resources Development Act.

Notes

1. Much of the discussion of the national health insurance bills in this chapter relies heavily on this type of detailed information presented in *National Health Insurance Proposals–Provisions of Bills Introduced in the 93rd Congress as of February 1974,* compiled by Saul Waldman, U.S. Social Security Administration, Office of Research and Statistics (March, 1974). See also, *National Health Insurance Resource Book,* prepared by the Staff of the Committee on Ways and Means for the Use of the Committee (U.S. Government Printing Office: Washington, D.C., 1974).

2. See Bruce C. Stuart, "National Health Insurance and the Poor," *American Journal of Public Health,* Vol. 62, No. 9 (September, 1972), 1252-1259. In his study of the impact of national health insurance on the poor versus the present role of the Medicaid program, Stuart suggests the utility of employing more analytical distinctions among the national health insurance proposals to

assess the impacts of certain program characteristics. At the time of his study, only two national health insurance proposals would actually abolish any part of or all the present Medicaid program.

3 The Distribution of Income in the United States

Few statistics reveal as much about the operation of an economy as do those on income distribution. Although the levels of living that are possible in any society are prescribed by the size of the national product, a given output can be distributed in many different ways. It can provide palaces for live kings and pyramids for dead ones, but hovels and hunger for the mass of mankind; or it can be widely distributed and provide reasonably uniform levels of living for all.[1]

The essence of this statement is applicable to the national policy decisions directed at the current distribution of the supply of health services and the demand for health services by persons in the various income levels.

Direct efforts to reduce the inequalities in the distribution of income may not be politically and fiscally possible at this time. However, alternative and indirect means provide additional options for relieving the inequality that is known to exist. First, indirect means are available to redistribute the goods and services to those persons whose income level denies them the necessities of daily living. In this manner, the overall economic status and quality of life of large numbers of families and individuals can be improved. Second, the current structure of personal taxes frequently not only places undue burdens on low- and middle-income groups, but also allows for relatively favorable tax incidence for the higher-income groups. Each of these two means of redistribution of income exist as inherent opportunities for consideration within a national health insurance plan. The extent to which these possibilities are realities in the various national health insurance proposals is the question at hand.

This chapter outlines the variation in the distribution of income among families and unrelated individuals according to economic, social, and demographic factors. The purpose of this chapter is to assess the inequality of the distribution of income by employing various measures of inequality. In subsequent chapters, the distribution of income is a central part of the overall framework for evaluating the national health insurance proposals. The proposals are analyzed in terms of their potential for altering income inequality through the redistribution of health services and/or the restructuring of the present system of financing health care. Since much of the data presented in later chapters on the utilization of and expenditures for health services and the implied benefits and costs of a national health insurance program focuses on the family as the decisionmaking unit for the consumption of health care, more attention is directed at an analysis of the pattern of family income distribution.[2]

Current Patterns of Income Distribution

The distribution of total money income in the United States in 1972 for families and unrelated individuals is given in Table 3-1. Median money income for families (that income class which divides the higher- and the lower-income groups into halves) was $11,116 in 1972, an increase of more than 8 percent from the median level for 1971. When adjustment is made for the increase in consumer prices, the 1972 median income for families in *real* terms increased by only 4.6 percent from the 1971 median. The median income for unrelated individuals was approximately $3,500 in 1972 and as few as 25 percent of all unrelated individuals received an annual income of $7,000 or more.[3]

Tables 3-2 and 3-3 present the percentage and cumulative distribution of money income for families and unrelated individuals for 1972. These distributions show great differences in the concentration of the numbers of families and

Table 3-1
Number of Families and Unrelated Individuals by Total Money Income in 1972[a]

Total Money Income ($)	*Number of Families*[b]	*Number of Unrelated Individuals*[c]
Total	54,373,000	16,811,000
Under 1,000	683,000	1,638,000
1,000-1,999	1,183,000	3,030,000
2,000-2,999	2,018,000	2,715,000
3,000-3,999	2,494,000	1,749,000
4,000-4,999	2,670,000	1,369,000
5,000-5,999	2,735,000	1,144,000
6,000-6,999	2,828,000	874,000
7,000-7,999	3,030,000	889,000
8,000-9,999	6,063,000	1,342,000
10,000-11,999	6,245,000	800,000
12,000-14,999	7,947,000	623,000
15,000-19,999	8,597,000	465,000 (15,000-24,999)
20,000-24,999	3,899,000	
25,000 and over	3,982,000	174,000
Median income	$11,116	$3,521

[a]Families and unrelated individuals as of March, 1973.

[b]The term "family" refers to a group of two or more persons related by blood, marriage, or adoption who reside together.

[c]The term "unrelated individuals" refers to persons 14 years old and over who are not living with any relatives. An unrelated individual may constitute a one-person household or may be part of a household including one or more other families or unrelated individuals.

Source: U.S. Department of Commerce, Bureau of the Census, "Money Income in 1972 of Families and Persons in the United States," *Current Population Reports: Consumer Income,* Series P-60, No. 87 (June, 1973), Table A.

Table 3-2
Family Money Income, Percentage and Cumulative Distributions of Families, by Income Level, 1972

Total Money Income ($)	*Percentage*	*Cumulative*
Under 3,000	7.2%	7.2%
3,000-4,999	9.4	16.6
5,000-6,999	10.2	26.8
7,000-9,999	16.8	43.6
10,000-11,999	11.5	55.1
12,000-14,999	14.6	69.7
15,000 and over	30.3	100.0

Source: U.S. Department of Commerce, Bureau of the Census, "Money Income in 1972 of Families and Persons in the United States," *Current Population Reports,* Series P-60, No. 90 (December, 1973), Table 2.

Table 3-3
Unrelated Individual Money Income, Percentage and Cumulative Distribution of Unrelated Individuals, by Income Level, 1972

Total Money Income ($)	*Percentage*	*Cumulative*
Under 1,500	17.9%	17.9%
1,500-2,999	26.0	43.9
3,000-4,999	18.5	62.4
5,000-6,999	12.0	74.4
7,000-9,999	13.2	87.6
10,000 and over	12.3	99.9[a]

[a]Due to rounding.

Source: U.S. Department of Commerce, Bureau of the Census, "Money Income in 1972 of Families and Persons in the United States," *Current Population Reports,* Series P-60, No. 90 (December, 1973), Table 8.

unrelated individuals in the income groups and reflects inequality in levels of living. In 1972, more than 26 percent of the families in the United States received income of less than $7,000, while 30 percent received more than $15,000. Unfortunately, the general public and, perhaps even at times those in public office, are conditioned to accept only information on levels and changes in median or per capita income, figures which do not portray the economic hardships faced by many families and individuals.

Those persons designated as "unrelated individuals" comprise only about one-tenth of the total population, but they face the effects of great inequality imposed by the present levels and distribution of income, as is shown in Table 3-3. (Note that the total money income categories listed here with the percentage and cumulative income distributions for unrelated individuals are smaller at the low income levels than for the data presented for family income.) Whether they be the elderly persons living on social security benefits, the youths who can find only part-time or temporary employment, or the individuals who have no family survivors, 17.9 percent of all persons "living on their own" received less than $1,500 in 1972. Further, in 1972 almost 44 percent of the unrelated individuals received less than $3,000 and about 62 percent received less than $5,000.

Income Levels Measured by Economic Fifths

One means of measuring the inequality in the distribution of income and describing the possible gains and losses by family units and unrelated individuals due to a change in the distribution of income over time is to employ the concept of economic fifths. Table 3-4 presents the percentage share of money income received by each fifth of the population for families and unrelated individuals, ranked by total money income for selected years from 1950 to 1972. If all inequality in the distribution of income was eliminated over time, then each fifth of the population would have received a fifth of the total income in 1972. In fact, the data indicate that significant inequality remains in the distribution of income for both families and unrelated individuals.

The claim is frequently made that within the last decade the changes in the distribution of income have benefited most those families at the lower levels of income. However, any increases in absolute dollars of income received must be assessed in terms of how these increased dollars affect the family's relative position in the distribution of income to determine any actual gains in income status. For example, if a family's income increased by $2,200 in *absolute* terms from 1962 to 1970, its relative position in the income distribution may not have altered, simply due to its initial level of income in 1962 and the increases in income that occurred for all other families by 1970. Assuming a family is at the median income level of $7,600 in 1962, then this $2,200 increase is merely sufficient to *maintain* a median money income level for the family in 1970, estimated at approximately $9,800. They are, in fact, no better off in *relative* terms.

By 1972, families whose incomes placed them in the top 20 percent or the highest fifth of the population received 41.4 percent of total income; the top 40 percent of all families received 65.3 percent of total income. The top 5 percent received almost 16 percent of total income in 1972, up 1.5 percentage points from 1970 or an increase in income received by this highest-income group which resulted in greater concentration and greater inequality in the distribution of income. In this same year, the families in the lowest fifth of the population, ranked by income, received only 5.4 percent of total money income, a slight decline from the 1970 level of 5.5 percent, indicating again a movement toward greater inequality.

Table 3-4
Percentage Share of Aggregate Money Income Received by Each Fifth of Families and Unrelated Individuals, Ranked by Income, Selected Years, 1950, 1960, 1970, and 1972[a]

Income Rank	*1950*	*1960*	*1970*	*1972*
Families				
Lowest fifth	4.5	4.9	5.5	5.4
Second fifth	12.0	12.0	12.0	11.9
Third fifth	17.4	17.6	17.4	17.5
Fourth fifth	23.5	23.6	23.5	23.9
Highest fifth	42.6	42.0	41.6	41.4
Top 5 percent	17.0	16.8	14.4	15.9
Unrelated Individuals				
Lowest fifth	2.3	2.6	3.3	3.3
Second fifth	7.0	7.1	7.9	8.2
Third fifth	13.8	13.6	13.8	13.8
Fourth fifth	26.5	25.7	24.5	23.9
Highest fifth	50.4	50.9	50.5	50.9
Top 5 percent	19.3	20.0	20.5	21.4

[a]Money income includes the following sources: (1) money wages and salaries; (2) net income from nonfarm self-employment; (3) net income from farm self-employment; (4) Social Security benefits; (5) dividends, interest (on savings or bonds), income from estates or trusts, or net rental income; (6) public assistance or welfare payments; (7) unemployment compensation, government employee pensions, or veterans' payments; and (8) private pensions, annuities, alimony, regular contributions from persons not living in household, and other periodic income.

Source: U.S. Bureau of the Census, "Income in 1970 of Families and Persons in the United States," *Current Population Reports*, Series P-60, No. 80 (1971), Table 14; and "Money Income in 1972 of Families and Persons in the United States," Series P-60, No. 90 (1973), Table 16.

The percentage shares for unrelated individuals, given in Table 3-4, indicate an even greater maldistribution of income than for family income. Throughout this twenty-year period, the highest fifth or top 20 percent of all unrelated individuals received more than 50 percent of this group's total income, while the top 5 percent received as much as 21 percent of the total income in 1972. No major improvements in terms of redistribution of income occurred during this period, with perhaps the exception of the small recent gains for the members of the second highest fifth. Indeed, the "losses" by this group actually meant "gains" in income received by the highest fifth or a reinforcing of inequality in the distribution of income received by unrelated individuals.

Figure 3-1 presents in graphic form the distributions of income for families and unrelated individuals and their deviations from a distribution with absolute

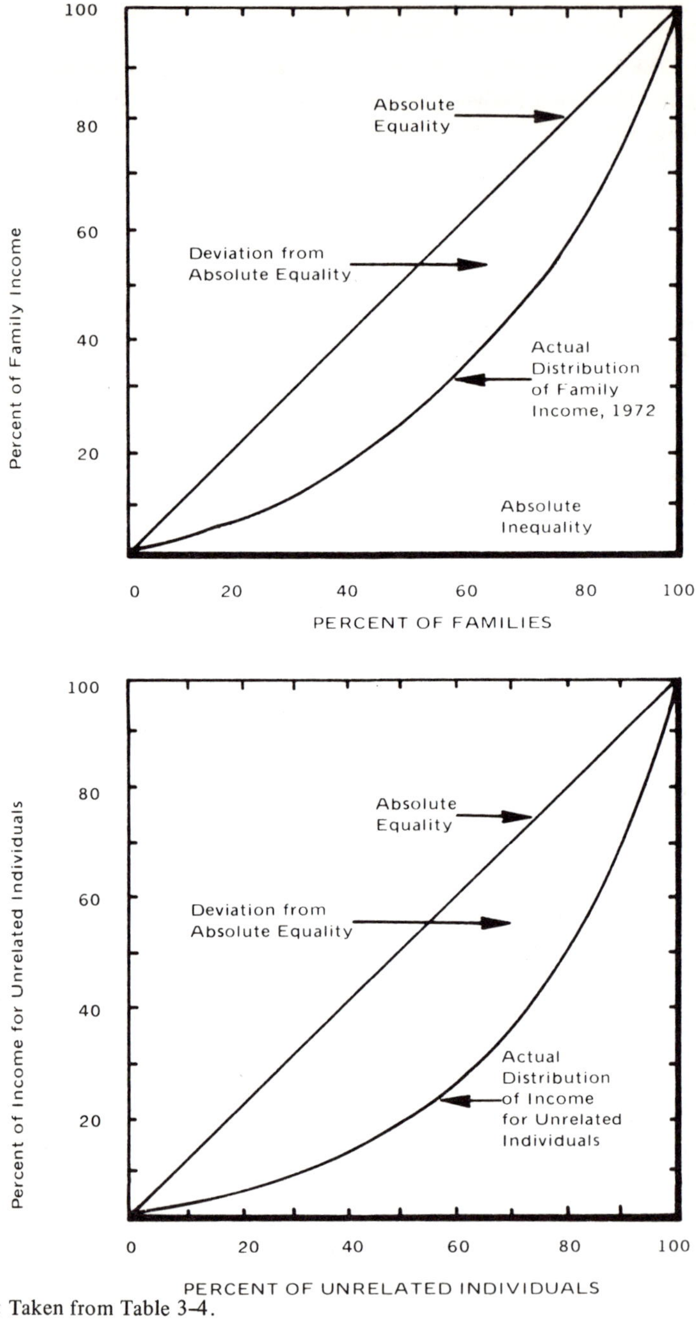

Source: Taken from Table 3-4.

Figure 3-1. Distribution of Income for Families and Unrelated Individuals, 1972

equality of income for these recipient groups.[4] The economic fifths for the respective populations are plotted against the cumulative percentage shares of total income received. The measure of the extent of inequality is then the deviation of the curve that connects the points of the actual distribution of income from the straight line of absolute equality, which designates each fifth of the population receiving one-fifth or 20 percent of total income. For example, when the curves for families versus unrelated individuals are compared, the existence of greater inequality for unrelated individuals is apparent. Of primary interest, however, is the fact that significant inequality remains in the current distribution of income and that some form of redistribution of income would be necessary to shift the curves closer to the line of perfect equality of income. The incidence of the benefits and costs of a national health insurance program on the various income groups can alter the distribution of income. While the question of the extent to which a particular type of plan will measurably redistribute income is critical, a more immediate concern may be the apparent neglect of this kind of criteria. Such neglect could, in fact, result in negative impacts on the distribution of income.

Poverty Levels

The poverty level of income, specified as $4,275 in 1972 for a four-person, nonfarm family, is an arbitrary and absolute policy measure.[5] The poverty level simply dichotomizes the population into groups of "poor" and "non-poor"; it implies nothing about the actual distribution of income.

On the subject of defining "poverty levels", Bronfenbrenner writes:[6]

> Social workers and social economists have attempted many statistical definitions of poverty, without avoiding elements of arbitrariness. Sometimes these are frank and open; as an example, a historian wrote, "I will abandon the commonly accepted $2,000 a year—a criterion unchanged despite the postwar inflation—and take the more realistic $3,000."[7]

More often, the arbitrary element is concealed under one or another more sophisticated approach. One traditional procedure, associated with wealth or assets rather than with income, has been to draw up a list of commonplace amenities, i.e., so many square feet of floor space per person, so many calories of food per day, etc. When a family lacks a certain proportion of these items, it is defined as living in poverty, even if the family's income would permit their purchase. Conversely, even if the family has sufficient necessities of life, but subsists by depending on the charity of friends and relatives, by selling assets and drawing down savings, or by incurring debt, the family may not be found to be in need of public assistance.

Table 3-5 presents historical data on the number of poor, their percentage of the total population, and poverty line statistics. In 1972, 24.5 million persons or 12 percent of the population were below the designated poverty level of income, according to these statistics. However, when the increases in the poverty level of income are compared with the increases in the median family income level, the growth trend of the latter far exceeds the increases in the poverty income level that have been permitted in the past twelve years. In fact, the 1972 poverty level ($4,275) as a percentage of median family income ($11,116) is 38.6 percent, the *lowest* percentage for all years reported in Table 3-5.

In conclusion, definitions of the poverty level of income are arbitrary and are known to be largely meaningless for programs directed at the redistribution of income. National health insurance proposals that rely on current definitions of the "poor" and "near poor" for the distribution of the benefits and costs of their plans may have direct negative effects on the distribution of income. Under these definitions, large numbers of families and individuals will be omitted from programs established for persons in need of some financial support for health care services. In order to meet these kinds of criteria, more appropriate definitions of "need," possibly defined at several different income levels and based on *increasing* percentages of median income, may prove necessary. More equitable plans would, therefore, include preferential provisions for all who are poor or medically indigent, and those persons at income levels below the median income who may bear a higher cost relative to benefits received within the alternative national health insurance proposals.

Notes

1. U.S. Bureau of the Census, *Income Distribution in the United States*, by Herman P. Miller (A 1960 Census Monograph) (Washington, D.C.: Government Printing Office, 1966), p. 1.

2. Personal income is defined here to include: social security benefit payments; government employee pensions; public assistance; veterans benefits; and unemployment insurance benefits and workmen's compensation. For a discussion of the redistributive effects of these transfer payments, see Benjamin Bridges, Jr., "Redistributive Effects of Transfer Payments among Age and Economic Status Groups," U.S. Department of H.E.W. Social Security Administration, Office of Research and Statistics, Staff Paper No. 10 (October 1971).

3. Excluded from the discussion of income distribution here are the redistributive effects of inflation and the distribution of wealth. The analysis of the redistributive effects of inflation in the literature takes the form of two related hypotheses: (1) during inflationary periods, "money wages tend to lag behind prices; real wages fall, real profits rise, and the income distribution shifts against labor" and (2) business firms as such gain, on balance, from inflation." See

Table 3-5
Number of Poor, Percentage of Total Population, Poverty Line Statistics, and Median Income, 1960-1972

	Poor				All Families
Year	*Number of People (Millions)*	*Percentage of Total Population*	*Poverty Line for Four-person Non-farm Family*	*Poverty Line as Percentage of Median Income*	*Median Family Income*
1960	39.9	22.2%	$3,022	53.8%	$5,620
1961	39.6	21.9	3,054	53.2	5,737
1962	38.6	21.0	3,089	51.9	5,956
1963	36.4	19.5	3,128	50.0	6,249
1964	36.1	19.0	3,169	48.2	6,569
1965	33.2	17.3	3,223	46.3	6,957
1966	28.5	14.7	3,317	44.2	7,500
1967	27.8	14.2	3,410	42.8	7,974
1968	25.4	12.8	3,553	41.2	8,632
1969	24.1	12.1	3,743	39.7	9,433
1970	25.4	12.6	3,968	40.2	9,867
1971	25.6	12.5	4,137	40.2	10,285
1972	24.5	12.0	4,275	38.6	11,116

Sources: U.S. Bureau of the Census, "Income in 1970 of Families and Persons in the United States," *Current Population Reports,* Series P-60, No. 80 (1971), Table 11; "Characteristics of the Low-Income Population, 1971," Series P-60, No. 86 (1972), Tables L, 1, 2; "Money Income in 1971 of Families and Persons in the United States," Series P-60, No. 83 (1972), p. 3; "Money Income in 1972 of Families and Persons in the United States," Series P-60, No. 90 (1973), Table 8; and "Characteristics of the Low-Income Population, 1972," Series P-60, No. 91 (1973), p. 1 and Table L.

Martin Bronfenbrenner, *Income Distribution Theory,* (Chicago: Aldine-Atherton, Inc., 1971), p. 91. Our concern for "the effects of inflation on the personal income distribution" indicate that "within each major economic category, particular individuals are left behind." For example, Bach and Ando conclude that "the major losers from inflation on current income account—the relatively fixed-income groups—[are] clearly scattered throughout the economy as pensioners, insurance recipients, college professors, and others, rather than concentrated in major income size or occupation groups." See G.L. Bach and Albert K. Ando, "The Redistributional Effects of Inflation," *Review of Economics and Statistics* (February, 1957). "In any case, the simple theory that places labor on the losing end seems largely outmoded once labor has become organized and money illusions have been evaporated by experience in long or repeated inflations." (Bronfenbrenner, p. 92.)

As to the actual distribution of wealth, Smith finds that in 1969 "... people held in their own names gross assets of three and one-half trillion dollars; that is, in the neighborhood of $17,000 for each man, woman, and child, had it been distributed evenly." (Smith, p. 143.) However, "the super rich (defined as each having a net worth over $60,000 and numbering about 5 million individuals) accounted for 4 percent of the population age twenty and over, but they owned 33 percent of the net worth of all persons." (Smith, p. 148.) See James D. Smith, "The Concentration of Personal Wealth in America, 1969," *The Review of Income and Wealth,* Series 20, No. 2 (June, 1974).

4. The Lorenz or Gini curve is commonly employed as a statistical measure of concentration ratios. See Bronfenbrenner (pp. 49-50) for a list of the particular disadvantages of this measurement of inequality. For further discussion, see also George Garvy, "Inequality of Income: Causes and Measurement," *Studies in Income and Wealth,* (New York: National Bureau of Economic Research, 1952), 25-48; and James Morgan, et. al., *1961 Survey of Consumer Finances,* (Ann Arbor: University of Michigan, Survey Research Center, 1962).

5. See Miller, *op. cit.* and Mollie Orshansky, "Counting the Poor: Another Look at the Poverty Profile," *Social Security Bulletin,* Vol. 28 (January, 1965), pp. 3-29. For the discussion of an index to incorporate family circumstances such as family size and geographic location, see Harold W. Watts, "The Iso-Prop Index: An Approach to the Determination of Differential Poverty Income Thresholds," *The Journal of Human Resources,* Vol. 2, No. 1, 3-18. This criticism also holds, of course, for the definition of the "near-poor" income level which is simply defined at 125 percent of the poverty level.

6. Bronfenbrenner, op. cit. pp. 38-39.

7. Gabriel Kolko, *Wealth and Power in America* (New York: Praeger Publishers, 1962), p. 73.

4 National and Personal Health Expenditures

National health expenditures totaled more than $100 billion in fiscal year 1974, representing almost 8 percent of the gross national product.[1] On a per capita basis, more than $485 was expended in 1974 for the provision and financing of health services and supplies, including expenditures for medical research and facilities construction. Total health expenditures directly related to personal health care were more than $90 billion in fiscal year 1974, an increase of 10.6 percent from the 1973 level. The magnitude of these expenditures is evidence of at least the kind of commitment that our nation and its people are willing to make to health care.

This chapter presents a summary report of the level and trends in national and personal health expenditures by source of payment and by type of service. *National health expenditures* are defined broadly as the dollar amount spent for all public and private health care services and supplies and also medical research and facilities construction. Included in this definition are: expenditures for prepayment (the difference between premium income and benefit expenditures for private health insurance organizations or the net cost of insurance); administrative expenses (the cost of administration of federally funded programs that can be identified); and government public health activities. *Personal health expenditures* are defined as those public and private expenses incurred only as a direct result of personal health care received by individuals. Thus, expenditures for public health programs, prepayment, administration, and research and construction are omitted from this definition. The total health bill reflects the influences of several factors: (1) the growth of population; (2) the substantial increases in the price and cost of health services and supplies; (3) changes in the size and structure of the health care delivery system and the utilization of health services; and (4) technological advancements in medical diagnostic and treatment methods. A brief review of national health expenditures is followed by the more relevant discussion of personal health expenditures and the factors that affect these expenditures.

National Health Expenditures

The increases in the level of national health expenditures within the two decades from 1950 to 1970 represent a more than five-fold growth from $12 billion to $69 billion. In fiscal year 1974, total national health expenditures rose to

$104.2 billion. The percentage of the gross national product apportioned to national health expenditures was 4.6 percent in 1950 and by 1973 had risen to 7.7 percent. (See Figure 4-1.)

The trend in aggregate national health expenditures by public versus private source of funds and the percent of gross national product for fiscal years 1966 through 1974 is given in Table 4-1. During this recent period, total expenditures increased by approximately 150 percent, and in the case of per capita expenditures, the increase was almost 130 percent. In 1974, the private sector accounted

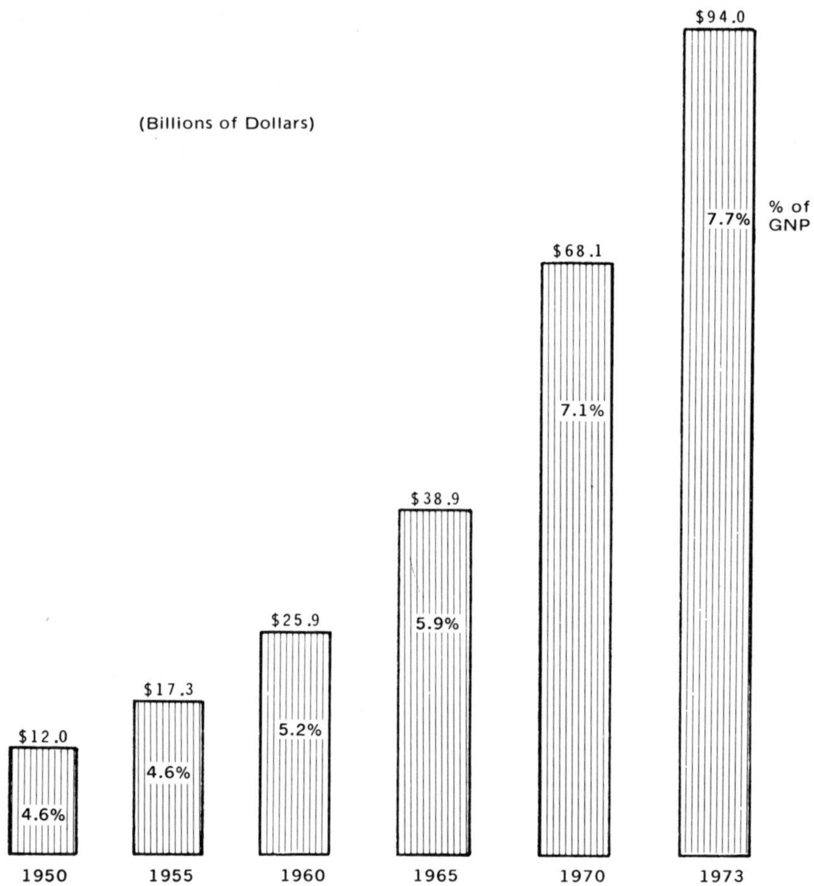

Source: Barbara S. Cooper, Nancy L. Worthington, and Paula A. Pino, "National Health Expenditures, 1929-73," *Social Security Bulletin,* Vol. 36, No. 3 (March, 1974), Table 1.

Figure 4-1. Total National Health Expenditures and Percent of Gross National Product, Selected Fiscal Years

Table 4-1
Aggregate and per Capita National Health Expenditures, by Source of Funds and Percent of Gross National Product, Fiscal Years 1966 through 1974

		Health Expenditures								
		Total			*Private*			*Public*		
Fiscal Year	*Gross National Product (in Billions)*	*Amount (in Millions)*	*Per Capita*	*Percent of GNP*	*Amount (in Millions)*	*Per Capita*	*Percent of Total*	*Amount (in Millions)*	*Per Capita*	*Percent of Total*
1966	$ 718.5	$ 42,109	$211.56	5.9%	$31,279	$157.15	74.3%	$10,830	$ 54.41	25.7%
1967	771.4	47,879	237.93	6.2	32,057	159.30	67.8	15,823	78.63	33.0
1968	827.0	53,765	264.37	6.5	33,727	165.84	62.7	20,040	98.54	37.3
1969	899.0	60,617	295.20	6.7	37,682	183.51	62.2	22,937	111.70	37.8
1970	954.8	69,202	333.57	7.2	43,964	211.92	63.5	25,238	121.65	36.5
1971	1,013.3	77,162	368.25	7.6	48,558	231.74	62.9	28,604	136.51	37.1
1972	1,100.6	86,391	408.31	7.8	53,365	252.22	61.8	33,025	156.09	38.2
1973	1,225.2	94,235	441.94	7.7	58,415	273.95	62.0	35,819	167.98	38.0
1974[a]	1,349.8	104,239	485.36	7.7	62,929	293.01	60.4	41,311	192.35	39.6

[a]Preliminary estimates.

Source: Nancy L. Worthington, "National Health Expenditures, 1929–74," *Social Security Bulletin*, Vol. 37, No. 2 (February, 1975), p. 5, Table 1.

for 60 percent of national health expenditures, a decline from the 75 percent level which was represented by the private sector in 1966. Private expenditures include: payment of private health insurance benefits, out-of-pocket payments by consumers, and other sources of payment, such as philanthropy and industry.[a] Public expenditures by federal, state, and local governments quadrupled from 1966 to 1974, when the total expenditures by governments reached $41 billion.[2] By comparison with private expenditures, public expenditures represented 40 percent of aggregate national expenditures in fiscal year 1974, an upward shift from the 1966 level of 25.7 percent. A major contributor to this increase in the proportion of total expenditures funded by public monies was the introduction of the Medicare and Medicaid programs in 1966, with 1967 being the first full year of implementation. Medicare—the largest government-administered health financing program—resulted in expenditures of $11.3 billion in 1974, with 10 percent of this total actually accounted for by premium payments by enrollees. Expenditures under the Medicaid program also reached a total of about $11 billion in 1974, including those Medicare supplementary insurance premiums paid under the State Medicaid "buy in" agreements. (A more complete discussion of the Medicare and Medicaid programs is given in Chapter 10.)

Estimates of national health expenditures by type of expenditure and by source of funds for fiscal year 1974 are given in Table 4-2. In general, the data show that hospital care and physicians' services have the highest expenditures for both private and public sources of funds. However, a relatively higher proportion of hospital care is paid for by public funds, while a substantially higher proportion of expenditures for physicians' services is met by private funds. Consumers, primarily with out-of-pocket payments, but also through third party or insurance benefits, still pay for almost all expenditures for drugs, drug sundries, and dentists' services. State and local governments currently fund about a third of the public expenditures for hospital care and about one-fourth of the public expenditures for physicians' services.

Personal Health Expenditures

Since 1950, expenditures for personal health care have risen from $10 billion to $90 billion in 1974. Additional significance is associated with the extent to which the proportions of this total health bill met by the various sources of funds have altered during this same period. Direct payments by consumers now are placed at 35 percent of all personal health expenditures, while in 1950

---

[a]Because the estimates of private expenditures do *not* exclude the effects of deductions for health insurance premiums and health care expenses allowed under the federal income tax system, these estimates are overstated.

Table 4-2

Estimates of National Health Expenditures, by Type of Expenditure and Source of Funds, Fiscal Year 1974 (In Millions)

		Source of Funds					
		Private			Public		
Type of Expenditures	*Total*	*Total*	*Con-sumers*	*Other*	*Total*	*Federal*	*State and Local*
Total	$104,239	$62,929	$58,043	$4,886	$41,311	$28,343	$12,968
Health services and supplies	97,183	59,815	58,043	1,772	37,369	25,335	12,034
Hospital care	40,900	19,272	18,759	513	21,628	14,845	6,783
Physicians' services	19,000	14,476	14,462	14	4,524	3,277	1,248
Dentists' services	6,200	5,858	5,858		342	210	132
Other professional services	1,990	1,629	1,591	38	361	226	136
Drugs and drug sundries	9,695	8,900	8,900		795	404	391
Eyeglasses and appliances	2,153	2,065	2,065		88	50	38
Nursing-home care	7,450	3,504	3,474	30	3,946	2,208	1,738
Expenses for prepayment and administration	4,224	2,934	2,934		1,290	1,042	247
Government public health activities	2,126				2,126	1,234	892
Other health services	3,445	1,177		1,177	2,268	1,840	428
Research and medical facilities construction	7,056	3,114		3,114	3,942	3,008	934
Research	2,684	205		205	2,479	2,395	84
Construction	4,372	2,909		2,909	1,463	613	850
Publicly owned facilities	1,112				1,112	277	835
Privately owned facilities	3,260	2,909		2,909	351	336	15

Source: Nancy L. Worthington, "National Health Expenditures, 1929-74," *Social Security Bulletin,* Vol. 37, No. 2 (February, 1975), Table 2.

consumers paid 68 percent of the total expenses. In 1950, benefit payments by the health insurance sector represented only 8.5 percent of total expenditures, but by 1974 such payments had increased to 25.6 percent. The public sector, as a source of funds for personal health care, expended in 1974 almost double its respective percentage in 1950, primarily because of the additional expenditures required under the Medicare and Medicaid programs. In 1974, these two programs accounted for more than half of the total expenditures made by federal, state, and local governments when public payments represented 38 percent of the total, compared with 20 percent in 1950. The relatively small proportion of expenditures made by philanthropy and industry of 1.4 percent in 1974 is, in fact, a decline from the 1950 level of 3.0 percent.

Table 4-3 gives the distribution of personal health care expenditures by source of funds on an annual basis from fiscal year 1966 to 1974. In this short-term period, the major growth of federal expenditures is quite evident, particularly if viewed by the trend in the percentage distribution, which shows an increase from 9 percent in 1966 to 25 percent in 1974. This upward trend in expenditures for federally funded programs is then offset by the decline in the proportion of expenditures met by direct consumer payments. Out-of-pocket consumer expenditures declined from 51 percent of total personal health expenditures in 1966 to 35 percent in 1974. Of interest also is the relative *constant* proportion of expenditures met by insurance benefits (25%) and by state and local governments (12%) during this period.

The trends in *per capita* expenditures indicate more than a doubling of personal health expenditures from $182 in 1966 to $420 in 1974. The largest portion of this increase is related to the rapid growth of public expenditures, $40 in 1966 versus $158 in 1974 on a per capita basis. While per capita private expenditures also increased during this period, the relative growth rate was much smaller, i.e., $142 versus $262, respectively. Direct, or out-of-pocket, payments actually experienced the smallest rate of increase, according to the data presented in Table 4-3, as the insurance benefits contribution grew from $45 per capita in 1966 to $108 in 1974. However, direct payments by consumers remain in 1974 the largest per capita dollar amount ($148) from among all possible sources of financing of health care.

Table 4-4 presents the percentage distribution of personal health expenditures by source of funds and by type of service for fiscal years 1966 to 1974. The largest portion of hospital care expenditures is met at present by public funds, with insurance benefits as the second largest source. The rankings were the reverse in 1966, when insurance benefits accounted for the highest percentage of hospital care expenditures. Prior to 1968, direct consumer payments represented more than half of total expenditures for physicians' services; by 1974, this proportion only declined to 39 percent of all payments for physicians' services. Indeed, the out-of-pocket consumer expenditures remain a larger percentage of total expenditures for physicians' services than the percentage met

Table 4-3
Distribution of Personal Health Care Expenditures, by Source of Funds, Fiscal Years 1966 through 1974[a]

		Source of Funds						
		Private				Public		
Fiscal Year	Total	Total	Direct Payments	Insurance Benefits[b]	Other	Total	Federal	State and Local
				Aggregate Amount (in Millions)				
1966	$36,216	$28,324	$18,668	$ 8,936	$ 720	$ 7,892	$ 3,349	$ 4,542
1967	41,343	28,883	18,786	9,344	753	12,461	7,471	4,991
1968	46,521	30,322	19,098	10,444	780	16,200	10,401	5,797
1969	52,690	33,987	20,597	12,206	824	18,705	12,283	6,421
1970	60,113	39,568	24,272	14,406	890	20,545	13,403	7,142
1971	67,228	43,999	26,307	16,728	964	23,229	15,401	7,827
1972	74,688	47,738	28,083	18,620	1,035	26,949	18,130	8,819
1973	81,281	51,886	30,193	20,568	1,125	29,972	20,182	9,789
1974	90,281	56,329	31,970	23,139	1,220	33,953	23,059	10,895

Table 4-3 (Cont.)

		Source of Funds						
		Private				Public		
Fiscal Year	Total	Total	Direct Payments	Insurance Benefits	Other	Total	Federal	State and Local
				Per Capita Amount				
1966	$182	$142	$ 94	$ 45	$4	$ 40	$ 17	$23
1967	205	144	94	46	4	62	37	25
1968	229	149	94	51	4	80	51	29
1969	257	166	102	59	4	91	60	31
1970	290	191	117	69	4	99	65	34
1971	321	210	126	80	5	111	74	37
1972	353	226	133	88	5	127	86	42
1973	384	243	142	96	5	141	95	46
1974	420	262	148	108	6	158	107	51

Table 4-3 (Cont.)

		Source of Funds						
		Private				Public		
Fiscal Year	*Total*	*Total*	*Direct Payments*	*Insurance Benefits*	*Other*	*Total*	*Federal*	*State and Local*
				Percentage Distribution				
1966	100.0	78.2%	51.5%	24.7%	2%	21.8%	9.2%	12.5%
1967	100.0	69.9	45.4	22.6	2	30.1	18.1	12.1
1968	100.0	65.2	41.1	22.5	2	34.8	22.4	12.5
1969	100.0	64.5	39.8	23.2	2	35.5	23.3	12.2
1970	100.0	65.8	40.4	24.0	2	34.2	22.3	11.9
1971	100.0	65.4	39.1	24.9	1	34.6	22.9	11.6
1972	100.0	63.9	37.6	24.9	1	36.1	24.3	11.8
1973	100.0	63.4	36.9	25.1	1	36.6	24.7	12.0
1974	100.0	62.4	35.4	25.6	1	37.6	25.5	12.1

[a]Personal health care expenditures include all expenditures for health services and supplies other than: (1) expenses for prepayment and administration; (2) government public health activities; and (3) expenditures of private voluntary agencies for other health services.

[b]Includes any insurance benefits and expenses for prepayment (insurance premiums less insurance benefits).

Source: Nancy L. Worthington, "National Health Expenditures, 1929-74," *Social Security Bulletin,* Vol. 37, No. 2 (February, 1975), Table 6.

Table 4-4
Percentage Distribution of Personal Health Care Expenditures, by Source of Funds and Type of Expenditures, Fiscal Years 1966 through 1974[a]

		Private Funds				
Fiscal Year	*Total*	*Total*	*Direct Payments*	*Insurance Benefits*[b]	*Other*	*Public Funds*
			Hospital Care			
1966	100.0	62.1%	18.4%	41.4%	2.2%	37.9%
1967	100.0	50.1	12.3	35.8	2.0	49.9
1968	100.0	46.8	10.4	34.7	1.8	53.2
1969	100.0	47.0	10.4	35.1	1.6	53.0
1970	100.0	49.2	12.3	35.5	1.4	50.8
1971	100.0	48.1	10.2	36.5	1.4	51.9
1972	100.0	46.3	9.0	35.9	1.3	53.7
1973	100.0	47.8	11.1	35.4	1.3	52.2
1974	100.0	47.2	10.4	35.4	1.3	52.9
			Physicians' Services			
1966	100.0	93.3	62.1	31.1	0.1	6.7
1967	100.0	85.5	55.6	29.8	0.1	14.5
1968	100.0	78.1	48.0	30.0	0.1	21.9
1969	100.0	77.4	45.7	31.7	0.1	22.6
1970	100.0	78.2	44.9	33.2	0.1	21.8
1971	100.0	78.2	43.8	34.2	0.1	21.8
1972	100.0	77.9	42.7	35.0	0.1	22.1
1973	100.0	77.3	40.5	36.7	0.1	22.7
1974	100.0	76.2	38.8	37.3	0.1	23.8
			All Other Services[c]			
1966	100.0	85.6	80.4	2.2	3.0	14.4
1967	100.0	82.2	76.1	3.4	2.8	17.8
1968	100.0	78.4	72.1	3.7	2.6	21.6
1969	100.0	77.4	70.8	4.1	2.5	22.6
1970	100.0	78.5	71.7	4.4	2.4	21.5
1971	100.0	79.1	71.9	4.8	2.4	20.9
1972	100.0	77.5	70.9	4.3	2.3	22.4
1973	100.0	74.8	67.8	4.8	2.3	25.2
1974	100.0	74.3	66.9	5.2	2.3	25.7

Notes for Table 4-4

[a]Personal health care expenditures include all expenditures for health services and supplies other than: (1) expenses for prepayment and administration; (2) government public health activities; and (3) expenditures of private voluntary agencies for other health services.

[b]Includes any insurance benefits and expenses for prepayment (insurance premiums less insurance benefits).

[d]Includes dentists' services, other professional services, drugs and drug sundries, eyeglasses and appliances, nursing-home care, and other health services.

Source: Nancy L. Worthington, "National Health Expenditures, 1929-74," *Social Security Bulletin*, Vol. 37, No. 2 (February, 1975), Tables 6 and 7.

by insurance benefits. The public sector accounts for only about 24 percent of expenditures for physicians' services, a portion that was established following the implementation of the Medicare and Medicaid programs.

All other services, including dentists' services, prescriptions and drugs, nursing-home care, etc.—the aggregate category given in Table 4-4—are largely paid for by direct consumer payments. However, any one of these service types may specifically be funded to a greater degree by other sources of financing, such as nursing-home care by public monies. While the proportion of expenditures for services other than for hospital and physician care met by direct consumer payments has declined in the past decade, in 1974 more than 66 percent of total expenditures for these other types of services were made directly by consumers. Insurance benefits presently cover only about 5 percent of expenditures for health services which are non-hospital- and non-physician-based, according to the recent estimates. The public sector, however, funds about 26 percent of this category of all other services, or more than double the percentage of these kinds of payments made with public monies in 1966.

The percentage distribution of *per capita* personal health expenditures by source of funds and by type of service for fiscal year 1973 is given in Figure 4-2. On the average, each person in the United States consumed about \$170 for hospital care in 1973; more than half of these payments for hospital care were met by the public sector. Private health insurance benefits covered about 36 percent of per capita expenditures for hospital care and the consumer made direct or out-of-pocket payments to meet about 10 percent of these expenditures. Per capita expenditures for physicians' services in 1973 were half as large as the expenditures for hospital care, or about \$85. Direct payments by the consumer were the largest source of funds for physicians' services, with insurance benefits covering only 35 percent of the average expenditures for physician care. Dentists' services, prescriptions, and drugs are presented in Figure 4-2 as separate categories from the all other services classification. In 1973, per capita expenditures for drugs and for dentists' services were \$41 and \$25, respectively. Relatively high proportions of consumer out-of-pocket expenditures pay for dentists' services

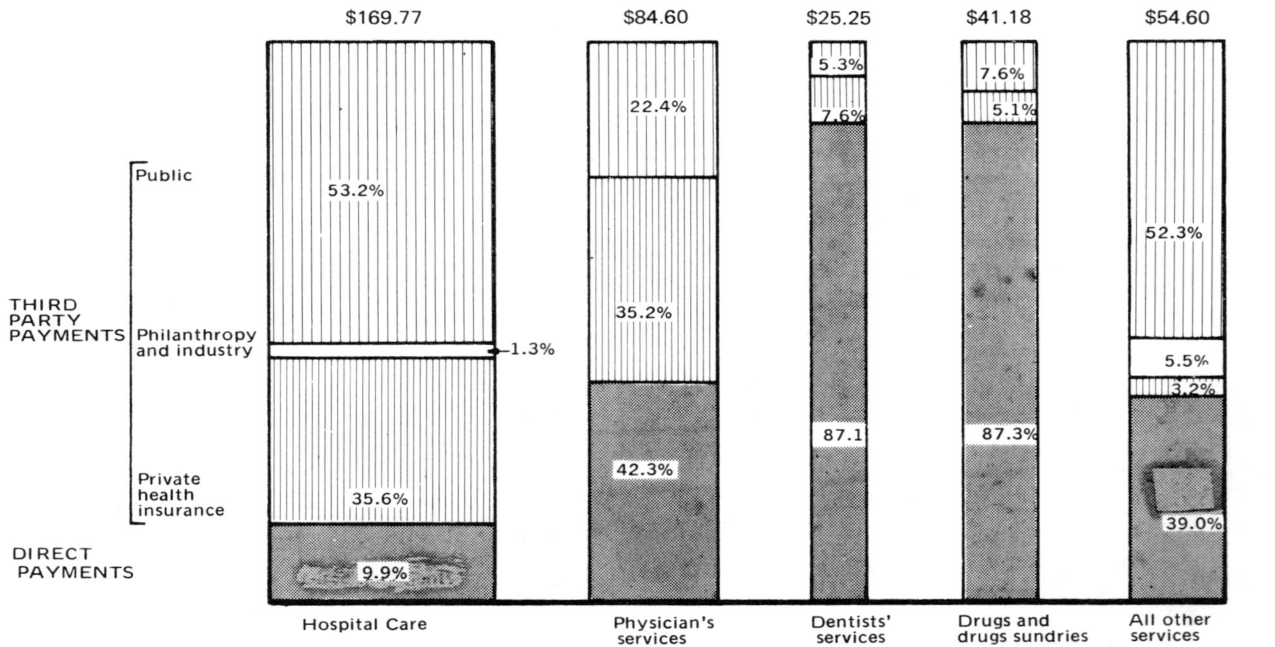

Source: Barbara S. Cooper, Nancy L. Worthington, and Paula A. Piro, "National Health Expenditures, 1929–73," *Social Security Bulletin,* Vol. 36, No. 3 (March, 1974), Chart 2.

Figure 4-2. Percentage Distribution of Per Capita Personal Health Care Expenditures, by Type of Expenditure and Source of Funds, Fiscal Year 1973

and drugs and drug sundries, with government and private health insurance funding slightly more than 10 percent of the total per capita expenditure for each of these two categories. Per capita expenditure for all other services—*excluding* dentists' services and drugs—totaled in 1973, to more than the per capita expenditure for physicians' services. Moreover, the greater porportion of the expenditures for these other types of services was met by consumer payments.

Factors Affecting Total Expenditures

Total health expenditures in a given year are a function of the growth of population, changes in the prices of health services, the rate of utilization of health services, and technological advancements in methods of medical diagnosis and treatment. While it is not always possible to isolate the exact contribution of each of these factors to increases in total health expenditures, some evidence does exist on the role of population growth and the impacts of increases in the prices and costs of health services.

One approach to isolating the influence of population growth on the level of health expenditures is to compare changes in per capita versus total expenditures over time. Data given in Table 4-3 indicate that the percentage increase in per capita personal health expenditures from 1967 to 1974 is not as great as the percentage increase in total expenditures. In fact, the growth of population accounted for 11.4 percent of the $49 billion increase in total expenditures or $7 billion over this eight-year period.

During the 1960s, the prices of personal health services increased almost twice as fast as the prices of all consumer items.[b] The price indices for selected health care items and for all consumer items for 1960 to 1974 are given in Table 4-5, using 1967 as the base year for the indices. Compared with the trends in the indices of other types of health services, semiprivate hospital room rates show the sharpest rise and contributed significantly to the inflation of the "all medical care items" price index beginning in the late 1960s. Since 1967, the index for semiprivate hospital room rates, as one measure of the inflation in the price of hospital care, has increased by more than 100 percent, while the price index for physicians' services increased by 50 percent. During this same period, the price index for all consumer items rose by about 47 percent. The prices of prescriptions and drugs, which have begun to stabilize, experienced a small increase again in 1974.

[b] The aggregate price index for all health care services reflects, of course, only the changes in prices for the selected health care items that are included in the index and is dependent, therefore, on the specific definitions of these items and their respective prices. In addition, no adjustments are made in the price indices to reflect changes in the quality of these health services.

Table 4-5
Price Indices (Annual Averages) for All Consumer Items and Selected Medical Care Items, 1960 to 1974[a]

Year	*All Consumer Items*	*Medical Care Items*	*Semi-private Hospital Room Rates*	*Physicians' Fees*	*Prescriptions and Drugs*
1960	88.7	79.1	57.3	77.0	104.5
1965	94.5	89.5	75.9	87.3	100.2
1967	100.0	100.0	100.0	100.0	100.0
1968	104.2	103.1	113.6	105.8	100.2
1969	109.8	113.4	128.8	113.3	101.3
1970	116.3	120.6	145.4	122.6	103.6
1971	121.3	128.4	163.1	131.4	105.4
1972	125.3	132.5	173.9	134.8	105.6
1973	133.1	137.7	182.1	139.5	105.9
1974	147.7	150.5	201.5	150.9	109.6

[a]Base year = 1967

Source: U.S. Department of Labor, Bureau of Labor Statistics, *Monthly Labor Review*, various issues.

Based on the increases in the price index for all medical care items, the rise in the prices of health services accounted for more than 50 percent of the increase in total personal health expenditures from 1967 to 1974.[3] This means that health services purchased in 1974 with a per capita expenditure of $420 would only have required an expenditure of $279 or almost $120 less if these services had been purchased at the 1967 level of health care prices.

With 11 percent of the increase in total personal health expenditures of $56 billion from 1967 to 1974 attributed to population growth and at least 50 percent merely reflecting the inflation of health care prices, only the residual 39 percent or $22 billion of the increase in total expenditures is, therefore, the result or greater utilization of health services and the introduction of advancements in medical techniques.

Notes

1. Nancy L. Worthington, "National Health Expenditures, 1929-74," *Social Security Bulletin,* Vol. 37, No. 2 (February, 1975), p. 3.

2. For past and current data on health expenditures under government programs, see the annual reports on social welfare expenditures in the *Social Security Bulletin.*

3. Price controls imposed on health care providers from August 1971 until October 1974 under the federal economic stabilization program are considered a factor in the slower rate of growth of price indices during this period. See Loucele A. Horowitz, "Medical Care Prices Change under the Economic Stabilization Program," *Social Security Bulletin,* Vol. 35, No. 6 (June, 1973), pp. 28-32.

5 Private Health Insurance

Probably every person, or at least a family member, relative, or friend, has experienced the need for medical services that resulted in major expenditures. Generally, the heaviest kind of financial burdens resulting from health problems are associated with a period of hospitalization, some types of surgery, or the process of rehabilitation due to illness or disease. In order to guard against such risks of high personal expenditures for health care, some people choose to purchase private health insurance coverage and the majority of covered persons have access to health insurance plans through their place of employment, with a portion of the cost of their insurance paid by the employers. However, the costs of enrollment in terms of monthly premiums for the individual or family are sufficiently high that not all persons who *want* and *need* health insurance coverage can afford it. This is true for persons employed in certain industries, e.g., construction and farming, for persons self-employed, and for unemployed persons. Moreover, for those persons who have coverage offered through employee plans or who can budget for the "basic" coverage—i.e., partial benefits for inpatient hospital services and certain surgical services—the purchase of supplementary medical benefit packages or "major medical" plans require additional premiums much beyond what their incomes will permit. In addition, major medical types of coverage actually only approach the concept of a comprehensive or all-inclusive benefit package.[a]

With private insurance options available to all, why, in fact, are the number and variety of national health insursurance proposals presently before the Congress? Probably the major reason why national health insurance is being given strong political consideration is the current status and role of the private health insurance industry in the United States.[1] Health care is no longer believed to be a privilege for only those who can afford it, but a right for all individuals, and private health insurance, in its present form, is inadequate as a financing mechanism to provide for this health care right.

This chapter examines the private health insurance sector in terms of enrollment, benefits, and costs. Its purpose is to review the levels and trends in enrollment in private health insurance plans, the types and amounts of benefits

[a]Major medical plans may include hospital and surgical costs not covered—or covered on a limited basis—by hospital and surgical policies, physicians' office and home visits, drugs, psychiatric care, dental care and optical care, depending on the provisions of the particular group contract (generally, employee plans).

received, and the cost of coverage, according to several characteristics of the population. Primary concern is placed on which groups within the population are enrolled in a variety of plans and which groups have limited private health insurance coverage or none at all. Of major interest is how enrollment, benefits, and costs are distributed across the income groups.

Many of the national health insurance proposals rely on the private health insurance sector for the structure and administration of the financial systems that these proposals would establish. In other cases, proposals permit the present private health insurance mechanisms to remain only somewhat intact by offering improvements in the structure and administration of their financing components. And, of course, the option of denying any role for the private health insurance sector in a national health insurance plan is also a viable alternative.

Enrollment

The gross enrollment in private health insurance plans for 1940 to 1970 is given in Figure 5-1. These trends indicate substantial continuous growth in gross enrollments for both hospital and surgical coverage during the more than thirty-year period. The most recent data for gross enrollment in 1972 indicates that approximately 221 million persons were enrolled in various plans for hospitalization coverage. A slightly lower number (201 million) were covered by surgical insurance plans. Estimates for *net* enrollment for 1972, made by adjusting for double-counting of multiple coverage by individuals under more than one policy, brings the *actual* number of persons enrolled in some type of hospital coverage plan within a range of 160 to 180 million. The net enrollment of persons with surgical coverage is also at a slightly lower level.[2] While the major portion of the market for voluntary health insurance is met by Blue Cross-Blue Shield plans, many private insurance companies offer health insurance coverage. The recent trend in enrollment for this group of companies reflects a more rapid growth than for the Blue Cross-Blue Shield plans.[3]

While this aggregate data gives a quick picture of the growth of enrollment in private health insurance plans, additional information on enrollment by particular groups within the population paints a somewhat different picture. Table 5-1 presents estimates of the net number of persons covered under private health insurance plans and the percent of the population covered by age groups and for specified types of health care services at the end of 1972. When all ages are included, the percent of the population covered for hospital care (70 percent) and surgical services (74 percent) is the highest proportion. About half of the population, presumably those covered also for hospital and surgical services, had some type of coverage for prescription drugs, private-duty nursing, and visiting nursing services. However, less than half of the population is covered by health insurance for physicians' office and home visits and as little as 22 percent for nursing-home care and 9 percent for dental care.[4]

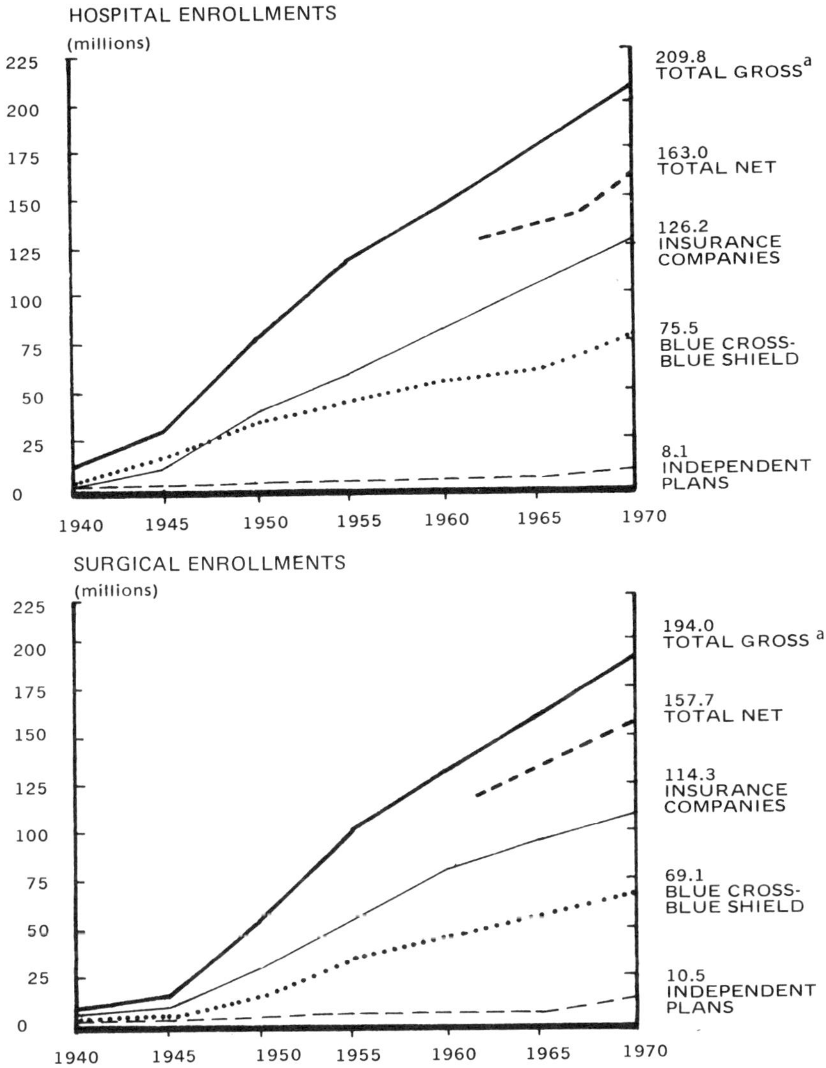

[a]Gross enrollment contains duplication because of multiple coverage of individuals through supplementary plans and policies. The net number of different persons covered (which eliminates duplication) is estimated for 1962 and 1967 by the Social Security Administration on the basis of household surveys. The 1970 estimate is derived by applying HIAA percentage increase in net enrollment to the 1969 estimate (not shown).

Source: Marjorie Smith Mueller, "Private Health Insurance in 1970: Population Coverage, Enrollment, and Financial Experience," *Social Security Bulletin*, Vol. 35, No. 2 (February, 1972), Tables 6 and 7.

Figure 5-1. Gross Enrollment under Private Hospital and Surgical Insurance Plans, 1940-1970

Table 5-1
Estimates of Net Number of Different Persons under Private Health Insurance Plans and Percent of Population Covered, by Age and Specified Type of Care, as of December 31, 1972

	All Ages		*Under Age 65*		*Aged 65 and Over*	
Type of Service	*Number (in Thousands)*	*Percent of Civilian Population*	*Number (in Thousands)*	*Percent of Civilian Population*	*Number (in Thousands)*	*Percent of Civilian Population*
Hospital care	159,526	77.0	148,285	79.7	11,270	53.2
Physicians' services						
Surgical services	153,326	74.0	143,525	77.1	9,813	46.3
Inhospital visits	149,734	72.2	141,579	76.1	8,155	38.5
X-ray and laboratory examinations	149,444	72.1	141,694	76.1	7,750	36.6
Office and home visits	99,914	48.2	95,568	51.3	4,346	20.5
Dental care	17,904	8.6	17,608	9.5	296	1.4
Prescribed drugs (out of hospital)	111,374	53.7	107,855	58.0	3,519	16.6
Private-duty nursing	108,959	52.6	105,518	56.7	3,441	16.3
Visiting-nurse service	115,904	55.9	111,416	59.9	4,488	21.2
Nursing-home care	45,460	21.9	39,987	21.5	5,473	25.8
HIAA estimates						
Hospital care	181,602	87.6	169,555	91.1	12,047	56.9
Surgical services	166,261	80.2	156,646	84.2	9,615	45.4

Source: Marjorie S. Mueller, "Private Health Insurance in 1972: Health Care Services, Enrollment and Finances," *Social Security Bulletin*, Vol. 36, No. 3 (March, 1974), Table 1.

Comparison of categories by type of covered services for the "under sixty-five years" and the "sixty-five years and over" age groups shows relatively higher percentages for the former group and significantly lower percentages for the latter group. These data do not incorporate Medicare coverage, the federal health insurance program for the elderly, and it is reasonable to assume that at least the greater portion of the discrepancy in the extent of coverage for the elderly population is due to the role of the Medicare program.

The most recent data available for private health insurance enrollment by family income groups are from a 1968 survey. Table 5-2 presents the number and percent of persons under sixty-five years of age with hospital and surgical insurance coverage by family income for 1968. Relatively minor differences are shown between these two types of insurance coverage *within* any given income group, but substantial increases in the percent insured occur as total family income increases from a level of "under $3,000" to "$15,000 and over." The income group of $5,000-$6,999, for example, is associated with approximately the average percent of persons covered. However, the distribution of percentages is such that in the "under $3,000" category less than 40 percent of the persons are covered, while for persons with family income of $10,000 or more, the percent covered is greater than 90 percent.

Data for an earlier period, July 1962 to June 1963, given in Table 5-3, suggest that the increases in the percentage of the population covered by hospital and surgical insurance by family income groups have been rather small within the five-year period of comparison. Although obviously the population base itself has increased over time and other factors such as family size and employment situations have altered, the more recent levels of enrollment in private health insurance plans in terms of the percent covered in each family income group may rep-

Table 5-2
Number and Percent of Persons under 65 Years with Hospital and Surgical Insurance by Family Income, 1968

Family Income ($)	*Total Population*	*Hospital Insurance*		*Surgical Insurance*	
All incomes	177,051	138,485	(78.2%)	135,580	(76.6%)
Under 3,000	16,324	5,933	(36.3)	5,685	(34.8)
3,000-4,999	20,792	11,806	(56.8)	11,356	(54.6)
5,000-6,999	34,262	26,880	(78.5)	26,271	(76.7)
7,000-9,999	41,019	36,621	(89.3)	36,028	(87.8)
10,000-14,999	36,685	33,729	(91.9)	33,267	(90.7)
15,000 and over	18,795	17,484	(93.0)	17,044	(90.7)

Source: "Hospital and Surgical Insurance Coverage–1968," *Vital and Health Statistics*, Series 10, No. 66, Table 3.

Table 5-3
Percent of Persons under 65 Years with Hospital and Surgical Insurance by Family Income for July 1962 to June 1963

Family Income ($)	*Hospital Insurance*	*Surgical Insurance*
All incomes	72.5%	67.2%
Under 2,000	38.0	25.0
2,000-3,999	49.4	45.5
4,000-6,999	80.4	75.9
7,000-9,999	88.8	85.1
10,000 and over	90.0	85.5

Source: "Health Insurance Coverage, United States–July 1962-June 1963," *Vital and Health Statistics*, Series 10, No. 11, Tables 1 and 6.

resent a relatively stable percentage. (The family income categories are not the same in Tables 5-2 and 5-3 and must be taken into account when interpreting any differences.) When more significant increases have occurred in coverage over time, these increases have not, however, been concentrated in the lower-income groups with the lowest percentages of coverage.

From the 1968 survey, information is available on those persons with no health insurance and the reasons they gave for having no coverage. Forty percent of all persons under sixty-five years stated that they could not afford health insurance, while 17 percent gave as a reason that other type of assistance was available. However, when the level of family income is given consideration also, 56 percent in the "under $3,000" group and 48 percent in the $3,000-$4,999 group listed inability to afford insurance as their reason for not having coverage. For the $10,000-$14,999 group, only 9 percent have this reason, while 22 percent in the latter income group said other type of aid is available and 37 percent gave other reasons in general. It is interesting to note that relatively large numbers of persons in the higher income groups stated that health insurance is not available or not obtainable, that they did not "believe" in insurance, or had good health, although these kinds of reasons were given by a very small percentage of those in the lower- and middle-income groups.[5]

Age is a primary factor in describing the extent of health insurance coverage for persons in various family income groups. Figure 5-2 gives the percentage of children covered by hospital insurance for family income groups. In 1968, less than one-fourth of children under seventeen years of age in families with an income of under $3,000 were covered by hospital insurance; for family income of $3,000-$4,999, less than half of the children had hospital insurance coverage. While certainly these percentages are substantially affected by the implementation of the federal Medicaid program for the poor and medically indigent in

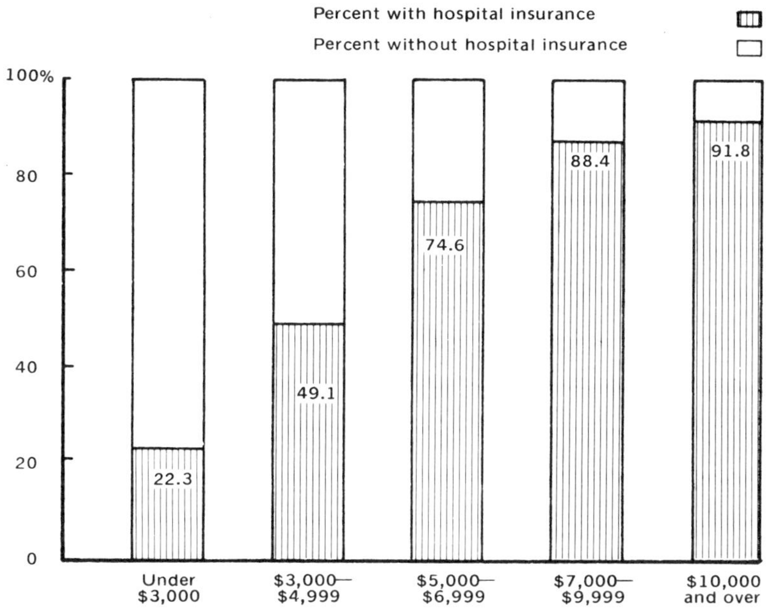

Source: U.S. Department of Health, Education and Welfare, Public Health Service, National Center for Health Statistics, *Monthly Vital Statistics Report,* Vol. 18, No. 11, Supp. 2 (February 2, 1970), Table 2.

Figure 5-2. Hospital Insurance Coverage for Children (under 17 Years of Age) by Family Income, 1968

1966, it does appear that without these and other types of health care programs literally millions of children in the United States can face the possibility of postponed hospitalization until the most critical stages of need occur and always with major financial burdens for the family. In addition, family size interacts with the age factors and the income level. Generally, less than complete health insurance coverage for all family members results as the family size increases.

Further, indices of health status, e.g., the proportion of the population with limitation on the amount of or kind of major activity due to chronic conditions, indicate that persons with higher incomes are healthier than those in the lower-income groups. Data collected in household interviews during 1969 and 1970 indicate that the proportion of the population with activity-limiting chronic conditions for the "under $3,000" income group is 14.7 percent and declines progressively to a level of 3.8 percent for the "$15,000 and over" income group.[6] The respective percentages for all age classes under sixty-five years show comparable unfavorable differentials for the low-income group of at least double that for the high-income group. Thus, the need for health insurance coverage is greater for the lower-income families.

Benefits

Benefit expenditures paid by all private health insurance organizations in 1972 totaled almost $20 billion. Of this total, more than $12 billion was benefits for hospital care and more than $6 billion for physicians' services. The proportion of the total benefits which represents expenditures for hospital care has declined almost continually since 1950 to a level of 62 percent in 1972. Benefit payments for physicians' services remained relatively stable at about 30 percent of the total benefits during these twenty years. The decline in the percentage distribution of benefits for hospital care was compensated for by an increase in the percentage of benefits that paid for dental care, drugs, private duty nursing, etc.[7]

In 1972, 42 percent of total consumer health care expenditures were actually paid by private health insurance benefits. (Consumer expenditures for health care include some items *not* covered by health insurance, i.e., nonprescription drugs, various drug sundries, and sunglasses, and do *not* include health insurance premiums.) Figure 5-3 presents the trend in the proportion of consumer expenditures for all health care services, hospital care, physicians' services, and other types of health care met by private health insurance for 1950 to 1972. The relatively low ratio of total insurance benefits to expenditures is due to: (1) the large amounts of expenditures made by those consumers who do not have private health insurance coverage; (2) the limitation on the kinds of health services which private insurance benefits cover; and (3) the amount of out-of-pocket expenditures that remains to be paid by the consumer who does have insurance coverage, but must also make coinsurance and deductible payments, forms of consumer cost sharing.

The upward trend in physicians' services benefits as a percentage of total expenditures indicates some acceleration. However, what is important is the fact that as recently as 1972, only 45.3 percent of consumer health care expenditures for physicians' services were covered by private health insurance benefits, particularly when it is considered that a large portion of the benefits received were for physician visits for inpatient hospital care. Benefits for all other types of care represented only 6.7 percent of the total consumer expenditures in 1972.

One author writes that "a gradually increasing share of expenditures going to non-hospital, non-physicians' services suggests a broadening and deepening coverage of health insurance plans over the years."[8] In the context of national health insurance and income distribution, the question then becomes one of broadening and deepening of coverage for whom. From the data available on private health insurance enrollment by income groups, the answer is probably for those high-income groups who already have high rates of enrollment in hospital, surgical, and major medical plans, rather than for low-income groups.

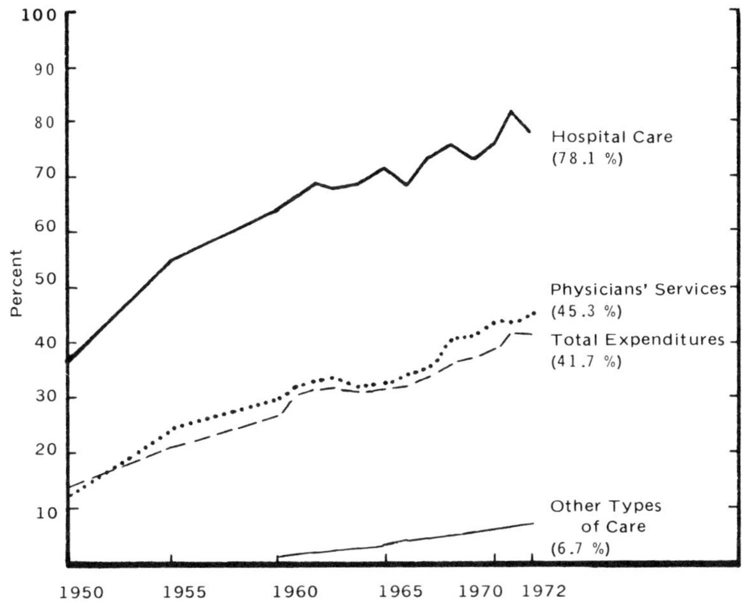

Source: Marjorie Smith Mueller, "Private Health Insurance in 1972: Health Care Services, Enrollment, and Finances," *Social Security Bulletin,* Vol. 37, No. 2 (March, 1974), p. 38.

Figure 5-3. Proportion of Consumer Health Care Met by Private Health Insurance, 1950-1972

Costs

The total net cost of private health insurance in 1972 was $2.8 billion, an increase of $900 million from the previous year. The net cost is the difference between earned premium or subscription income and benefit expenditures.[9]

For the family or individual who is enrolled in a private health insurance plan, the actual cost translates into an annual premium or subscription rate of several hundred dollars (for, at best, partial coverage of services and with coinsurance and deductibles built into the plan). Krizay and Wilson, in their study, use a range of annual premiums from $525 to $630 for a family of four when discussing "typical" plans offered by three different insurance companies.[10]

Most health insurance policies have some form of cost sharing for the consumer; it is expected that if the consumers must pay for part of the cost of services, they will consciously restrain their consumption of health care within rational behavior or at least not increase their consumption beyond what is necessary for purposes of good health. The two most common types of cost sharing schemes are deductibles and coinsurance. With a *deductible* scheme, the consumer pays all of some level of initial expenses, e.g., the first $100 is assumed as cost by the consumer, but hereafter total insurance benefit coverage begins. With a *coinsurance* scheme, the consumer pays some percentage of the expenditures no matter when the expenditures occur or no matter what the overall amount of the expenditures. With a *copayment* scheme, the consumer pays a fixed charge per unit of service, e.g., $2.00 is paid for each prescription, regardless of the actual cost. Also, *indemnity* payments are a form of cost sharing whereby the consumer receives a fixed payment per unit of service from the insurance company, regardless of the actual amount of the expenditures.[11] Therefore, the least expensive health insurance policy in terms of the annual premium may not ultimately result in lower actual out-of-pocket expenditures, since the effects of the cost sharing schemes must also be considered. Further discussion of the cost sharing arrangements that are incorporated into the various national health insurance proposals is given in Chapter 8.

The health care industry has not been spared the recent problems of inflation. In fact, the medical care component of the consumer price index has increased faster than the average of all goods and services, with hospital semiprivate room rates showing the largest increase. Although there are arguments that focus on the supply factors, such as hospital costs and shortages in the health labor force as major contributors to this inflation, there are also arguments that attribute the rapid inflation to demand factors, initiated by the Medicare and Medicaid programs and the growth and the role of private health insurance coverage. Any national health insurance plan must attempt to control the rising costs of health care by reliance on the lessons learned from the experiences of Medicare and Medicaid, the private health insurance industry, and the role of third-party payers. Simultaneous measures will also need to be considered in alleviating the inflationary effects of supply factors.[12]

Two further topics are of interest in a discussion of the costs of private health insurance—the special case of catastrophic illness coverage and the role of the medical deduction on personal income tax returns. The costs of catastrophic illness far exceed the regular expenses of more common brief periods of poor health and, moreover, are usually sudden and unpredicted. Health insurance policies often attach a limit to the overall dollar maximum that will be paid out to the insured person in the form of benefits. Because of the financial burdens placed on the family or individual faced with the costs of catastrophic illness, many of the national health insurance proposals include means to provide some type of financial support for these special cases.[13]

Mitchell and Vogel in their study of medical tax deductions report that:

> In 1970 the medical deduction under the personal income tax and the government's failure to tax health insurance premiums paid by employers reduced

federal revenues by $3.8 billion . . . The features of the present law (federal tax policy) create an IRS (Internal Revenue Service) plan whose benefit structure consists of a deductible proportional to income and a coinsurance rate that declines with income. The net result of this mixture of income-related cost-sharing provisions is an average benefit (subsidy) per taxpayer that *increases* with income.[14]

What this means then is that the taxpayers who do *not* have health insurance directly or through their employers or who do not have out-of-pocket expenditures in excess of 3 percent of adjusted gross income receive no subsidy. The tax subsidies instead are paid to families or individuals with health insurance coverage for reimbursement of health care expenses that are not covered by their insurance plan.

Employee Health Insurance Plans

In 1972, 70 percent of the estimated 46 million full-time workers in private industry and government jobs were covered by some type of group health insurance coverage through their employment. Those who were not enrolled were more likely to be: low wage earners; in the agricultural, construction, trade and service industries; self-employed; women, and nonwhite. About half of those workers covered on their job had hospital, surgical, and medical protection; the majority of the others had only hospital and surgical coverage. For about a third of these workers in group health insurance plans, their employer paid the full cost of coverage; another 47 percent of these workers shared a portion of the cost of the plan with their employers.[15]

Table 5-4 gives the trend in coverage and contributions under employee health insurance plans for the wage and salaried members of the labor force from 1950 to 1970. As is shown by the calculated percentages for covered employees, hospital and surgical insurance coverage reached a new level of about 80 percent of all wage and salaried workers in 1970. Twice as many workers were enrolled in regular medical plans as were enrolled in major medical plans. Therefore, a large proportion of these workers do not have comprehensive coverage, but rather partial benefits for particular types of health services only.

The total of both employer and employee contributions for health insurance as a percentage of total wages and salaries is also given in Table 5-4. The total costs of hospital insurance measured in these terms more than doubled from 1950 to 1970, when combined contributions represented 1.45 percent of total wages and salaries. The percentage contribution for surgical and regular medical coverage also increased during this same period. However, in 1970 this coverage was only about half as expensive as hospital insurance, given the marginal differences in the percent of employees covered for the different types of plans. Employee-employer contributions under the major medical plans as a percent of total wages and salaries have a higher growth rate than for the other types of

Table 5-4
Coverage and Contributions under Employee Benefit Plans, by Type of Benefit in Relation to Employed Wage and Salaried Labor Force Members–1950-1970[a]

Year	*Hospitalization*	*Surgical*	*Regular Medical*	*Major Medical*
	Covered Employees as Percent of All Wage and Salary Workers[b]			
1950	48.7%	35.5%	16.4%	
1955	60.0	54.7	37.0	4.0%
1960	68.9	65.5	50.2	16.5
1961	71.3	68.4	53.6	19.7
1962	71.5	68.5	54.5	21.2
1963	73.5	70.7	56.7	23.7
1964	73.8	71.2	58.3	24.8
1965	74.3	72.0	60.3	26.8
1966	73.0	70.8	60.1	27.7
1967	74.3	72.5	62.6	30.2
1968	75.7	73.6	63.9	31.6
1969	77.2	76.0	66.2	33.1
1970	80.2	79.2	71.1	35.8
	Employer and Employee Contributions as a Percentage of All Wages and Salaries[c]			
1950	0.40%	0.21%		
1955	0.69	0.38		0.02%
1960	0.96	0.49		0.18
1961	1.06	0.54		0.24
1962	1.11	0.56		0.26
1963	1.16	0.56		0.28
1964	1.21	0.58		0.30
1965	1.25	0.61		0.31
1966	1.20	0.61		0.31
1967	1.16	0.63		0.32
1968	1.23	0.65		0.36
1969	1.29	0.69		0.38
1970	1.45	0.77		0.44

[a]Plans whose benefits flow from the employment relationship and are not underwritten or paid directly by government (federal, state, or local). Excludes workmen's compensation required by statute and employer's liability.

[b]Coverage of private and public employees related to average number of private and government full-time and part-time civilian employees–74.3 million in 1970. See *Survey of Current Business* (July, 1971), Table 6.3 and the *National Income and Product Accounts of the United States, 1929-1965 Statistical Tables* (Supplement to the Survey of Current Business), 1966.

[c]Amounts for private and public employees related to private and government civilian wages and salaries–$552.0 billion in 1970. Data for surgical and regular medical benefits not available separately. See ibid., Table 6.2.

Source: Walter W. Kolodrubetz, "Two Decades of Employee-Benefit Plans, 1950-70: A Review," *Social Security Bulletin,* Vol. 34, No. 4 (April, 1972), p. 17.

plans. However, it appears from these data that if the same coverage rate for hospital insurance were applied to the major medical enrollment for employees, total cost as a percent of total wages and salaries would be lower than the contributions for hospital coverage.

Government's Role with Private Health Insurance

In fiscal year 1973, government (federal, state, and local) paid thirty-eight cents out of every dollar spent for personal health care services. These expenditures totaled more than $30 billion. Of this total, the federal government spent twice as much ($20 billion) as state and local governments ($10 billion). Prior to the introduction of the Medicare and Medicaid programs, the federal government and the state and local governments each assumed approximately half of the expenditures in the public sector.[16]

Under the structure of present health programs, the public sector through government agencies frequently contracts with private health insurance organizations to act as intermediaries or fiscal agents for such government health programs as Medicare, Medicaid, and CHAMPUS (Civilian Health and Medical Program of the Uniformed Services). These private health insurance organizations, primarily Blue Cross and Blue Shield plans and insurance companies,

> . . . pay hospitals, physicians and other providers of service for care rendered to the beneficiaries of these programs or [to] reimburse beneficiaries for provider charges paid directly. In this capacity, the intermediaries or fiscal agents assume no risk-taking or underwriting function; they are reimbursed in full by the responsible governmental agency for all payments made to providers of care or to beneficiaries and for their administrative expenses incurred in carrying on the work.[17]

While the advantages and disadvantages of government's role with private health insurance organizations continue to be debated in terms of cost, controls, flexibility, and overall efficiency, the use of these organizations as financial intermediaries and fiscal agents by the government represents a significant portion of the private health insurance industry's regular business.[18] (See Figure 5-4.) In 1968, 58 percent of total claims paid by Blue Cross ($8.6 billion) were for government programs and only 42 percent for their regular business. Of the $2.7 billion disbursements made by Blue Shield in 1972, 45 percent was for government business and the remainder for regular business. The seventeen private health insurance companies that also contracted as fiscal agents for government programs paid out 19 percent of their total payments for government business.[19]

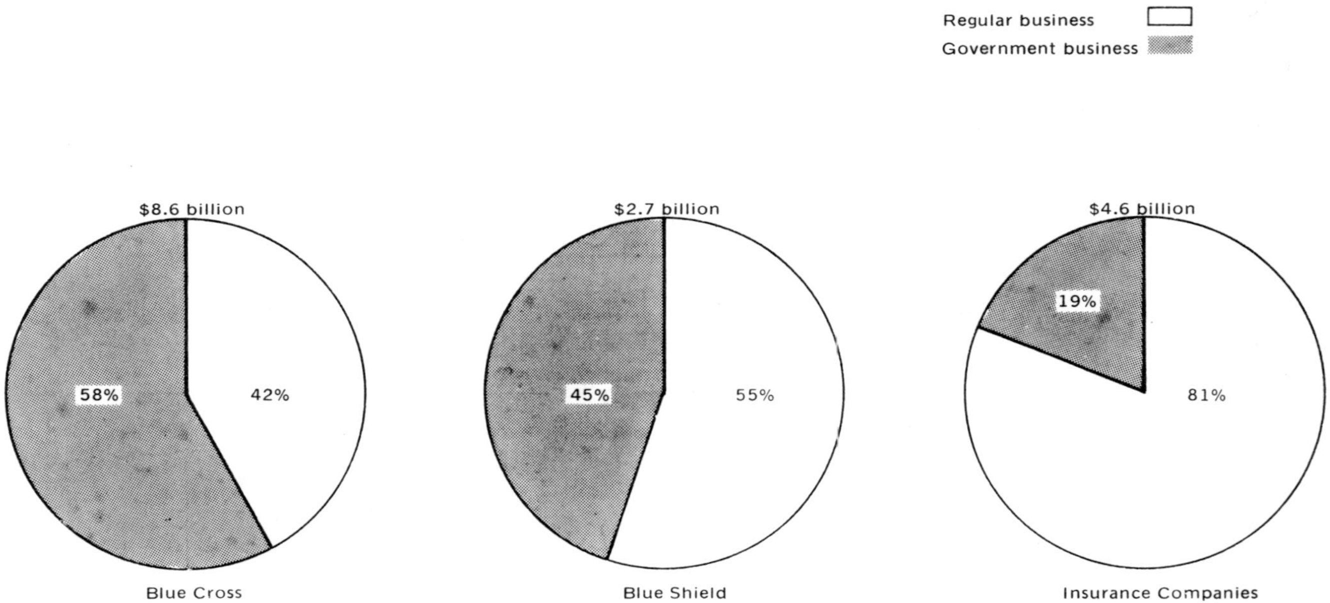

Source: Louis S. Reed, *Private Health Insurance Organizations as Intermediaries or Fiscal Agents under Government Health Programs,* Staff Paper No. 7, Office of Research and Statistics, Social Security Administration, Department of Health, Education, and Welfare (January, 1971), pp. 9–10, 12.

Figure 5–4. Portion of Private Health Insurance Business Serving as Intermediaries for Government Programs, 1968

Health Maintenance Organizations as an Alternative

The concept of the health maintenance organization (HMO) incorporates several components in providing for more efficient and effective delivery of health care services. These components are: (1) fixed population of enrollment, (2) comprehensive care services, (3) group medical practice, and (4) prepayment for services. Our concern here is with the prepayment for services as an alternative to the traditional fee-for-service system whereby the insured is reimbursed by third-party payers, i.e., Blue Cross-Blue Shield and private health insurance companies.

By 1972, approximately 11 million persons or about 6 percent of the population were enrolled in HMOs, primarily in the older and well-established ones, such as the Kaiser Plan in California or the Health Insurance Plan of Greater New York, but also in other "independent" plans.[20] As the consumer becomes more knowledgeable and informed of the alternative of HMO enrollment—and the growth of the number of HMOs provides more options for more consumers—it is predicted that HMO enrollment will greatly increase. Several recent developments will assist the process of growth of HMOs. First, the commitment on the part of the Administration and the Congress to the HMO concept as evidenced by the passing of Public Law 93-222, the Health Maintenance Organization Act of 1973. This act provides for grants, contracts, and loans for the initial operating costs of HMOs and formulates guidelines, goals, and requirements for HMOs. Second, Medicare and Medicaid recipients can now be included in an HMO enrollment. Third, the HMO Act mandates that employers with over twenty-five employees must offer the HMO as an option, where one is located within the community involved. Finally, the private health insurance organizations, and particularly Blue Cross-Blue Shield, have taken on the task of forming HMOs, and through this process the private health insurance industry will be able to offer to its subscribers the dual option of HMO or prepaid type of coverage versus indemnity insurance.

Notes

1. For a complete discussion of the private health insurance industry, see John Krizay and Andrew Wilson, *The Patient as a Consumer: Health Care in the United States,* (Lexington, Mass.: Lexington Books, 1974).

2. Marjorie S. Mueller, "Private Health Insurance in 1972: Health Care Services, Enrollment and Finances," *Social Security Bulletin* (March, 1974), Table 2.

3. "Blue Cross and Blue Shield are not private companies but nonprofit organizations whose tax-exempt status gives them some advantages in competing with the private carriers. Actually, Blue Cross-Blue Shield consists of 75 Blue Cross plans and 72 Blue Shield plans, each of which is autonomous, local, and only loosely affiliated nationally." See Krizay and Wilson, op. cit., p. 6.

4. In 1972, approximately 143 million persons wer enrolled in "regular medical expense" plans with Blue Cross-Blue Shield and insurance companies; only 80 million or 37 percent of the population had "major medical" policies with insurance companies. Major medical expense insurance is provided as a supplement to basic hospital-surgical or regular medical insurance policies, or as comprehensive protection where both basic and extended health care benefits are offered as a unit. See *Source Book of Health Insurance Data, 1973–74* (New York: Health Insurance Institute, 1974), pp. 23–24 and *Source Book of Health Insurance Data, 1971–72,* p. 24.

5. "Medical Care, Health Status and Family Income, United States," *Vital and Health Statistics,* Series 10, No. 9, Table 17.

6. "Limitation of Activity due to Chronic Conditions, United States, 1969 and 1970," *Vital and Health Statistics,* Series 10, No. 80, Table 3.

7. Mueller, op. cit., Table 19.

8. *Ibid*., p. 36.

9. The net cost of private health insurance is comprised of operating expenses and net underwriting gain or loss. It represents the retention by the carriers:

> . . . to cover operating expenses, profits, and such additions to reserves not accounted for by deductions from premium income or inclusion in claims expense. The net underwriting gain is used for additions to reserves and profits. In years when there is a net underwriting loss, part of the retention is a deficit that is met from previously accumulated reserves or by borrowing.

See *Social Security Bulletin* (March, 1973), pp. 37-38.

10. The typical Aetna plan ($630.72) pays 80 percent of all eligible expenses for both inpatient and outpatient care, over $50 per covered person per year and pays all of the first $1,000 for hospital expenses and all hospital expenses over $10,000. This plan has no internal maximums, no limits on hospital days, no surgical benefit schedule and no restrictions on the number of psychiatric visits. The lifetime maximum is $50,000, with an annual $2,000 restoration feature thereafter.

The typical Blue Cross-Blue Shield plan ($574.92) is a comprehensive plan which includes the basic plan for hospital-surgical coverage and a deductible of $100 for expenses covered by either supplementary or major medical plan.

The typical Prudential plan ($525.12) is also a basic first-dollar hospital-surgical coverage and a major medical supplement that has deductibles that vary according to the enrollee's income. The lifetime maximum is $100,000 but only 50 percent of the cost of psychiatric treatment is paid at only $20 per visit. Moreover, the amount of the deductible must be incurred within a ninety-day period. See Krizay and Wilson, op. cit., p. 24.

11. Paul B. Ginsburg and Larry M. Manheim, "Insurance, Copayment, and Health Services: A Critical Review," *Journal of Economics and Business,* Vol. 25, No. 3 (Spring-Summer, 1973), 142.

12. Bruce Stuart and Ronald Stockton, "Control over the Utilization of Medical Services," *Milbank Memorial Fund Quarterly* (Summer, 1973), 341-394.

13. Richard J. Zeckhauser, "Coverage for Catastrophic Illness," *Public Policy* (Spring, 1973), 149-172.

14. Bridger M. Mitchell and Ronald J. Vogel, *Health and Taxes: An Assessment of the Medical Deduction* (Santa Monica, Ca.: Rand Corp., August 1973), p. v.

15. Walter W. Kolodrubetz, "Group Health Insurance Coverage of Full-Time Employees, 1972," *Social Security Bulletin* (April 1974), p. 17.

16. Mueller, op. cit., p. 6.

17. Louis S. Reed, "Private Health Insurance Organizations as Intermediaries or Fiscal Agents under Government Health Programs," *Staff Paper No. 7,* Social Security Administration, Office of Research and Statistics (January 1971), p. 1.

18. Data available on the operating expenses of 74 Blue Cross plans and 73 Blue Shield plans from 1965 through 1969 show that nationally operating expenses, on a *per enrollee* basis, increased by 66 percent for Blue Cross and 61 percent for Blue Shield plans. In 1969, operating expenses per enrollee ranged from $1.18 to $8.74 among the Blue Cross plans. This inflation in the operating expenses of private health insurance warrants further assessment, and any national health insurance program that would rely on private health insurance organizations as fiscal intermediaries must, therefore, be carefully evaluated for this reason. See Robert J. Weiss, William H. Wiese, and Joel C. Kleinman, "Trends in Health-Insurance Operating Expenses," *The New England Journal of Medicine,* Vol. 287, No. 13 (September 28, 1972), 638.

19. Reed, op. cit., pp. 1-2.

20. Mueller, op. cit., p. 22.

6 The Utilization of Personal Health Services by Family Income Groups

The tenet that "health care is a right" grows out of the profound concern among citizens and policymakers with the distribution of health care services by geographic area, by age groups, and by socioeconomic status. Proposed national health insurance legislation as a major policy measure directed at the financing of health services portends to legitimize health care as a right for all persons, regardless of income, and not only as a privilege for those who can afford it. In order to understand the impact that the distribution of covered service benefits under the various national health insurance proposals will have on the utilization of health services across income groups, it is necessary first to examine the recent patterns of use of health services by income groups.

The utilization of personal health services is influenced by a number of different but often interrelated factors, such as age, race, income, health status, access to services, health insurance coverage, occupation, and education.[1] This chapter focuses discussion on the relationship between family income and the utilization of the two dominant types of services, i.e., hospital care and physician services. Chapter 7 then extends the investigation to the relationship between family income and the utilization of health services as measured by the expenditures made for health services. The data employed in these two chapters are primarily abstracted from the reports of national health surveys conducted by the Center for Health Administration Studies of the University of Chicago.[2]

In recent years, the pattern of use of health services across income groups has altered significantly. In this regard, most studies of the relationship of utilization of health services and family income have the major disadvantage of not employing current data. Possibly because of the long periods of time necessary to collect, analyze, and report information based on national surveys, commonly voiced facts and conclusions rely on out-of-date staistics that can misdirect policy. While there are a number of advantages to the data source employed in the discussion of this chapter, including the survey methodology and verification process, the current status of its information for a very large number of population characteristics is of significant relevance for setting forth policy options on the issue of national health insurance.

One difficulty in interpreting the data is the fact that the report of the survey includes unrelated individuals in the definition of family, as a family of size one. Hence, the lowest family income group includes many persons, sixty-five years and over, whose hospital care expenses, in particular, are covered by the Medicare program. To the extent that information is also available on the utilization of health services by family income *and* by age, the effects of this family classification scheme can at least be partially ameliorated. In addition, the discussion in Chapter 7 of expenditures for health services by family income groups will directly investigate the sources of payments for health services, including the Medicare program.

In the discussion that follows, the use of hospital care and the use of physician services are reviewed as two distinct types of health services, although in an economic sense they might be considered as either complements or substitutes in a specified demand function for health care. The concluding remarks attempt to indicate the possible interrelationships between the utilization of these two types of health services across income groups.

Utilization of Hospital Care

This section describes the pattern of hospital care utilization by family income groups in 1970.[3] Historical data on the use of hospital care are presented to permit comparisons of the relationship between the use of hospital care services and family income over time. Several different measures of utilization are specified in order to test the consistency of the relationship.

Hospital Admissions

The rate of hospital admissions *per person per year* by family income groups is given in Table 6-1. The most recent data for 1970 indicate an inverse relationship between family income levels and the rate of hospital admissions. That is, as the level of family income increases, the rate of hospital admissions decreases. However, a number of changes in the pattern of hospital admissions have occurred as reported in the data for the earlier three survey years. In 1953, persons at all income levels had approximately the same rate of hospital admissions, i.e., 12 admissions per 100 person-years. By 1958, increases in the rates for two lower-income groups occurred, while the rates for the higher-income groups indicated a slight decline. Similar kinds of changes resulted in 1963, but with the differences between the rates for the lowest-income class and the highest-income classes widening. A clearly defined inverse relationship across income groups is not apparent in the 1963 data alone.

By 1970, the pattern of use of hospital care measured by the rate of admissions shows the lowest-income class with a rate more than double the rate for the highest-income class. While the significant increases in the rates for the low-income groups might be partially explained by the introduction of the Medicare and Medicaid programs in 1966, the longer historical trend in the data suggests that the tendency for the low-income groups to have higher rates was present for several years prior to the establishment of these programs. In order to better

Table 6-1
Hospital Admissions per 100 Person-years by Family Income—1953, 1958, 1963, and 1970

	Hospital Admissions per 100 Person-years			
Family Income ($)	*1953*	*1958*	*1963*	*1970*
0- 1,999	12	14	16	19
2,000- 3,499	12	12	12	16
3,500- 4,999	12	14	12	17
5,000- 7,499	12	12	14	16
7,500- 9,999			14	15
10,000-12,499			11	12
12,500-14,999	11	10		11
15,000-17,499			10	11
17,500 and over				9

Source: *Health Services Use: National Trends and Variations, 1953-1971,* Ronald Andersen, Study Director, Department of Health, Education and Welfare, Health Services and Mental Health Administration (October, 1972), Table 12.

describe the trends in the relationship between family income and use of hospital care services, the rates of hospital admissions by family income and by age groups are discussed below.

Hospital Admissions by Age Groups

Data on hospital admissions per 100 person-years by family income and by age groups is given in Table 6-2. For the 0-17 age group, the direct relationship of utilization of hospital care and family income in 1963 changed to an inverse relationship in 1970, when children in the lower-income groups experienced rates of hospital admissions double the rates for children in the higher-income groups. For the 18-54 age group, the largest increases in the rate of hospital admissions from 1963 to 1970 occurred for the lower-income classes. The $5,000-$9,999 income groups experienced a slight decline in the rate, with the two higher-income groups maintaining about the same rate over this time period on the average. Therefore, for this age group also, the rate of hospital admissions for the lowest-income group is double the rate for the highest income groups. Since this age group is not eligible for Medicare coverage, there appear to be other reasons for the upward trend in hospital admissions for the low-income groups.[4] The 55 years and over age group has a somewhat consistent rate of admissions across family income levels in 1970. This recent pattern of use of hospital care occurred due to large increases in the rate of hospital admissions for the middle- and high-income groups, together with the slight decline in the

Table 6-2
Hospital Admissions per 100 Person-years by Family Income and Age Groups, 1963 and 1970

<table>
<tr><th></th><th colspan="6">Age</th></tr>
<tr><th></th><th colspan="2">0-17</th><th colspan="2">18-54</th><th colspan="2">55 and over</th></tr>
<tr><th>Family Income ($)</th><th>1963</th><th>1970</th><th>1963</th><th>1970</th><th>1963</th><th>1970</th></tr>
<tr><td>0- 1,999</td><td>5</td><td>11</td><td>20</td><td>27</td><td>21</td><td>20</td></tr>
<tr><td>2,000- 4,999</td><td>6</td><td>8</td><td>15</td><td>22</td><td>14</td><td>19</td></tr>
<tr><td>5,000- 9,999</td><td>7</td><td>9</td><td>19</td><td>18</td><td>19</td><td>23</td></tr>
<tr><td>10,000-14,999</td><td rowspan="2">7</td><td>4 } 5</td><td rowspan="2">12</td><td>15 } 13</td><td rowspan="2">15</td><td>23 } 21</td></tr>
<tr><td>15,000 and over</td><td>7</td><td>9</td><td>19</td></tr>
<tr><td>Total</td><td>7</td><td>7</td><td>16</td><td>16</td><td>18</td><td>21</td></tr>
</table>

Source: *Health Services Use: National Trends and Variations, 1953-1971,* Ronald Andersen, Study Director, Department of Health, Education and Welfare, Health Services and Mental Health Administration (October, 1972), Table 13.

rates for the lower-income groups from 1963 to 1970. The largest increase in the rate, from fifteen to twenty-one admissions per 100 person-years, was for the combined income category of $10,000 and over.

Hospital Surgical Procedures

The recent inverse relationship between hospital care and family income is also largely supported by the data on the number of inhospital surgical procedures performed in 1970. (See Table 6-3.) This pattern of utilization is again a change from a more direct relationship in 1963 for the rate of surgical procedures across family income groups. The historical trends in the rates for the different levels of family income suggest that either unmet need was present for the low-income groups or overutilization of services occurred for the high-income groups in 1963, since the expected illness pattern across income would have the low-income groups probably requiring proportionately more hospitalization for surgery than the high-income groups. It seems reasonable, therefore, to associate some of these patterns of utilization with the variation in health insurance coverage, particularly since most health insurance provides some inhospital surgical benefits even for the minimum medical coverage plans. For example, the obvious differences in the number of surgical procedures per 100 person-years for the family income groups below $5,000 and the family income groups above $5,000 in 1963 could be related to the relatively high percentage of persons in the higher-income groups with health insurance coverage. The smaller surgical rates for the lower-income classes in the early sixties might be explained

Table 6-3
Inhospital Surgical Procedures per 100 Person-years by Family Income—1958, 1963, and 1970

<table>
<tr><th></th><th colspan="6">Procedures per 100 Person-years</th></tr>
<tr><th>Family Income ($)</th><th>1958</th><th colspan="2">1963</th><th colspan="3">1970</th></tr>
<tr><td>Under 2,000</td><td>5</td><td colspan="2">3</td><td colspan="3">7</td></tr>
<tr><td>2,000- 3,499</td><td>4</td><td colspan="2">4</td><td colspan="3">6</td></tr>
<tr><td>3,500- 4,999</td><td>5</td><td colspan="2">4</td><td colspan="3">7</td></tr>
<tr><td>5,000- 7,499</td><td>5</td><td colspan="2">6</td><td colspan="3">7</td></tr>
<tr><td>7,500- 9,999</td><td rowspan="5">4</td><td>7</td><td rowspan="5">6</td><td colspan="2">5</td><td rowspan="5">5</td></tr>
<tr><td>10,000-12,499</td><td>5</td><td colspan="2">6</td></tr>
<tr><td>12,500-14,999</td><td rowspan="3">4</td><td colspan="2">5</td></tr>
<tr><td>15,000-17,499</td><td>4</td><td rowspan="2">5</td></tr>
<tr><td>17,500 and over</td><td>5</td></tr>
</table>

Source: *Health Services Use: National Trends and Variations, 1953-1971,* Ronald Andersen, Study Director, Department of Health, Education and Welfare, Health Services and Mental Health Administration (October, 1972), Table 14.

by the low percentage of persons in these income groups that had health insurance coverage and other sources of payment, resulting at times in possible unmet needs for this type of hospital care. Similarly, the recent large increases in the number of surgical procedures associated with the lower-income groups may be affected by the benefit structure of the Medicare and Medicaid programs, although improved access to care should not be eliminated from any explanation of these patterns of utilization.[5]

Number of Hospital Episodes

Table 6-4 presents data on the number of persons hospitalized in 1968 by the number of hospital episodes across family income groups. Based on this data from the National Health Interview, not only do the lower-income classes have a relatively higher overall rate of hospital admissions, but also a greater proportion of persons in the lower-income groups have more than one hospital admission within a year.[a] The data show that more than twice as many persons in the "under $3,000" than in the "$10,000 plus" income class had two hospital episodes in 1968. A similar comparison of utilization by these two income groups for the three-plus hospital episode category finds the respective ratio almost three to one.

[a]The National Health Survey also employs a definition of family which includes unrelated individuals and measures family income by the definition given in note 3 of this chapter.

Table 6-4
Number of Persons Hospitalized per 1,000 Population per Year by Number of Hospital Episodes and by Family Income, 1968

	Number of Persons Hospitalized per 1,000 Population per Year			
		Number of Hospital Episodes		
Family Income ($)	*None*	*1*	*2*	*3 plus*
Total	904.4	81.9	10.4	3.3
Under 3,000	877.5	99.6	16.4	6.5
3,000-4,999	893.3	89.7	12.4	4.6
5,000-6,999	902.6	84.9	9.6	2.9
7,000-9,999	906.4	81.3	9.6	2.8
10,000 and over	918.2	71.3	8.1	2.3

Source: "Persons Hospitalized by Number of Hospital Episodes and Days in a Year, 1968," *Vital and Health Statistics*, Series 10, No. 64 (December, 1971), Table 1.

Length of Hospital Stay

The relationship between hospital care utilization and family income is further complicated by the variable influence of length of stay. Figure 6–1 gives the periods of hospital length of stay in 1968 by the percentage of persons with more than one short-term hospital episode and by family income. These data indicate a decrease in the percentage of persons hospitalized for the longer periods of stay as family income increases. Some slight increases do occur in the percentage of persons hospitalized at the higher-income levels for lengths of stay of 8-14 days and 15-30 days. Persons in the lower-income groups, because of limited or no insurance coverage or lack of alternative sources of financing, may postpone their expressed need for medical care until some more acute or critical stage of the illness and necessarily then require a longer period of hospitalization. Persons in the higher-income groups are more likely to have hospital insurance coverage and thus may, at times, take advantage of the "free" hospital services by extended hospital stays simply for the sake of convenience.

Physician Visits

The average number of physician visits per person-year by family income and by age groups in 1970 is given in Table 6–5. This recent data indicates a decline in the average number of physician visits for the total of all age groups as income

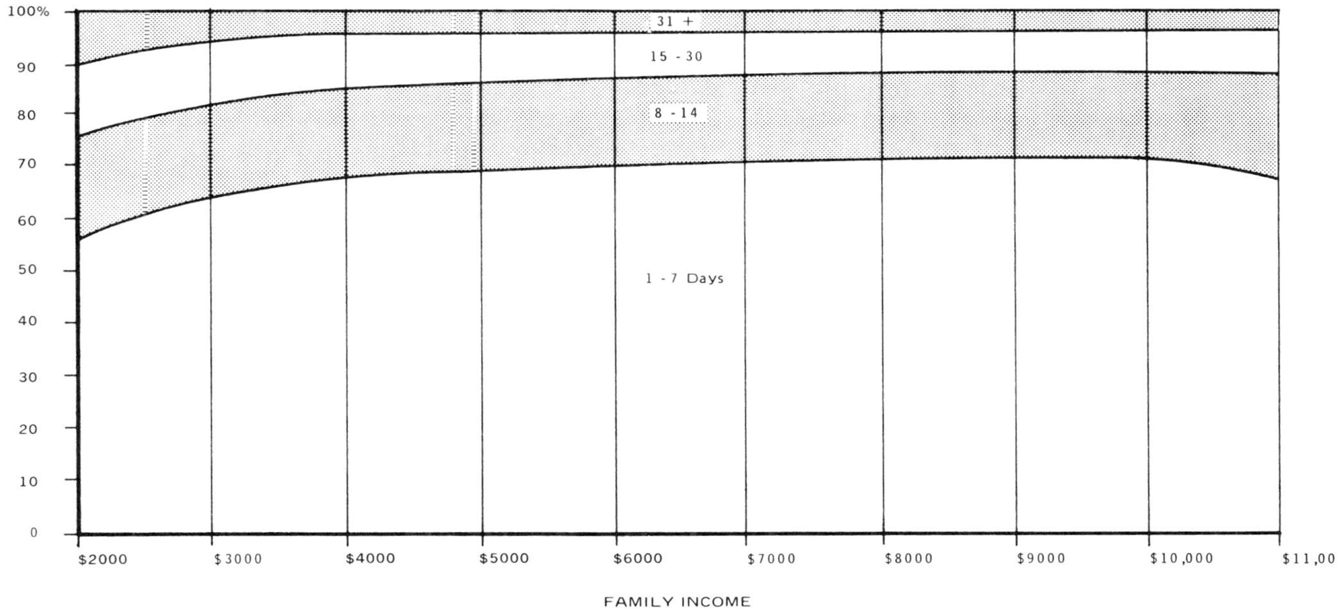

Source: "Persons Hospitalized by Number of Hospital Episodes and Days in a Year, 1968," *Vital & Health Statistics,* Series 10, No. 64 (December, 1971), Table 18.

Figure 6–1. Periods of Hospital Length of Stay by Percentage of Persons with More Than One Short-term Hospital Episode by Family Income, 1968

Table 6-5
Mean Number of Physician Visits by Age and by Family Income, 1970

	Visits per Person-year			*Visits per Person Seeing Physician*		
Age	*Low Income*	*Middle Income*	*High Income*	*Low Income*	*Middle Income*	*High Income*
0- 5	3.2	4.4	4.6	4.0	5.1	5.1
6-17	1.7	2.2	2.4	3.4	3.8	3.3
18-34	5.2	4.2	3.9	7.5	6.0	5.5
35-54	5.1	4.0	3.7	7.8	6.0	5.4
55-64	7.1	6.3	5.5	9.8	8.3	7.5
65 and over	6.3	6.4	6.7	8.6	7.4	7.9
Total	4.9	3.9	3.6	7.3	5.7	5.1

Source: *Health Services Use: National Trends and Variations, 1953-1971,* Ronald Andersen, Study Director, Department of Health, Education and Welfare, Health Services and Mental Health Administration (October, 1972), Table 8.

increases from low- to middle- to high-income levels.[b] When age and income class are both taken into account, the inverse relationship between family income and physician visits as a particular type of health service is not always confirmed. For example, the mean number of physician visits is greater for the middle- and high-income groups than for the low-income groups for children in both the 0-5 years and the 6-17 years age categories. Also, the number of visits per person-year for the sixty-five years and over age group is greater for the high-income groups than for either the low- or the middle-income groups. For all other age categories, persons in the low-income groups have the highest average number of visits and an inverse pattern of utilization is evident across the family income groups.

Table 6-5 also presents data on the average or mean number of physician visits for persons who had seen a physician during the year 1970. These data show, again with the critical exception of the number of visits by children, that the low-income groups have visit rates that are greater than for the middle- and high-income groups. That is, not only do low-income persons, on the average, utilize more outpatient physician services than do persons in the higher-income groups, but also those low-income persons who do see a physician have a greater number of visits within a year than comparable members of the higher-income groups.

[b]Income represented by each family income level:

	Low	*Middle*	*High*
1963	\$0–3,999	\$4,000– 6,999	\$ 7,000 plus
1970	\$0–5,999	\$6,000–10,999	\$11,000 plus

Table 6-6 presents historical data on the average number of physician visits per person by family income groups. In fiscal year 1963-64, the number of physician visits per person per year was directly related to family income levels. In fiscal year 1966-67, the relationship was bimodal, with the highest physician visit rate associated with the lowest and the highest income groups, i.e., 4.6 visits per person per year. All other income groups show a decline in their visit rate during this four-year period, such that a utilization pattern resulted that has at or below average physician visits for the middle-income groups and above average visits for the two extreme income groups. Comparison with the 1970 data, given in Table 6-5, shows further increases in the average number of physician visits for the low-income group and declines for the middle- and high-income groups.

In Table 6-7, the mean number of physician visits per person is given by family income, by age, and by race for the year 1970. Across all age categories, the average number of visits for nonwhites is lower than for whites for all three income classes. The mean number of visits for nonwhite children is also lower than for white children in all income groups. However, of those nonwhite low-income children who do see a physician, the number of visits is greater than for the white low-income children. In addition, the average number of physician visits for nonwhite low-income persons in the 18-64 years and the 65 years and over age groups is greater than for whites in the same age and income groups. Primarily because of the differential between the adult white and nonwhite groups in the number of visits per person seeing a physician, the overall average of visits per person seeing a physician is greater for the nonwhites in all age and income groups (6.0) than the comparable average for whites (5.8).

Table 6-6
Number of Physician Visits per Person per Year by Family Income for 1963-1964 and 1966-1967

	Number of Physician Visits per Person per Year	
Family Income ($)	*July 1963-June 1964*	*July 1966-June 1967*
Total	4.5	4.3
Under 3,000	4.3	4.6
3,000-4,999	4.5	4.1
5,000-6,999	4.5	4.2
7,000-9,999	4.7	4.3
10,000 and over	5.1	4.6

Source: "Volume of Physician Visits, United States, July 1966-June 1967," *Vital and Health Statistics*, Series 10, No. 49 (November, 1968), Table A.

Table 6-7
Mean Number of Physician Visits by Age, by Family Income, and by Race: 1970

		Visits per Person-year		*Visits per Person Seeing Physician*	
Age	*Family Income*	*White*	*Nonwhite*	*White*	*Nonwhite*
0-17	Low	2.3	1.7	3.6	3.8
	Middle	3.0	1.9	4.4	3.3
	High	3.0	1.5	4.0	1.9
18-64	Low	5.6	6.1	8.1	9.3
	Middle	4.5	3.6	6.5	5.6
	High	4.0	2.9	5.7	5.2
65 and over	Low	6.0	8.8	8.2	11.9
	Middle	6.1	a	7.1	a
	High	6.8	a	8.0	a
All ages	Low	5.0	4.4	7.2	7.7
	Middle	4.0	3.1	5.7	5.0
	High	3.7	2.3	5.1	3.7
	Total	4.1	3.6	5.8	6.0

[a]Based on fewer than 25 unweighted observations.

Source: *Health Services Use: National Trends and Variations, 1953-1971,* Ronald Andersen, Study Director, Department of Health, Education and Welfare, Health Services and Mental Health Administration (October, 1972), Table 9.

Summary and Conclusions

Inadequate income is a common barrier to the consumption of many essential goods and services by the lower-income groups. In the particular case of the consumption or utilization of personal health services, the extent to which national health insurance can eliminate or mediate the effects of income barriers is largely dependent on the type of benefit structures specified and the criteria for determining eligibility.

When the relationship between the utilization of both hospital care and physician services and family income *only* is analyzed, employing the most recent data on a national basis, an inverse relationship is found. The traditional concern has been that the low-income groups are faced with the problem of "underutilization" of personal health services, if the rates associated with the high-income groups are set as guidelines for adequate demand or need. The policymaker, in addition to the researcher, must go beyond the simple relationship between health care use and income or socioeconomic status to understand the underlying nature of the problems for not only the low- but also the middle-income groups. Of particular importance is the differences in utilization patterns that occur for the various age goups. As will be shown in Chapter 7, the influence of family size on family and individual health expenditures is critical to the more complex relationship that includes both income and age as variable factors in describing the use of health services.

Some of the evidence presented here appears to indicate that the more recent patterns of utilization of hospital care and physician services across family income groups is toward an equalization of opportunities.[6] However, the total evidence does not suggest that all health care needs for members of all income groups have been or can be met by the present system of financing and delivery of personal health care services.

Differences in the rate of utilization for the various family income groups are shown also to depend strongly on age factors. For example, children in low- and middle-income families are found to have relatively lower physician visit rates than both adult members of the same income groups and children in high-income groups.[7] This holds true even if analysis controls for any differences in disability status.[8] The use of personal health care services by the members of the various income groups are also linked to the particular type of service, race, and place of residence, although the above discussion did not review all factors in detail.

There is evidence, for example, that the traditional direct relationship between health services utilization and family income is present for dental care.[9] The percentage of the population within respective income groups who visited a dentist in 1970 increases as family income increases, from 23 percent for the less than $2,000 category to 67 percent for the $17,500 and over income category. While these percentages are generally higher than those found in the earlier surveys for 1953 and 1963, there are some indications of a relative decline for the middle-income groups. The direct relationship with income is common among all age groups, but the lowest percentages are given for children under five and persons sixty-five and over.

The data on the use of prescription drugs is limited.[10] Information from a 1964-1965 survey indicates that an indirect relationship was generally present for the number of prescriptions per person and family income. The rate is given at 6.4 prescriptions for the under $2,000 income group and 4.6 for the $10,000 and over class. For the age group under sixty-five years, the rates are the lowest for the low middle-income groups and the highest-income group has the largest number of prescriptions per person, i.e., 4.4. As would be expected, the sixty-five years and over age group had significantly larger rates, although there is no direct relationship across income groups within this age group. The elderly in the lowest-income group had a rate of 12.2 prescriptions per year.[11] (More recent data is available on the use of prescription drugs by the elderly under the Medicare program and is discussed in Chapter 10.)

The use of hospital care may actually be a result of substitution for physician outpatient care. This possibility of substitution of types of care is likely to affect the pattern of utilization for the low income-groups in particular for several reasons. First, because of income and price barriers, members of the low-income groups and to some extent the middle-income groups also cannot afford preventive care and must, therefore, rely on the health care system primarily for curative care. It is frequently because of limited financial resources or the lack of adequate health insurance coverage that their *expressed* need for health care is postponed until some more acute or critical stage of illness. A period of hospitalization may necessarily result. Persons in high-income groups are more financially able to afford to spend some portion of their income on physician visits and regular check-ups and to purchase adequate health insurance coverage or have it available through their place of employment. Most empirical studies indicate that the price of particular health services has only a relatively small effect on the demand for the service.[c] Some substitution of the types of services may, however, occur based on relative prices. The decision to substitute services, for example, may depend on the extent of insurance coverage. The patient or the physician may decide to use hospital care instead of outpatient services when the former is a covered service and the latter is not. The opposite situation could occur if the patient has no hospital insurance coverage, i.e., outpatient services may be substituted for any additional days of hospitalization.

Second, the substitution of hospital care for physician services and vice versa may also occur as the result of individuals' patterns of access to a regular source of care. For example, the increases in the demand for health services linked to the Medicare and Medicaid programs resulted in greatly expanded use of the hospital emergency room as a source of care, simply because these programs did not provide for appropriate accommodations in the supply and delivery of health services.

Reported survey findings show that several changes in the regular source of care for the various family income groups have occurred between 1963 and 1970.[12] In general, the proportion of the population who named a hospital or health center or clinic as their regular source of care increased considerably between 1963 and 1970. The proportion that named a particular physician declined accordingly. Over all income groups, those who claimed no regular source of care decreased slightly during this period.

However, changes in the source of regular care varied considerably according to family income. The proportion of the population in the low- and middle-income groups who named a particular physician as their regular source of care decreased significantly, while the proportion for the high-income groups remained the same. The proportion who named a clinic as their regular source of care increased for all income groups. In 1970, 16 percent of the low-income groups had no regular source of care, compared with 8 percent for the high-income groups.

---

[c]Estimates of price elasticity, however, indicate that the demand for physician and dental services are highly responsive to changes in the prices of these services.

Since 1963, the differences in the pattern of regular source of care according to family income has, in fact, become more extreme, with not only the poor or low-income groups, but also the middle-income groups, less likely to have a regular physician and more likely to have no regular source of care.

Some discussion was given of differences in the patterns of health care utilization experienced by whites and nonwhites. These patterns were shown to depend also on family income, but, in addition, particularly on age factors and place of residence. The survey report finds that the following results may indicate some equalization of opportunities for health care across race: (1) for those persons who see a physician, the mean number of visits by nonwhites is about as large as the mean for whites, and the mean number of visits for central city residents exceeds the overall national average number of visits; (2) there is little difference in the use of physician services between whites and nonwhites according to reported types of disabilities; and (3) whites are twice as likely as nonwhites to see a dentist in a given year.

The findings with regard to the relationship between the utilization of services, family income, age, and race are further complicated by factors associated with the place of residence. While the specific data on utilization and residence was not presented here, the survey results offer these kinds of findings that indicate the lack of equal opportunities for health care across geographic areas: (1) a smaller percentage of children living in central cities and rural areas have a physician visit in a year than is found for other children in the population; (2) members of the rural farm population are not only less likely to see a physician than the rest of the population, but also those who do see a doctor have a fewer number of visits; and (3) pregnant women in the central cities are less likely to see a physician during the first trimester of pregnancy than other pregnant women who live elsewhere.[13]

Notes

1. For a discussion of the approaches and findings of studies of the demand for health care services, see Hyman Joseph, "Empirical Research on the Demand for Health Care," *Inquiry,* Vol. 86 (March, 1971), 61-71. See also, Michael Grossman, *The Demand for Health: A Theoretical and Empirical Investigation,* NBER Occasional Paper 119 (New York: Columbia University Press, 1972). Grossman, in his recent study, presents a model of the demand for health. The demand for health care services is only one aspect of his overall framework of analysis. In most earlier studies, the demand for health care services is assumed to be dependent on prices, income, and tastes, as in the case of consumer demand for a final product. In Grossman's model, the state or level of health is chosen by the consumer, as in the case of the demand for a consumer durable good.

2. For a complete discussion of the survey and the data sources used in this chapter, see *Health Services Use: National Trends and Variations – 1953 to 1971,* Ronald Andersen, Study Director, Department of Health, Education and Welfare, Health Services and Mental Health Administration, (October, 1972). The data are based on four similar studies of random sample surveys of the utilization of health care services by families in the United States. The most recent study is based on survey information obtained in early 1971 for the use of health services in calendar year 1970.

3. Family income is defined as total family income before taxes for the survey year. Income from wages, salaries, own business or farm, professional work or trade, pensions, rents, welfare payments, unemployment compensation, alimony, regular contributions from friends or relatives, dividends, interest, and similar sources are included. Income in kind, such as the value of free rent or noncash benefits, is excluded. Total family income is the sum of all earned and unearned income of each person 14 years of age and older in the family. *(Health Services Use,* ibid., p. 38.) Individuals are assigned to family income class according to their own income if they live alone, and to a total family income if they are part of a family living together. See *Expenditures for Personal Health Services – National Trends and Variations, 1953-1970,* Ronald Andersen, Study Director, Department of Health, Education and Welfare, Health Resources Administration, (October, 1973), p. 16.

4. For further discussion, see *Health Services Use,* op. cit., pp. 15-17, 27.

5. One study of access to physician care and the utilization of services by socioeconomic class finds that although distance (measured by the number of miles from residence to the nearest Kaiser facility) affects the initial contact for physician care, "it is clear from these data that social class is the more powerful variable." The authors conclude further that distance influences the nature of the health care process in different patterns, depending on its interaction with the social class variable. See James Weiss and Merwyn Greenlick, "Determinants of Medical Care Utilization: The Effect of Social Class and Distance on Contacts with the Medical Care System," *Medical Care,* Vol. 8, No. 6 (November-December, 1970), 456-462. Also see *Health Services Use,* op. cit., pp. 3-7 for a discussion of findings from the survey on the regular source of care, some of which are presented later in this chapter.

6. See Thomas W. Bice, Robert L. Eichhorn, and Peter D. Fox, "Socio-Economic Status and Use of Physician Services: A Reconsideration," *Medical Care,* Vol. 10, No. 3 (May-June, 1972), 261-271. In their study of socioeconomic status and the use of physician services, Bice et. al. find that "since 1957, rates (number of physician visits per person per year) have remained rather stable in the low-income group and the attenuation of the relationship of family income and physician use has been due primarily to decreasing average use among the high-income persons." (p. 269).

7. The findings from the survey employed in the analysis is largely supported by data for several different measures of utilization from another source.

These data are based on the National Health Interview Survey. The reported data on the number of physician visits per person per year, by age and by family income for 1969 is given here because of the particular significance of this relationship.

Family Income	*Under 17 years*	*17-44 years*	*45-64 years*	*65 years and over*
Under $3,000	2.7	4.5	5.5	6.0
$3,000-3,999	2.8	4.7	5.5	5.9
$4,000-6,999	3.1	4.1	4.8	6.3
$7,000-9,999	3.7	4.1	4.7	6.0
$10,000 and over	4.2	4.2	4.3	7.5

See "Age Patterns in Medical Care, Illness and Disability, United States, 1968-69," *Vital and Health Statistics,* Series 10, No. 70, Table H.

8. Bice et. al., find that: "Controlling for disability status, differences in utilization persist for children in the three [income] classifications for which data are available; children from families with annual income of $10,000 or more have rates roughly 50 percent higher than those from families with incomes under $5,000." Bice et. al., *op. cit.,* 264-265.

9. See *Health Services Use,* op. cit., Tables 16 and 17.

10. For a discussion of the utilization of and expenditures for prescription drugs, see Donald D. Jones and J. F. Follman, Jr., *Health Insurance and Prescription Drugs* (New York: Health Insurance Association of America, 1971).

11. See "Cost and Acquisition of Prescribed and Non-Prescribed Medicines, United States, July 1964-June 1965," *Vital and Health Statistics,* Series 10, No. 33.

12. See *Health Services Use,* op. cit., p. 1 and, especially, Table 1.

13. For a list of findings, including those given here for race and place of residence, see *Health Services Use,* op. cit., pp. 33-34.

7 Expenditures for Personal Health Services by Family Income Groups

One appropriate measure of the potential benefits of a national health insurance plan and their distribution across family income groups are the dollar value of covered services received by members of the various defined income groups. In Chapter 6, analysis of the most recent survey data available on the utilization of hospital care and physicians' services outlined the nature of the relationships between the use of services and family income. This chapter employs data from this same survey source to examine the types of relationships that exist for expenditures for health services per family and per person and family income.[a]

The survey data makes the distinction between "free" and "non-free" sources of payment for health care services. This permits analysis of the trends in expenditures by comparing the most recent data for 1970 with the data from three previous surveys. *Non-free* expenditures are those the consumer makes either directly by out-of-pocket payments or indirectly through some third party to whom a premium is paid by the individuals or by others on their behalf. They include all types of expenditures reported in the earlier surveys, plus expenditures under the Medicare program.[1] Although Medicare did not exist in 1963, expenditures under this program are included in the non-free category, "since it [Medicare] is in large part a substitute for voluntary health insurance and no requirements regarding income levels are involved in its use," the program is funded through Social Security contributions, and coverage for Part B (the medical insurance plan) requires payment of premiums.[2] CHAMPUS, the armed forces dependents' coverage, is also considered as a non-free source in both the 1963 and 1970 survey reports.

Free expenditures are those expenses incurred for personal health care received by individuals and families at no direct cost or at substantially reduced rates and without benefit payments from any type of health insurance policy. These expenditures are reported only for the 1970 survey and not for the earlier surveys. Expenditures under the Medicaid program are included in the free category, since Medicaid was established to meet the needs of public assistance recipients and has fairly stringent income eligibility requirements. Health care

[a]All definitions of variables employed in the discussion of Chapter 6 on utilization also apply where appropriate to the data discussed here on expenditures. Of particular importance is the fact that unrelated individuals are included in the definition of a family and that family income is defined in the commonly accepted terms. Again, the surveys provide the most recent data on health expenditures according to a number of population characteristics and health services variables and facilitates analysis over the time period from 1953 to 1970.

given by tax-supported hospitals and clinics when no other source of payment is available is included in free expenditures, together with care for vocational rehabilitation, care provided by the Office of Economic Opportunity, and care provided by the federal government for members of the armed forces.

Expenditures per Family by Family Income

One measure of the level of family expenditures for health services is the average or mean expenditures for all services received by all family members. In order to indicate the distribution of expenditures across income groups, Table 7-1 presents the respective mean expenditures for all personal health services *per family* by given family income classes. Employing the definitions given above for the classification by particular source or type of payment, non-free and free expenditures are reported separately from total expenditures.

The relationship between mean *non-free* family expenditures and family income is basically a direct one; mean non-free expenditures increase as family income increases, with the notable exception of mean expenditures for the $7,500-$9,999 family income group. The relationship between mean *free* family expenditures and family income is, in general, an inverse one, as would be expected, with two exceptions. First, families with under $2,000 income are aided less by free sources of care than are those in the next income group, $2,000-$3,499. Second, a significantly higher level of free expenditures is

Table 7-1
Mean Expenditures for All Personal Health Services per Family by Family Income, 1970

	Mean Expenditures		
Family Income ($)	*Non-free*	*Free*	*Total*
Under 2,000	$343 (70%)	$146 (30%)	$ 489
2,000- 3,499	403 (69)	180 (31)	583
3,500- 4,999	496 (82)	106 (18)	602
5,000- 7,499	644 (87)	97 (13)	741
7,500- 9,999	606 (88)	69 (12)	675
10,000-14,999	686 (82)	153 (18)	839
15,000 and over	999 (98)	25 (2)	1,024
Below near-poverty	432 (69)	199 (31)	626
Above near-poverty	708 (90)	78 (10)	786
Total	636	108	744

Source: *Expenditures for Personal Health Services: National Trends and Variations, 1953-1970,* Ronald Andersen, Study Director, Department of Health, Education and Welfare, Health Resources Administration (October, 1973), Table 2.

reported for families in the $10,000-$14,999 income group, as compared with free expenditures for families in lower-income groups.

The reasonable hypothesis would have free services represent a large proportion of total expenditures for the low income groups. However, free expenditures actually are a surprisingly modest proportion of total expenditures—about 30 percent for those with incomes up to $3,500. In addition, since evidence shows that lower-income groups are generally found to have poorer health status, equitable opportunities for meeting health care needs across income groups would have the lower-income groups or those families at or below the near-poverty income level with larger total expenditures than families in the higher-income groups. Indeed, the level of *non-free* expenditures, on the average, for the lowest family income group ($343) is about a third as large as for the highest-income group ($999) and *total* expenditures for the lowest-income group ($489) are half as large as those for the highest-income group ($1,024).

Some of the discrepancy in the level of expenditures per family across income groups may be attributed to the effect of variable family size. In order to account for the possible influences of family size in addition to family income, the survey also defines a "near-poverty" level of income. This measure incorporates criteria of designated income levels and family size in judging whether a reported family income is below or above the estimated poverty income levels.[3] (See also the discussion of poverty levels in Chapter 3.) The adjustment to the data is particularly important, since elderly persons living alone are more concentrated in the low-income groups, and large families are more concentrated in both the low- and middle-income groups.

Regarding the role of family size in describing family expenditures for health services, one report finds:

> In general, as size of family increased, the annual amount spent for health services rose accordingly. However, . . . the rise in expense was not constant with increased family size. Average annual spending for medical services for a two-person family was more than twice that of an individual. *As family size increased from two to six or or more members, the increment of increase was considerably less than for one to two persons.*[4] (Emphasis added.)

While, in fact, this relationship between family size and changes in level of family expenditures for health services needs further verification, it is quite likely that children in large families are denied necessary health care for reasons of insufficient family income, in addition to other reasons.

The adjustment process greatly reduces the differences between the level of expenditures for the low- and the high-income groups, although certainly much less so for non-free expenditures than for total expenditures. (See Table 7-1.) The difference between non-free expenditures for families who are below the near poverty level ($432) and for those who are above the near poverty level ($707) remains so large that income effects appear present, whether purchase of health services is direct through out-of-pocket payments or indirect through private health insurance or the Medicare program. However, even adding free expenditures fails to bring *total* expenditures for families below the near poverty level ($626) up to the average family's *non-free* expenditures ($636), much less to the level of total expenditures. Other factors—the shifting of expenditures to alternative free sources, e.g., to Medicaid coverage, price differentials, access to care, etc.—must also be considered. Even while cautious interpretations must be made of all poverty income measures that fix arbitrary limits on the designated income levels, inequities in the dollar amount of services received, adjusted for family size, imply that families in the lower-income groups are at a disadvantage financially in meeting their health care needs.

Other significant findings of the survey that reinforce concern about poorer families' access to health care and the financial burden it imposes on them are:

1. While free health care accounted for a portion of the total health care expenditures for low-income families, as many as 70 percent of those in the lowest-income groups received *no free* health care;
2. The percentage of the population with *no* health care expenditures of any kind increases as family income decreases;
3. The combined income group of $3,499 or less had a higher percentage of persons with expenditures of $2,000 or more than did any other income group.[5]

The historical trends in the mean non-free expenditures for family income groups have varied considerably over the past two decades. These trends in expenditures for non-free personal health services per family are given in Table 7-2, together with the respective average annual percentage increases in the expenditures. According to this series of surveys, the average annual percentage increase in mean non-free expenditures per family across family income groups was 5.7 percent for the period 1953–1963 and 8.0 percent for the later period 1963–1970.[b] Comparisons of the trends for the particular income groups show that the largest annual percentage increases occurred for the lower-income groups. For the earlier period, the highest percentage increase was experienced by the lowest-income group. Since there is a proportionately higher number of elderly in this "under $2,000" category, and since expenditures for services

[b]Certainly price increases during the time period are also present in this trend data, although it is reasonable to assume that the *rate* of price inflation in health services was the same for consumers in all income groups, even if particular price differentials dependent on income levels do exist. The problem of the role of family size can largely be ignored in investigating these trends, since over this short period of time, the relationship between size of family, income levels, and income changes can be assumed to hold relatively constant. Thus, while average family size may be different at different family income levels, no changes in the nature of the relationship of any significance should have occurred.

Table 7-2
Mean Expenditures for Non-free Personal Health Services per Family by Family Income: 1953, 1963, and 1970 and Average Percentage Increases

	Mean Non-free Expenditure			*Average Annual Percent Increase*[a]	
Family Income ($)	*1953*	*1963*	*1970*	*1953-1963*	*1963-1970*
Under 2,000	$130	$228	$343	5.5%	6.0%
2,000- 3,499	156	245	403	4.4	7.4
3,500- 4,999	207	289	496	3.2	8.0
5,000- 7,499	259	409	644	4.4	6.7
7,500- 9,999	}	}	606 }	}	}
10,000-14,999	} 353	} 480	686 } 763	} 3.0	} 6.8
15,000 and over	}	}	999 }	}	}
Total	207	370	636	5.7	8.0

[a]Average annual percent increases in this report are computed according to the technique outlined by G. Barclay (*Techniques of Population Analysis*, New York: Wiley, 1958, pp. 28–33) using logarithms to the base 10. The shifts in proportion of the population represented by each income category make it possible for the average annual increase for all families to equal or exceed the computed increase for any income category.

Source: *Expenditures for Personal Health Services: National Trends and Variations, 1953–1970,* Ronald Andersen, Study Director, Department of Health, Education and Welfare, Health Resources Administration (October, 1973), Table 1.

received under the Medicare program are included in the definition of non-free expenditures, it is surprising that the lowest-income group shows the smallest increase for the later period. It is possible that the relatively higher annual increases for the next two low-income groups actually reflect the greater effect of Medicare expenditures for the aged population, although no age breakdowns are given here to enable any definite isolation of these kinds of effects. By far the greatest percentage increase for the 1963–1970 period occurred for the income category of $3,500–$4,999, despite the impacts of the Medicaid program for the poor and medically indigent, which should have shifted a portion of these expenditures to the "free" classification of source of payment.

Another measure of the impact of the level of health expenditures on the various family income groups is the dollar amount of total family outlays or out-of-pocket expenditures expressed as a percentage of the respective average family income.[6] These percentages are given in Table 7-3 for the four survey years from 1953 to 1970.[7] These data show for each survey year that aggregate family outlays for personal health services represent a *larger proportion* of family income as family income decreases. (A graphic presentation of the relationship is given in Figure 7-1 for 1970.) Of particular importance to policy-making is the fact that the percent of outlays to total income has continually increased for the income groups below $7,500 throughout this period of almost

Table 7-3
Aggregate Family Outlays for Personal Health Services as a Percent of Family Income, by Income Group—1953, 1958, 1963, and 1970

	Aggregate Outlay as a Percentage of Family Income				
Family Income ($)	*1953*	*1958*	*1963*	*1970*	
Under 2,000	11.8%	13.0%	15.7%	14.5%	
2,000- 3,499	6.1	8.4	8.5	9.3	
3,500- 4,999	5.4	6.4	6.8	7.7	
5,000- 7,499	4.7	5.4	5.6	6.1	
7,500- 9,999				4.6	
10,000-14,999	3.0	3.9	3.8	3.8	3.7
15,000 and over				3.3	
Total	4.8	5.5	5.0	4.4	

Source: *Expenditures for Personal Health Services: National Trends and Variations, 1953-1970,* Ronald Andersen, Study Director, Department of Health, Education and Welfare, Health Resources Administration (October, 1973), Table 5.

twenty years. Despite any expansion in the enrollments in private health insurance plans and despite the implementation of Medicare and Medicaid, there is an apparent need for families in *all* low-income groups to spend increasing proportions of the their family income directly on health care.[8]

The data on the trends in aggregate outlays as a percentage of family income for the higher income groups appear to indicate some leveling-off or possible decline. However, since data are not available for the smaller categories of family income above $7,500 for the earlier survey years, a cautious interpretation of the more aggregate trends is necessary. The "under $2,000" category, which has a large representation by the elderly, does show some decline in the percentage for 1970 from the pre-Medicare level of 1963.[9] But, because of the size of the percentage increase for this lowest income group as compared with the other income groups, the relative decline must certainly be considered minor.

As would be expected, a comparison of the proportion of the respective mean expenditures met by alternative sources of payment indicates significant differences for the various family income groups. In Table 7-4, mean expenditures are classified by four sources of payments: (1) the Medicaid program and other welfare or free care received under circumstances of inability to pay; (2) the Medicare program for the elderly; (3) benefits paid by voluntary insurance plans; and (4) direct out-of-pocket payments by the consumer. Mean expenditures per family under Medicaid and other welfare programs are inversely related to the level of family income, as is the case with the expenditures under the Medicare program. These two types of sources of payment each represent approximately one-quarter of mean expenditures for the two lowest

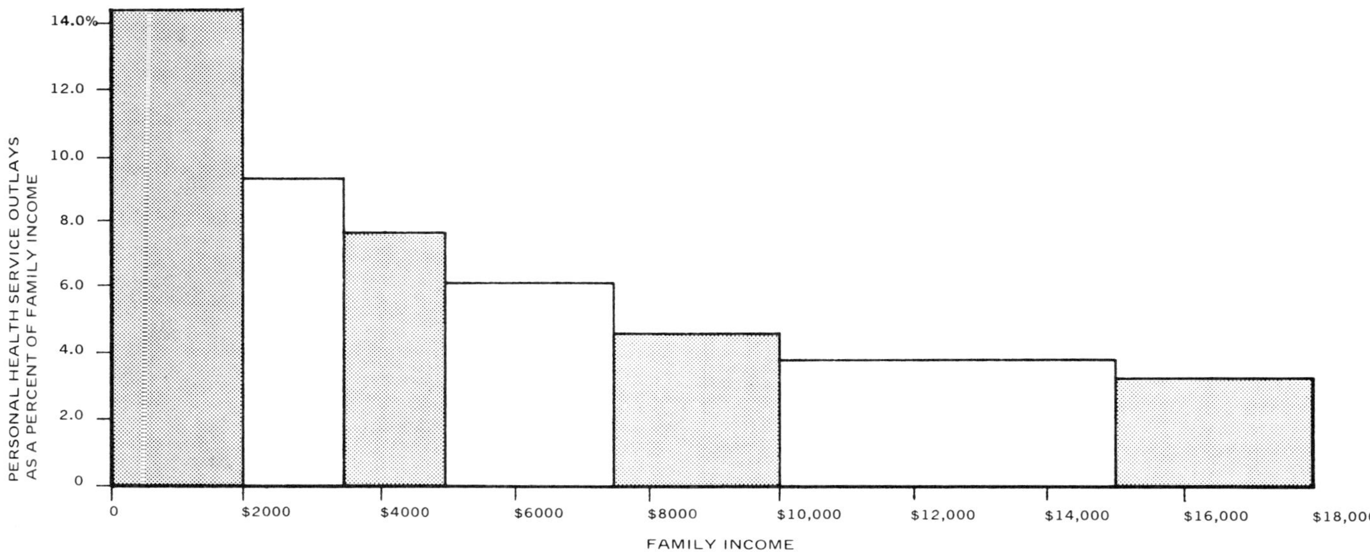

Source: Taken from Table 7-3.

Figure 7-1. Total Family Outlays for Perscnal Health Services as a Percent of Family Income, 1970

Table 7–4
Mean Expenditures for All Personal Health Services per Family by Family Income and Source of Payment, 1970

	Mean Expenditure by Source									
	Medicaid, Welfare Free Institutions		*Medicare*		*Voluntary Insurance*		*Out of Pocket*		*Total*	
Family Income ($)	*Mean*	*Percent of Total*	*Mean*	*Percent of Total*	*Mean*	*Percent of Total*	*Mean*	*Percent of Total*	*Mean*	*Percent of Total*[a]
Under 2,000	$133	27%	$113	23%	$ 49	10%	$180	37%	$ 489	100%
2,000– 3,499	160	27	142	24	62	11	192	33	583	100
3,500– 4,999	83	14	64	11	159	26	268	45	602	100
5,000– 7,499	60	8	78	11	243	33	316	43	741	100
7,500– 9,999	36	5	19	3	261	39	320	47	675	100
10,000–14,999	15[b]	2[b]	18	2	245	29	398	47	839	100
15,000 and over	10	1	19	2	386	38	583	57	1,024	100
Below near-poverty	171	27	113	18	102	16	211	34	626	100
Above near-poverty	20[b]	3[b]	36	5	265	34	395	50	786	100
Total	59[b]	8[b]	56	8	223	30	348	47	744	100

[a]The percents for the various sources do not add up to 100 because certain additional sources of payment included under both the "free" and "non-free" definitions are excluded from the components.

[b]The reported estimate does not include observations for extremely high-weighted expenditures.

Source: *Expenditures for Personal Health Services: National Trends and Variations, 1953–1970,* Ronald Andersen, Study Director, Department of Health, Education and Welfare, Health Administration Resources (October, 1973), Table A–1.

income groups. Adjusting for family size makes no difference in the percentage of mean expenditures under Medicaid and other welfare programs for the low-income groups, but decreases the comparable percentage met under Medicare, reflecting the disproportionate number of poor elderly living alone.

The proportion of mean expenditures that results from benefits received under voluntary health insurance plans is directly related to the level of family income. Insurance benefits represent the largest percentage of mean expenditures for the \$7,500-\$9,999 family income group; as little as 10 percent of the mean family expenditures for the lower-income groups was met by private insurance in 1970.

Of particular interest is the fact that even at the lowest family income levels, the estimates—including those which adjust for family size—show that as much as one-third of mean total expenditures are made directly by the consumer through out-of-pocket payments. Although the percentage of these total expenditures met by out-of-pocket payments increases with family income, the differences in the respective percentages are quite small over the range of family income from \$3,500 to \$15,000.

Expenditures per Person by Family Income

Estimates are also available for mean expenditures for personal health services on a *per person* basis according to family income groups. No well-defined relationship between mean expenditures per person and family income appears evident initially. In Table 7-5, which reports mean expenditures per person by family income, persons in the higher-income groups have mean *total* expenditures that are in some cases larger and in other cases smaller than for persons in the lower-income groups. Of particular interest is the finding that members of the lower end of the middle-income group (\$7,500-\$9,999) have the smallest expenditures for both the *non-free* and *total* expenditures classifications. Mean *free* expenditures per person, in general, appear to decrease as family income increases, although a significantly larger amount of free expenditures is given for the \$10,000-\$14,999 income group than for the lower middle-income group.

The estimates reported for *total* expenditures per person for family income levels below and above near-poverty income indicate a narrowing of the difference in the respective mean total expenditures (\$229 versus \$254) when family size is taken into account. Clearly, therefore, a major role must be attributed to the size of the family and related factors in describing the relatively higher unadjusted level of total expenditures for the low-income groups. Again, one obvious reason is that many members of the low-income groups are the aged, who are more likely to live alone or in smaller families and who use a larger number of health services—frequently more expensive inpatient or

Table 7-5
Mean Expenditures for All Personal Health Services per Person by Family Income, 1970

		Mean Expenditures	
Family Income ($)	*Non-free*	*Free*	*Total*
Under 2,000	$225 (70%)	$97 (30%)	$322
2,000- 3,499	195 (69)	86 (31)	281
3,500- 4,999	221 (86)	35 (14)	256
5,000- 7,499	228 (87)	34 (13)	262
7,500- 9,999	171 (89)	20 (11)	191
10,000-14,999	198 (83)	42 (17)	240
15,000 and over	258 (97)	6 (3)	264
Below near-poverty	158 (69)	71 (31)	229
Above near-poverty)	229 (90)	25 (10)	254
Total	213	35	248

Source: *Expenditures for Personal Health Services: National Trends and Variations, 1953-1970,* Ronald Andersen, Study Director, Department of Health, Education and Welfare, Health Resources Administration, (October, 1973), Table 8.

institutional type of care. Thus, the unweighted averages, such as the $322 for the lowest-income group, are much higher than for the mean expenditures that account for family size. It should be noted that with the adjustment for family size, mean total expenditures are shown to be *lower* for the below poverty income classification than for the above poverty income category.

Adjusting *non-free* expenditures per person for family size results in a similar decline in the level of expenditures for low-income persons. In this instance, the larger difference between the non-free expenditures for below and above near-poverty levels ($158 versus $229) reflects the variation in the major sources of payment for health services for the low- and the high-income groups, in addition to the influence of variable family size. Expenditures under the Medicare program are included in the category of non-free expenditures and, therefore, account for a large part of these expenditures for low-income persons, because of the large number of elderly people in small families and living alone. By adjusting mean *free* expenditures, changes again occur in the respective expenditures for below and above near-poverty income groups, but with the differential still favoring the low-income persons ($71 versus $25). Although the adjustment lowers the expenditure level as compared with the averages given for the two lowest-income groups, as would be expected because of the role of the elderly persons, the next two income groups—$3,500-$4,999 and $5,000-$7,499—have unweighted expenditures as small as half the value adjusted for family size. The estimates of $35 and $34, respectively for these two income groups, as compared with the adjusted below near-poverty level of free expenditures of $71, imply that members of larger families probably have lower free expenditures per person than the average or mean expenditures. In addition, persons in families with below poverty level income had twice as many non-free expenditures as free expenditures for health services in 1970.

The relationship between expenditures per person and family income is largely clarified when the expenditures are classified by the more specific source of payment, as given in Table 7-6. In general, an inverse relationship with mean expenditures per person decreasing as family income increases is valid for payments made under the Medicaid program, by other welfare sources, and under the Medicare program. For expenditures met by private health insurance, this relationship appears to be direct, as would be expected, given the relatively greater proportion of persons in the higher-income groups whose services are covered by voluntary insurance plans. However, very little variation occurs across income groups in the level of mean expenditures per person made directly by consumers and classified as out-of-pocket expenditures.

Table 7-6
Mean Expenditures for All Personal Health Services per Person, by Family Income and by Source of Payment, 1970

	Mean Expenditure by Source				
Family Income ($)	*Medicaid, Welfare, Free Institutions*	*Medicare*	*Voluntary Insurance*	*Out of Pocket*	*Total*[a]
Under 2,000	$87	$74	$32	$118	$322
2,000- 3,499	77	69	30	93	281
3,500- 4,999	35	28	67	114	256
5,000- 7,499	21	30	84	112	262
7,500- 9,999	10	6	72	91	191
10,000-14,999	4[b]	11	68	111	240
15,000 and over	3	6	83[b]	150	264
Below near-poverty	63	41	37	77	229
Above near-poverty	7[b]	15	84	127	254
Total	28[b]	21	73	116	248

[a]The means for the various sources do not add up to the total because certain additional sources of payment included under both the "free" and "non-free" definitions are excluded from the component.

[b]The reported estimate does not include observations for extremely high-weighted expenditures.

Source: *Expenditures for Personal Health Services: National Trends and Variations, 1953-1970,* Ronald Andersen, Study Director, Department of Health, Education and Welfare, Health Resources Administration (October, 1973), Table A-4.

Family size appears to have a strong influence on the distribution of expenditures per person across income groups in the case of all sources of payment, with the exception of voluntary insurance benefits. Of particular interest is the fact that for both categories of families below and above the near-poverty levels, the largest proportion of mean expenditures per person is met by out-of-pocket payments.

Expenditures per Person by Type of Service

Survey data with respect to the mean expenditures per person for the various types of health care services are given in Tables 7-7 to 7-10. The discussion focuses on expenditures across family income groups and by source of payment for four types of services: hospital care, physicians' services, dental services, and drugs.

Table 7-7
Mean Expenditures for Hospital Services per Person, by Family Income and by Source of Payment, 1970

	Mean Expenditure by Source				
Family Income ($)	*Medicaid, Welfare, Free Institutions*	*Medicare*	*Voluntary Insurance*	*Out of Pocket*	*Total*[a]
Under 2,000	$56	$58	$28	$31	$175
2,000- 3,499	49	53	18	11	140
3,500- 4,999	23	19	48	15	112
5,000- 7,499	13	23	43[b]	17	117
7,500- 9,999	5	8	51	10	78
10,000-14,999	3[b]	10	40	12	103
15,000 and over	2	5	42[b]	7[b]	103
Below near-poverty	40	32	26	15	121
Above near-poverty	4[b]	11	55	13[b]	104
Total	20[b]	16	48	17	108

[a]The means for the various sources do not add up to the total because certain additional sources of payment included under both the "free" and "non-free" definitions are excluded from the component.

[b]The reported estimates does not include observations for extremely high-weighted expenditures.

Source: *Expenditures for Personal Health Services: National Trends and Variations, 1953–1970,* Ronald Andersen, Study Director, Department of Health, Education and Welfare, Health Resources Administration (October, 1973), Table A-5.

Table 7-8
Mean Expenditures for Physicians' Services per Person, by Family Income and by Source of Payment, 1970

	Mean Expenditure by Source				
Family Income ($)	*Medicaid, Welfare, Free Institutions*	*Medicare*	*Voluntary Insurance*	*Out of Pocket*	*Total*[a]
Under 2,000	$26	$15	$ 8	$34	$85
2,000- 3,499	18	14	11	26	71
3,500- 4,999	10	10	12	29	64
5,000- 7,499	5	6	22	32	72
7,500- 9,999	2	2	19	32	58
10,000-14,999	1	1	21	33	61
15,000 and over		1	21[b]	36	65
Below near-poverty	16	8	9	22	57
Above near-poverty	1	3	23	36	67
Total	5	4	20	33	65

[a]The means for the various sources do not add up to the total because certain additional sources of payment included under both "free" and "non-free" definitions are excluded from the component.

[b]The reported estimate does not include observations for extremely high-weight expenditures.

Source: *Expenditures for Personal Health Services: National Trends and Variations, 1953-1971,* Department of Health, Education and Welfare, Health Resources Administration (October, 1973), Table A-7.

The survey results largely support the conclusions of Chapter 6, i.e., lower-income groups have a relatively higher rate of utilization of hospital services than do middle- and high-income groups, according to the estimates of mean expenditures per person for *hospital services* across family income groups.[10] The significantly low level of mean expenditures for persons in the $7,500-$9,999 income group is again present. Medicaid and other welfare payments, together with expenditures under the Medicare program, are the primary sources of payment for hospital services for the lower-income groups, while private health insurance benefits represent the major source of payment for the higher-income groups. (See Table 7-7.) However, voluntary insurance was also a significant source of payments for hospital services for the lower middle-income families—those above the poverty level, but below the national median family income (approximately $11,000 in 1970). Despite the reliance of the lower-income groups on Medicaid and Medicare for payment of hospital care, the estimate for their per person mean out-of-pocket expenditures adjusted for family size ($15) is greater than the estimate for above near-poverty income groups ($13).

Table 7-9
Mean Expenditures for Dental Services per Person, by Family Income by Source of Payment, 1970

	Mean Expenditures by Source			
Family Income ($)	*Medicaid, Welfare, Free Institutions*	*Voluntary Insurance*	*Out of Pocket*	*Total*[a]
Under 2,000	$4		$11	$15
2,000- 3,499	5		8	13
3,500- 4,999	4	$2	16	23
5,000- 7,499	1		20	23
7,500- 9,999	2	1	16	20
10,000-14,999		3	28	32
15,000 and over		1	43	45
Below near-poverty	5		9	14
Above near-poverty	1	2	30	33
Total	2	1	25	28

[a]The means for the various sources do not add up to the total because certain additional sources of payment included under both the "free" and "non-free" definitions are excluded from the component.

Source: *Expenditures for Personal Health Services: National Trends and Variations, 1953-1970,* Ronald Andersen, Study Director, Department of Health, Education and Welfare, Health Resources Administration (October, 1973), Table A-10.

Much of these high out-of-pocket expenditures may be represented by deductible and coinsurance payments under the Medicare program by the elderly in the lower-income brackets.

In Table 7-8, mean expenditures per person for *physician services* are reported by family income and by source of payment.[11] The total mean expenditures for all sources of payment approximates an inverse relationship with family income. This finding implies conclusions similar to those presented in Chapter 6 on the pattern of utilization of physician services across family income groups.[12] That is, the number of physician visits per person is inversely related to family income, as is the case here for total mean expenditures per person for physician services. However, the pattern of utilization of physicians' services by family income *and* by age categories indicated that the number of physician visits for children in the low-income groups is significantly less than for children in the higher-income groups. The pattern of total mean expenditures across family income adjusted for family size also supports this finding. The estimates of expenditures for the individual in a family with below near-poverty income ($57) is lower than the respective estimate for above near-poverty

Table 7-10
Mean Expenditures for Drug Services per Person, by Family Income and by Source of Payment, 1970

	Mean Expenditures by Source			
Family Income ($)	*Medicaid, Welfare, Free Institutions*	*Voluntary Insurance*	*Out of Pocket*	*Total*[a]
Under 2,000	$9		$31	$43
2,000- 3,499	7		33	42
3,500- 4,999	1	$3	40	45
5,000- 7,499	2	3	29	35
7,500- 9,999		1	22	23
10,000-14,999		2	25	28
15,000 and over		3	26	30
Below near-poverty	5	1	23	30
Above near-poverty		2	28	32
Total	2	2	27	32

[a]The means for the various sources do not add up to the total because certain additional sources of payment included under both the "free" and "non-free" definitions are excluded from the component.

Source: *Expenditures for Personal Health Services: National Trends and Variations, 1953-1970,* Ronald Andersen, Study Director, Department of Health, Education and Welfare, Health Resources Administration (October, 1973), Table A-9.

income ($67). This unfavorable differential in mean expenditures per person, after adjusting for family size, most likely reflects the relatively low expenditures on physicians' services for those children in the below or near-poverty income groups and, particularly, for individual children in large families.

Again, with expenditures for physicians' services, Medicaid, welfare programs, and Medicare are the primary sources of payment for the lower-income groups. However, the actual dollar amount of the mean per person expenditures for each of these sources of payment is *smaller* than the estimate given for out-of-pocket payments. For the higher income groups, voluntary insurance benefits are *only* the second largest source of payment, with out-of-pocket expenditures financing the largest proportion of their physicians' services.

The direct relationship presented by the data on the use of dental services and family income is reinforced by the data given in Table 7-9 on the mean expenditures per person for *dental services.*[13] The estimates adjusted for family size do not alter this relationship. Medicaid and other free sources of payment for dental care were responsible for the smaller proportion of expenditures for the lower-income groups. Although out-of-pocket expenditures for dental services were significantly larger for the higher-income groups, this type of payment also remains the largest source of payment for the lower-income groups. Private insurance benefits represented very minor expenditures for dental care for persons in the higher-income groups, since these types of benefits are generally not included in the limited types of coverage provided for under most voluntary insurance plans.

Total mean expenditures per person for *drug services* as reported in Table 7-10 show relatively *larger* expenditures for the lower-income groups than for the higher income groups.[14] A marked change in the level of mean expenditures per person occurs with the decline from $45 to $35 when family income increases to $5,000-$7,499 and with the further decline from $35 to $23 when family income increases to $7,500-$9,999. However, the estimates for expenditures per person in the below and above near-poverty level of income, which adjusts for family size, appear to bring the level of expenditures for these broader income groups into relatively close alignment.

By far the largest source of payment for drugs for all income groups is the direct out-of-pocket consumer payments. A smaller proportion of expenditures for drugs are covered by the Medicaid and other welfare programs for the low-income groups; voluntary insurance benefits represent the source of payment for marginal amounts of the expenditures by members of the middle- and high-income groups.

Summary and Conclusions

The evidence presented in the discussion of Chapter 7 highlights the kinds of inequities in the present structure of health expenditures across the distribution of income. The evidence also suggests the types of accommodations that must be available in the benefit structures of proposed national health insurance plans if in fact financial benefits are to be distributed more equitably. Major findings regarding expenditures for families by family income are:

1. As little as 30 percent of the mean total expenditures for families below the poverty level (adjusted for family size) is reflected in free sources of payment.

2. As many as 70 percent of those in the lowest-income groups had *no free* health care in 1970.

3. There are relatively small differences in the percentage of total expenditures met by out-of-pocket payments for income groups, adjusted for family size, from $3,500 to $15,000.

4. Aggregate family outlays represented a *larger* proportion of family income as family income decreases.

5. Expenditures under Medicaid and other welfare programs and expenditures under the Medicare program each represented approximately one-quarter of total mean expenditures for the two lowest-income groups.

6. The proportion of mean expenditures resulting from private health insurance benefits is directly related to the level of family income.

7. The differential between non-free expenditures for families below and above the poverty level is almost $300, and is most probably directly linked to income, either in the form of little or no private health insurance coverage or constraints on out-of-pocket expenditures.

8. While average annual expenditures for health care for a two-person family are more than twice that for an individual, the increment of increase in expenditures as family size increases beyond two members is significantly smaller than for one to two persons. Therefore, children in large families, and particularly those in low-income families, appear less likely to receive necessary health care because of financial circumstances.

Major findings regarding expenditures per person—including expenditures for particular types of services—by family income are:

1. The largest proportion of mean expenditures per person is met by out-of-pocket payments for both families below and above the poverty level.

2. Family size appears to have a strong influence on the distribution of expenditures per person across income groups for all sources of payment except voluntary insurance benefits.

3. As would be expected, Medicare, Medicaid, and other welfare programs are the primary sources of payment for hospital services for the lower-income groups; private health insurance benefits are the primary sources of payments for the higher-income groups. However, voluntary insurance is also a significant source of payment for the lower middle-income families—those above the poverty level, but below median family income.

4. The estimates of the level of expenditures for physicians' services for an individual in a family below poverty income is *less* than the respective estimate for a person in the above poverty income family. This finding most likely reflects the relatively low expenditures for children, particularly children in large families, for physicians' services. Thus while aggregate data on the use of physicians' services by different income groups support an inverse relationship with family income, the pattern of use of physicians' services by income *and* by age group indicates that the number of physicians' visits for children in low-income groups is significantly less than for children in higher-income groups.

5. The actual dollar amounts spent on physicians' services by low-income persons are *smaller* for Medicaid, other welfare programs, and Medicare than for out-of-pocket payments. Much of the relatively high out-of-pocket expenditures for the lower-income groups are probably deductibles and coinsurance payments under the Medicare program by the elderly and expenses for uncovered services, such as drugs.

6. For higher income groups, out-of-pocket expenditures are also the largest dollar source of payment for physicians' services, with voluntary insurance benefits being only the second largest source.

7. Expenditures per person for dental services across income groups indicate a direct relationship with family income, as is also the case for the utilization of dental services. The majority of payments for all income groups is made out-of-pocket for dental services. Private health insurance represents a very minor source of expenditures for the high-income groups, as is the case with respect to Medicaid and other free sources for the low-income groups.

8. Expenditures for drugs show a *larger* per person expenditure for low-income groups than for high-income groups. Again, the largest source of payment for all income groups is direct out-of-pocket payments.

Notes

1. *Expenditures for Personal Health Services: National Trends and Variations, 1953–1970,* Ronald Andersen, Study Director, U.S. Department of Health, Education and Welfare, Health Resources Administration (October, 1973), p. 2.

2. Ibid., p. 3.

3. Poverty level income is adjusted for size of family based on Bureau of Labor Statistics figures. A family is at poverty level or below if their reported income is less than these amounts given by family size:

Family Size	*Weekly*	*Monthly*	*Yearly*
1	$ 50	$220	$2,600
2	70	310	3,700
3	85	370	4,500
4	110	470	5,700
5	130	550	6,600
6	145	620	7,500
7+	175	760	9,100

See *Expenditures for Personal Health Services,* op. cit., p. 56.

4. "Family Health Expenses, United States–July-December, 1962," *Vital and Health Statistics,* Series 10, No. 41, p. 6.

5. *Expenditures for Personal Health Services,* op. cit., p. 21.

6. Aggregate family outlays include out-of-pocket expenditures which have actually been directly made by the family, payment of health insurance premiums (excluding any premium payments made by employers), and payments made by family members for the health care of another person outside the defined family group. Outlays exclude any payments made by third-party payers, payments which remain outstanding, payments made on a family

member's behalf by someone outside the family, and accident or liability insurance payments made for health care. See *Expenditures for Personal Health Services,* op. cit., p. 56.

7. Because of the self-weighting scheme employed in the reporting of the survey data, certain extremely high-weighted expenditures can bias the estimates given in any one income-expenditures cell. When the total weighted expenditures were $200,000 or more and the weighted expenditures in a given cell accounted for 15 percent or more of the total weighted expenditures in that cell, the survey sample observation was excluded from one of the two series of estimates. The series that excludes the high-weight case or cases is reported in this and other tables in this chapter. These estimates, therefore, indicate the level of expenditures as if the omitted observation had not occurred. Ibid., see expository footnote for Table A-1 and pp. 57-59.

8. The most recent report of the surveys gives the following factors as possibly also influencing the level of health expenditures as a percentage of family income: (1) proportionately fewer families are represented by the lower-income groups in the later surveys; (2) members of the lower-income groups are more likely to have illnesses of a serious nature, with family income then reduced at the same time as health expenses increase; and (3) the effect of the cost of employer contributions to insurance premiums. Ibid., pp. 12-13.

9. Aggregate family outlays for personal health services as a percent of family income were also calculated separately for families whose oldest member is 65 years and over and whose oldest member is under 65 years. The results show that for families with at least one member 65 years and over the percentages are higher than for the aggregate of families for all income levels, except for the lowest-income group. The reverse results are found in the case of families whose oldest member is under 65 years, that is, the expenditures are lower for all income groups, except for the lowest-income group. Ibid., p. 13.

10. A hospital is defined as either a short-term or long-term institution, including nursing homes and extended care facilities. The term hospital services refers only to inpatient care. Expenditures for outpatient and emergency services are included under physicians' services. Charges included in hospital expenditures are for: hospital room and board, laboratory fees, drugs, X rays, operating and delivery room fees, and other usual inpatient hospital charges. Fees for pathology, radiology, and anesthesiology services are included only when these are not billed for separately. Private-duty nursing fees are always excluded. Ibid., p. 24 and p. 53.

11. Physicians' services expenditures include: (1) charges made by a physician for surgery or delivery performed in a hospital; (2) charges for physician visits to a hospitalized inpatient or for the ancillary hospital services of an anesthesiologist, pathologist, or radiologist if the patient is not billed directly by the hospital; (3) charges for outpatient surgery by a physician; (4) charges for outpatient physician visits in the physician's office, the patient's home, or in a

clinic, including all charges for visits to a hospital outpatient or emergency room; and (5) charges for visits to an ophthalmologist for eye care, but not for eyeglasses. A physician is defined as a medical doctor or an osteopath. Charges for surgery performed by an intern or resident are included in the expenditures for hospital care. Charges for oral surgery performed in a hospital by a dental surgeon are, however, included in physician expenditures. Ibid., pp. 53-54.

12. In their study, Andersen and Benham analyze several factors that might bias estimates of the relationship between family income and the utilization of health services. Among these factors is *permanent income* or the family's expected regular income and *transitory income* or those negative or positive components of income that are not anticipated.

They conclude from their estimates of respective elasticities that physician expenditures are not consistent with the permanent income hypothesis, but dental expenditures are quite consistent. A second hypothesis tested is that illness simultaneously increases physician expenditures and produces a negative transitory component in family income. However, the study finds that the observed income elasticity for physician expenditures does not appear to be negatively affected by the transitory loss of income due to illness. See Ronald Andersen and Lee Benham, "Factors Affecting the Relationship between Family Income and Medical Care Consumption," in *Empirical Studies in Health Economics,* Herbert Klarman, ed. (Baltimore: Johns Hopkins Press, 1970).

13. Dental expenditures include charges for dentists' services and the services of ancillary personnel, e.g., a dental hygienist, and for dental appliances. Other charges included are for work requested by dentists but performed by dental laboratories and dental manufacturers. Excluded from the definition are charges for surgery performed by a dentist in a hospital or hospital outpatient department, since these are included under physician services expenditures. Ibid., p. 54.

14. Drug expenditures include payments for both prescribed and nonprescription drugs. Excluded are charges for drugs administered by a physician or dentist, as well as drugs received in the hospital, when these charges are included in the physician, dentist, or hospital bill. Ibid., p. 54.

8 The Benefit Structure of National Health Insurance

This chapter reviews and assesses the benefit structure of selected national health insurance plans by focusing on: (1) the respective eligibility criteria established by the various proposed programs; (2) the range of and limits on the types of covered services; (3) consumer cost sharing components attached to certain benefits; and (4) the role of catastrophic coverage.[a] In general, the majority of the debate concerning any differences in the various approaches to the structure of benefits has emphasized the issue of cost sharing factors in the alternative proposals. Cost sharing has impact on all consumer health care expenditures and, unless the cost sharing is directly linked to income levels, has proportionately greater impact on the relative expenditures for lower- and middle-income families and individuals. The differences in the other aspects of the benefit structures are perhaps less evident at first comparison. But, even marginal differences in the eligibility criteria and the scope and limits for covered services become important to a complete understanding of the distribution of benefits across income groups.

Data on the utilization of and expenditures for health services by different income groups suggest a number of ways in which distributional effects can be present in the structure of benefits under alternative proposals. Of paramount importance is whether eligibility is linked to income and, if so, what is the nature of the particular relationship between eligibility requirements for designated recipient groups and their level of income. For example, eligibility criteria for enrollment in proposed publicly funded plans for the poor and low-income groups may be reliant on a measure of poverty income, an approach that ignores the needs of the lower middle-income groups who presently lack sufficient financial means for the direct purchase of health care or comprehensive health insurance coverage and who may not always have employee insurance plans available to them. In addition to income criteria, other factors are also significant in evaluating the structure of benefits and eligibility criteria. The findings presented earlier stress the importance of family size and age as intervening variables in describing the nature of the relationship between health services use and expenditures and family income.

The variation in the patterns of utilization and expenditures across family income groups for the different types of health services also implies the need for

[a]In almost all cases, the detailed information presented in this chapter is cited in the written legislation for each of the respective proposals as they relate to the structure of benefits.

analysis of the amounts and kinds of services covered under the alternative approaches to the structure of benefits. The consideration here is whether those services covered under proposed programs are directly related to income, e.g., dental care, or whether these services are ones that low- and middle-income groups consume relatively more frequently than do high-income groups and/or have higher direct or out-of-pocket expenditures associated with their use, e.g., outpatient physician visits.

Arguments for attaching consumer cost sharing provisions to the benefit structures of all or some programs that would be established by proposed national health insurance legislation are broadly based in concerns regarding allocation of costs and services. The primary arguments relate to (1) the need for placing limits on the cost of such programs funded by public monies and (2) the role of cost sharing in providing for a more efficient and appropriate allocation of health care services. Two basic assumptions underlie these kinds of arguments. First, consumers have insufficient information and knowledge of their choices among providers and types of alternative services to make rational decisions with respect to the costs of services and the benefits of their insurance coverage. Second, cost sharing in the form of deductibles and coinsurance payments will discourage the use of inappropriate and unnecessary services and will encourage the choice and use of more efficient, low-cost providers.

Arguments against the imposition of cost sharing provisions stress the role of deductibles and coinsurance as barriers to health care, particularly with the large unmet demand for certain types of services, and refute the relevancy of cost sharing in any rationalization of consumer choices in health care. Those who argue for no cost sharing in national health insurance suggest other means for controlling the overall costs and the prices and utilization of individual services, such as regulation and utilization review.

Eligibility Criteria

In this section, eligibility criteria for enrollment under the different types of programs that would be established are reviewed and compared for those selected proposed plans that do not provide for universal eligibility. The Corman-Kennedy Bill and the Young Bill are excluded from the discussion, therefore, since both of these proposals would provide for universal coverage of the resident population of the United States under one program. The discussion focuses on eligibility criteria for proposed programs as differentiated for four population groups: (1) employee-employer groups; (2) the poor or low-income groups; (3) the medically indigent; and (4) the aged.

Employee-Employer Groups

Employees generally would be covered as a separate group by "qualified" policies that their employers voluntarily or by requirement offer through private health insurance organizations. Differences in the structure of the alternative proposed employee plans are:

1. The definition of an employer—usually given by the number and types of employees;
2. The inclusion of federal, state and local government employees;
3. The inclusion of self-employed persons;
4. The inclusion of part-time employees;
5. The inclusion of unemployed persons and persons receiving unemployment compensation;
6. The continuation of coverage during interim periods of unemployment; and
7. The eligibility of employed persons for coverage under any programs for the low-income and medically indigent groups.

Burleson-McIntyre Bill. The employee plan under the Burleson-McIntyre Bill asks only for the *voluntary* participation of employers in offering qualified private health insurance policies to their employees and families. Such a plan, however, must make *both* full-time and part-time employees and their dependents eligible. A part-time employee is defined as one who works at least twenty hours per week for twenty-six weeks in a year. All new employees would be covered after the first three months of employment. Continuation of coverage under this plan varies with the different reasons for any temporary or permanent termination of employment, with a minimum of two months of coverage for permanent termination to thirty months of coverage for absence due to illness or disability.

To accommodate the needs of those who are not eligible for either the employee plan or the State plan, such as self-employed and unemployed persons, this bill would also structure an individual plan whereby individuals can voluntarily purchase a qualified policy for themselves and their families.[b] The State plan under this bill sets reasonable limits for income eligibility requirements, and thus most employed and self-employed persons with low incomes would be eligible.

Fulton-Duncan Bill. Under the provisions of the Fulton-Duncan proposal, employers would be *required* to offer qualified private health insurance policies to employees and their families, with participation for the employee being optional. All full-time and part-time employees who work a regular twenty-hour week

[b]The entire premium cost would be incurred by the policyholder under the individual plan. However, income tax deductions would be provided as an incentive to encourage the purchase of nongroup insurance with specified benefits.

would be eligible for this coverage. Included in the definition of a part-time employee is the person who is expected to work at least twenty hours per week for twenty-six weeks during the next year or who has actually worked at least twenty hours per week during the previous year. Because of the mandatory participation of all employers in this program, "small" employers would receive federal assistance in the form of a subsidy, if the costs to the employer of this new program would increase their payroll by a substantial amount.

New employees would be eligible after the first month of employment, and coverage would continue for thirty days after termination of employment. For those persons who are temporarily unemployed, between jobs, and receiving unemployment compensation, a special program would be established whereby the federal government would pay the full premium cost for continuation of coverage under the employee's prior group plan.

Unemployed and self-employed persons could also purchase qualified private health insurance policies through a second type of program structured for the poor and medically indigent, with federal subsidies, based on income, to help defray the cost of the premium, as is also the case for the employee program. Employed persons are not eligible for enrollment in the program for the self-employed and unemployed for administrative reasons, since the share of the premium met by the enrollee for either program would be the same for a given level of income.

Ullman Bill. The Ullman proposal's plan for employees *requires* all employers who are currently subject to the payroll tax, including nonprofit organizations or employers who elect to participate in the social security program on a voluntary basis, to offer qualified insurance policies to all their employees. Federal, state and local government employees are *not* eligible for this employee plan (or for the federally contracted plan for low-income and medically indigent groups). Enrollment in the plan for the poor and medically indigent is also not available to any other employed persons, even though they may meet the income requirements for the plan and participation in the employee plan is voluntary.

The provisions for continuation of coverage under the employee plan are: (1) for fourteen days for the employee whose employment is terminated involuntarily and (2) for 30 days at the option of the employee, with the employee incurring the entire cost of the premium when termination is voluntary. Self-employed persons and other unemployed persons who are not eligible for the federal assistance plan can enroll in the employee plan on a voluntary basis through state administration of federally regulated guidelines for this component of the employee program.

Long-Ribicoff Bill. The program for employees and the self-employed under the Long-Ribicoff proposal is *voluntary,* whereby private health insurance policies are approved by the Secretary of HEW as meeting certain minimum requirements with respect to eligibility, covered services, and the benefit or pay-out ratio. The provisions of this bill would also promote the formation of "pools" of insurers offering certified policies. The scope of benefits, including the conditions for cost sharing, is the same as those provided for under the catastrophic program.

Any such employee-employer plan is required to make all employees and their families eligible. This requirement does not include: (1) employees who work less than twenty-five hours per week, (2) temporary employees, and (3) employees covered under the Medicare program. Federal, state and local government employees would be covered under these kinds of qualified private plans. The premium payments under an employee plan are completely the cost of the employer. No financial participation in the cost of the program is to be required or permitted of the enrollee. Coverage would begin after thirty days of employment and would continue for ninety days after any termination of employment.

Poor and Medically Indigent Groups

For those proposals under discussion here that focus on the poor and medically indigent groups through separate plans (excluding therefore the Corman-Kennedy and Young bills again), income eligibility criteria vary considerably. The Burleson-McIntyre bill offers a plan closely aligned with the current Medicaid program, i.e., cash assistance recipients are automatically eligible. Medically indigent persons could enroll voluntarily and the requirements for individuals and families of different sizes for meeting income eligibility are fairly liberal. This State plan would be financed by state and largely federal general revenues and by premiums paid by enrollees.

The Fulton-Duncan proposal for coverage under private qualified health insurance policies relies heavily on employee-employer plans for the broadest eligibility. This proposal's plan for the poor and medically indigent is basically directed at the unemployed and self-employed, with eligibility extended in some cases to low-income workers. Federal subsidization of private coverage is through a tax credit system.

The Ullman bill proposes a program of coverage for the aged, low-income, and medically indigent whereby the Federal government contracts with private insurance carriers. The aged population currently covered by Medicare would be automatically eligible without regard for income, but the present Medicare payroll tax revenues would be used toward financing this program. Eligibility for the medically indigent is defined by several income categories based on family size, and enrollees would pay premiums according to their income level.

The plan for the poor under the Long-Ribicoff proposal does not define a medically indigent class of eligibles. Although the working poor, in addition to cash assistance recipients, are eligible, the income cut-off is sufficiently low so as to include only those at subsistence level. Further details on the eligibility of poor and medically indigent groups for each of these proposals follows.

Burleson-McIntyre Bill. The Burleson-McIntyre proposal for a state health insurance plan would provide coverage for the poor and the medically indigent, in addition to the uninsurables and other special groups. The costs of this State plan would be joint federal and state general revenues in combination with premiums paid by the enrollees. All public assistance recipients would be automatically eligible without regard for income. The medically indigent could *voluntarily* enroll if they are not eligible for a qualified employee plan and if their adjusted gross income, as defined for federal tax purposes, is less than these amounts:

Individual	$5,000
Family of two	$7,500
Family of three or more	$10,000

Uninsurables may also enroll on a voluntary basis, if they have made applications to three insurance carriers to obtain a qualified plan and either have been refused a policy, usually for reasons of poor health or preexisting conditions, or were offered a policy at a premium greater than twice the premium under the State plan. Other persons–such as dependents of members of the armed forces and institutionalized persons–are also eligible for enrollment under the State plan on a group basis, since a substantial amount of their medical care is currently provided for through federal and state programs. Persons sixty-five years and over, covered under the Medicare program that is retained under this proposal, could also enroll in the State plan when certain conditions are met. Those unemployed because of work lay offs who meet the income requirements for two consecutive months would also be eligible for the State plan.

Fulton-Duncan Bill. The approach of the Fulton-Duncan proposal is to treat the poor and medically indigent through a program basically structured for the unemployed and self-employed. All persons who are not eligible for coverage under the employee-employer plan would be eligible for participation in this federally subsidized system of providing qualified private health insurance coverage. Persons who are sixty-five years and over and eligible for coverage under the Medicare program would also be eligible for subsidies for the purchase of a supplemental insurance policy.

Under the system of tax credits, the federal government would pay the full premium for those eligibles who have no income tax liability because of their low level of annual income. The Federal government would also assist in the payment of premiums for qualified health insurance policies for other eligibles, but in smaller proportions as the amount of income tax liability increases. A certificate of entitlement could be issued by the federal government that would be redeemable for insurance coverage with insurance carriers and would be in lieu of the tax credits against income tax payments.

The value of the certificate of entitlement or tax credit for a benefit year is determined by multiplying the amount of the premium by a given percentage factor designated by a schedule of income tax liabilities in the base year.

Income tax liability in base year	Percentage factor
$0	100%
$191-200	80%
$391–400	60%
$591-600	40%
$791-800	20%
$891 or over	10%

A benefit year is any twelve-month period beginning in the year immediately following the close of the base year. The value of the tax credit as measured by income tax liability is also subject to an adjustment for "special income" received by eligible individuals and families during the base year. Special income is defined as that income not subject to tax under the Internal Revenue Code, with the exception that pensions and annuity payments or social security benefit payments are only included in the definition, if, singly or in combination, they exceed $4,000 in any taxable year. For each full $100 of special income, the appropriate percentage factor based on income tax liability is reduced by one percentage point. In no case, however, will this reduction of the allowable tax credit be below 10 percent of the premium cost.

At least three other important provisions are built into this plan for the poor and medically indigent. First, in those cases when the individuals' or families' tax credit is greater than the respective income tax liability, any excess can be claimed as though it were an overpayment of income tax for the taxable year. Second, each insurance carrier that offers an employee-employer plan under this proposal must also offer qualified individual policies for the unemployed and self-employed. In addition, the premium rate for such individual policies can not exceed 125 percent of the estimated average premium paid in the state for qualified insurance for groups of employees with an enrollment of more than 100 members. Third, low-income workers can also be eligible for a certificate of entitlement or a tax credit, if the premium for insurance under an employee plan is greater than what would be paid for a comparable policy under the plan for the unemployed and self-employed.

Ullman Bill. Under the provisions of the Ullman Bill, federally contracted insurance with private carriers would provide a program of coverage for the aged, low-income, and medically indigent individuals and families. Aged persons would be automatically eligible without regard for income. Eligibility for low-income and medically indigent persons is based on family income and family size, as indicated by the income classes given below. Class 1 is defined as the low-income group; Class 2, 3, and 4 are defined as the medically indigent groups.

Income class	Individual	Family of 2	Family of 3	Family of 4 or more
1	$0-2,000	$0-3,000	$0-4,500	$0- 6,000
2	$2,001-3,000	$3,001-4,500	$4,501-6,000	$6,001- 7,500
3	$3,001-4,500	$4,501-6,000	$6,001-7,500	$7,501- 9,000
4	$4,501-6,000	$6,001-7,500	$7,501-9,000	$9,001-10,500

Long-Ribicoff Bill. The medical assistance plan for low-income persons under the Long-Ribicoff proposal actually replaces the present Medicaid program. Eligibility for benefits is based on family income and family size. The benefits of the program are available to persons whose annual family income is below the following specified amounts:

Individual	$2,400
Family of 2	3,600
Family of 3	4,200
Family of 4	4,800
Family of 4 or more	4,800 plus $400 for each additional family member

Both working persons and those receiving public welfare cash assistance would be eligible for coverage under this plan. The definition of income for determination of eligiblity would include both earned and unearned income. Eligibility would continue during any given year, unless income increases by more than 20 percent above the eligibility income requirements.

While no justification is given in the legislation as to why the above specified levels of income were selected as "cut-off" points, the amounts are in the general range of the commonly employed poverty income levels. Moreover, this plan does not provide for the eligibility of a medically indigent group, although the availability of coverage for some of the working poor does extend the benefits to a limited, but additional, few.

Aged Population

Three of the selected proposals for national health insurance would, in fact, retain the current program of hospital and medical insurance for persons sixty-five years and over under Medicare. These proposals are: the Burleson-McIntyre Bill, the Fulton-Duncan Bill, and the Long-Ribicoff Bill. The Burleson-McIntyre proposal attempts to deal with the problem of the limited covered services under Medicare by allowing persons sixty-five years and older to enroll in its State plan for the poor and medically indigent, if the aged person is already enrolled in Part B of Medicare, the voluntary medical insurance plan. All benefits would first be paid as covered services under Medicare. If the aged person's income is below the specified limits for the State plan, the premium for Medicare-Part B coverage would be paid through state general revenues; if above these income limits, the enrollee would be required to pay the premium for the State plan coverage, reduced by the amount of the premium for Part B. The Long-Ribicoff proposal offers similar provisions for the low-income elderly by assuming the premium cost of Medicare-Part B and paying all coinsurance and deductible payments for the enrolled elderly persons under its medical assistance plan.[c] The benefits for the low-income aged would thereby be extended to include: all medically necessary hospital care, skilled nursing-home care, intermediate nursing-home care, and unlimited home health care services. The Fulton-Duncan proposal would also retain the present Medicare program, but would offer tax credits or a certificate of entitlement to elderly persons for the cost of purchasing a qualified supplementary insurance policy.

Both the Corman-Kennedy Bill and the Young Bill would eliminate the Medicare program and would also repeal the payroll tax for the hospital insurance plan (Medicare-Part A). The Ullman Bill, as cited above, would have persons sixty-five years and over automatically eligible for the proposed plan, which is also directed at the poor and medically indigent groups. The aged population would be eligible without regard for income and would not assume any premium costs for coverage under the program of federally contracted private insurance policies. The Medicare payroll tax would, however, be maintained, and these earmarked revenues and those general revenues currently allocated to insurance for the elderly under Medicare would be applied to the financing of this program.

Covered Services

Many of the less evident differences in proposed national health insurance plans are related to the range of types of services covered as benefits. At one extreme of what can be viewed as a continuum in terms of the range of covered services

---

[c] Aged persons who are not eligible or fail to enroll in Medicare-Part B can enroll in the plan for low-income persons, but with a reduction of $250 in benefits payments or an assumption of this amount as a deductible. For those persons 65 years and over who are not covered by Medicare, the current rate of premium required for enrollment in the hospital insurance plan, Medicare-Part A, would be reduced by 50 percent under the Long-Ribicoff proposal.

is the comprehensive care benefit package, which implies coverage for *all* types of services, including preventive services and social services related to health care. To the extent that a plan provides coverage for a more complete range of services than another plan, it can be designated as "more comprehensive." At the other extreme is the limited benefit package, which would extend the present general level of coverage under private health insurance plans to include an additional, but marginal, complement of services not already covered. It is important to recognize in reviewing the proposed range of benefits that the use of services will also be limited by an imposition of cost sharing factors attached to all or specified types of services. General comments on the nature of cost sharing in the different proposals are given below, with a more detailed review presented in the section to follow.

Corman-Kennedy Bill

From among the proposals under discussion, approaches to the financing of health care services on the most comprehensive basis are exemplified by the Corman-Kennedy Bill and the Young Bill. The services covered by the structure of benefits under these two national health insurance plans include a full range of institutional care, personal services, and ancillary services and supplies, *without* any provisions for consumer cost sharing. The specific types of covered services in each of these categories is given below for the Corman-Kennedy Bill, as a guideline for analyzing the benefits in other proposals (an asterisk indicates that there is some limitation on those services):

Institutional Services

- General hospital inpatient care
- *Psychiatric hospital inpatient care
- Hospital outpatient care
- *Skilled nursing home care

Personal Services

- Physicians' services
  - Physical checkups
  - Immunizations
  - Well-child care
  - Family planning
- *Physicians' psychiatric services
- *Dentists' services
- Podiatrists' services
- Home health services
- Laboratory and X-ray services

*Other personal services, i.e., psychological, physiotherapy, nutritional, social work, health education, and other related services

Other Services and Supplies

Optometrists' services, including eyeglasses

*Medical and therapeutic devices, appliances, and equipment

Ambulance services

*Prescription drugs

Four types of services and supplies are not specifically covered in the range of benefits offered under the Corman-Kennedy Bill, but they are covered under at least one of the other proposals reviewed here. These services and supplies are: hearing care services and hearing aids; blood and blood products; speech therapy; and intermediate care nursing-home services.

The limitations on the amount of certain services that are covered under the Corman-Kennedy Bill restrict benefits by the number of days or visits, by age group, and by type of provider. First, psychiatric hospital inpatient care is limited to forty-five consecutive days for an episode of illness. Second, outpatient mental health services are limited to twenty visits per episode if the services are provided by a psychiatrist, but are without limitation as to the number of visits when these services are provided by nonphysician personnel in an HMO, hospital outpatient department, or mental health clinic under contract with the plan. Third, the benefits for skilled nursing-home care would be limited to 120 days for an episode of illness.[d] Fourth, dentists' services would be covered in the first year of the program for children under fifteen years of age, and the coverage would be extended to persons two years older in each year thereafter until persons twenty-five years of age are eligible.[e] Fifth, other personal services are only covered if provided by an institution, HMO, or provider under contract with the plan. Sixth, benefit expenditures for therapeutic devices, appliances, and equipment would be limited to 2 percent of the total program expenditures. Seventh, prescription drugs would be without limitation if prescribed by a physician through an HMO or medical foundation, but coverage would be limited to drugs for chronic conditions

---

[d]Skilled nursing homes must meet the Medicare certification standards as they currently exist. All professional services provided in a nursing home must be by staff affiliated with a hospital or health maintenance organization (HMO). These kinds of provisions are generally required under all proposals discussed here.

[e]Once a person is eligible for coverage of dental services, this benefit would then continue for a lifetime. Consideration would also be given to the possibility of phasing in coverage for the entire population after the initial implementation stage according to the provisions of this proposal. Preferences would probably be given to enrollees of approved HMOs and those in already organized dental insurance plans.

and for other specified conditions and personal circumstances if provided otherwise.

Young Bill

The scope of benefits offered by the provisions of this bill are very comprehensive and closely aligned with those benefits provided by the Corman-Kennedy Bill. No cost sharing factors are attached to any of the covered services under this proposal, but a small number of services are limited by the amount of services covered or by the type of provider. These limitations on home health services, skilled nursing care services, and mental health services are indicated in the following list of covered services under the Young proposal:

Inpatient hospital services
Physicians' services, including well-baby, prenatal, and family planning, in the office, clinic or at home
Medical supplies and other health services, such as prostheses, laboratory and X-ray services, ambulance services, etc.
Home health services (limited to 180 visits per year)
Posthospital extended care services (limited to 180 days per year)
Specified drugs and biologicals on an outpatient basis
Routine dental services
Vision care and eyeglasses
Hearing exams and hearing aids
Routine physical exams (defined by regulation)
Mental health services
  Inpatient services (limited to forty-five full days or ninety partial days in a psychiatric hospital)
  Outpatient services in a community mental health center (limited to the cost of fifty visits to a private practitioner)
  Outpatient services with a private practitioner (limited to two-thirds of the costs of fifty visits)

Burleson-McIntyre Bill

The Burleson-McIntyre Bill would phase in benefits over two time periods for each of the three groups covered under the employee, individual, and State plans. This proposal has both deductible and coinsurance factors attached to its benefits, in addition to limits placed on the extent of covered services for certain categories.

At the time of the initial implementation of this proposal, the enrollees in all three types of plans would be covered for the following services:

Inpatient and outpatient hospital services for both medical and psychiatric care
Skilled nursing-home care (limited to 180 days)
Physician services and all professional services at the direction of a physician for diagnosis and treatment (other than dental and mental services)
Outpatient mental health visits (limited to first twenty visits)
Home health care services (limited to 270 days)
Prescription drugs and contraceptives
Diagnostic laboratory and X-ray services
Oral surgery
Family planning counseling
Well-baby care and immunizations (limited to children under five years)
Dental examination (limited to one exam per year for children under thirteen years)
Eye examination (limited to one exam per year for children under thirteen years)
Radiation therapy, oxygen, anesthetics, prostheses, medical equipment
PAP smear (limited to one test every two years for women nineteen years and over)

In the second phase of the Burleson-McIntyre proposal, the following covered services are added to the benefits for the three separate programs of insurance:

Physical therapy
Speech therapy
Dental care services for fillings and extractions
Other dental services and prostheses, except orthodontia
Eye examination (limited to one exam every three years)
Eyeglasses (limited to one pair per year for persons under nineteen years and to one pair every three years for persons over nineteen years)
Hearing examination (limited to one exam every three years)
Hearing aids (limited to one every three years for persons under nineteen years and to one during a lifetime for persons over nineteen years)
Physical examination (limited to one exam every five years for persons five years or older)

Ullman Bill

The Ullman Bill also employs a phase-in process whereby more "comprehensive" health care benefits are eventually achieved for the defined recipient groups over a five-year period. However, in the determination of which groups would receive what range of covered services first, persons in the medically indigent groups are given the lowest priority. The result is that, during the initial six months of the proposed programs, present benefits under the Medicare program and catastrophic coverage are extended to employees, the self-employed, persons receiving unemployment compensation, the aged (with automatic coverage for medical insurance under Medicare–Part B and catastrophic coverage for the low-income aged) and all low-income persons. These same benefits are not made available to the medically indigent groups (who are not covered under the above plans) until more than two years later.

The Ullman proposal, for most covered services, has cost sharing components attached only after the limitations fixed on the benefits has been reached. Several types of services, however, do have cost sharing attached from the initial benefit stage. A broader range of benefits is achieved in the second phase of covered services, but with a more stringent role for cost sharing. The covered services in the initial (Medicare) benefit period are:

Hospital inpatient services (limited to sixty days with cost sharing after sixty days)
Skilled nursing facility (limited to twenty days with cost sharing after twenty days)
Physicians' services–in home, office and outpatient centers and in hospitals or in other institutions (no limit on the number of visits, but with cost sharing for all visits)
Diagnostic services–no limit, but with cost sharing for all services
Home health services (limited to 200 visits)
Prosthetic devices and medical equipment (by regulation and with cost sharing on all supplies)
Ambulance services–no limit, but with cost sharing for all services

In the initial phase, no benefits are provided for physical examinations, immunizations, well-baby care, dental services, vision care, and prescription drugs.

In the second benefit phase of this proposed plan, the intention is to offer a more comprehensive package of covered services. However, in some cases, cost sharing payments for the user are increased for particular benefits, although a broader range of types of services are covered. This second stage of benefits includes:

Hospital inpatient services (limited to ninety days with cost sharing per day)
Skilled nursing facility (limited to thirty days with cost sharing per day)
Intermediate care nursing facility (limited to ninety days with cost sharing per day)

Physicians' services

In hospital or other institution—no limit and with reduced cost sharing

In home, office, and outpatient centers (limited to ten visits per year, but with cost sharing)

Diagnostic services—no limit, but with cost sharing

Immunizations

Well-baby care (limited to eight visits per year for children under one year of age; four visits per year for children age one to two years; two visits per year for children age two to five years

Home health services (limited to 100 visits and with cost sharing)

Dental services (limited to one visit per year for children to age seven years and routine dental care by regulation and with cost sharing; once child is covered, then these benefits continue to age twelve years)

Prescription drugs (limited to drugs for specific conditions by regulation and with cost sharing)

Prosthetic devices and medical equipment (by regulation and with cost sharing)

Vision services (limited to one visit per year for children to age twelve years with no cost sharing; one pair of eyeglasses per year for children to twelve years, with cost sharing)

Medically necessary ambulance services—no limit, but with cost sharing

Fulton-Duncan Bill

Under the provisions of the Fulton-Duncan proposal, all persons who voluntarily enroll in qualified private health insurance plans would be covered for the same benefits, including employees, the poor, the medically indigent, and the aged. All covered services have a coinsurance rate of 20 percent attached to them, although limits are placed on the total amount of cost sharing expenses incurred by the consumer according to the level of income. The benefits under a qualified health insurance policy include:

Inpatient hospital services

Skilled nursing care services (limited to 100 days of inpatient care)

Emergency or outpatient hospital services

Physician or osteopath services, including diagnostic, therapeutic, and preventive services, regardless of where such services are delivered

Home health services (no limit for persons under the care of a physician)

Dental care (no limit for children age two to six years; emergency dental services and oral surgery for all persons)

Ambulance services (limited to medically necessary services)

Long-Ribicoff Bill

Under the Long-Ribicoff proposal, a different benefit package in terms of the range of covered services is given for the catastrophic plan and for the medical assistance plan. The benefits under the catastrophic plan would be the same as under the present Medicare program, but there would be no limit on the number of hospital days. These same covered services would be provided for by the qualified or certified private health insurance policies under the voluntary program for basic coverage. The medical assistance plan for low-income persons would replace the Medicaid program and offer a somewhat broader range of services.

The catastrophic plan would cover all medical services after the first $2,000 of direct consumer expenses in the form of cost sharing *or* all hospital expenses after sixty days of hospitalization for these covered services:

Institutional services
- Hospital inpatient services
- Posthospital extended care services

Personal services
- Physicians' services
- Laboratory and X-ray services
- Home health services
- Outpatient physical therapy services

Other services and supplies
- Medical supplies and appliances
- Ambulance services

Mental health benefits would cover: inpatient services in an accredited medical institution; partial hospitalization in or by an accredited medical institution or in a qualified mental health center; and outpatient services by a qualified community mental health center or a psychiatrist. Not included are: any outpatient services provided by a psychiatrist for purposes of diagnosis or treatment of acute psychosis in excess of five visits plus any additional approved visits; blood and blood products; experimental procedures and treatment. In addition, there would be no payment for covered extended care services during any period for which an individual is entitled to hospital insurance benefits under Part A of Medicare.

The medical assistance plan would provide for the following covered services:

Inpatient hospital services (limited to sixty days of necessary services during a benefit period)

Medical and other health services

Skilled nursing facility services
Home health services
Intermediate care services
Mental health services
Prenatal and well-baby care
Family planning counseling, services, and supplies
Early and periodic screening, diagnosis, and treatment (limited to eligible children under eighteen years)

This plan is the only one that would cover intermediate care nursing-home services from among all the various plans and programs offered by the six proposals reviewed here, except for limited coverage under the Ullman plan.

Under the voluntary certification program for private health insurance largely directed at employee groups and the self-employed, the provisions of the Long-Ribicoff proposal would require that at least those basic covered services offered as benefits under the plan for catastrophic coverage, and similar to the benefits under the Medicare program, be included in a qualified policy. Certain limits on the amount of services covered as benefits would exist under these types of qualified plans, and deductibles and coinsurance payments would be permitted with certain guidelines.

Cost Sharing

For those four proposals under discussion here that include cost sharing factors for the consumers of health services covered by their benefit structures, the general approaches to cost sharing differ in terms of the particular forms employed, i.e., deductibles, coinsurance, and copayments and in terms of the amounts of payment required for the consumer. Detailed information on the role of cost sharing in the Burleson-McIntyre, Fulton-Duncan, Ullman, and Long-Ribicoff proposals is given below. The Corman-Kennedy and the Young proposals are not included in this discussion, since the structure of benefits under their respective universal programs for national health insurance are free of any cost sharing components.

The structure of cost sharing found in the Burleson-McIntyre bill, which is endorsed by the Health Insurance Association of America (HIAA), employs a deductible and coinsurance factors. The maximum deductible allowed for a qualified policy is $100. For the poor and medically indigent eligible for the State plan, this deductible is adjusted downward, based on adjusted gross income and family size. With two exceptions, all the covered services offered in the first phase of the programs for the three different groups of enrollees have a coinsurance of 20 percent attached to them. These exceptions are the first twenty outpatient mental health visits and dental services other than fillings and extractions that have a 50 percent coinsurance rate attached to them. The coinsurance factors remain in effect for benefits in the second phase of this national health insurance proposal, excluding: diagnostic X rays and laboratory tests; well-baby care; dental examination for children under thirteen years; eye examinations for children under thirteen years; family planning counseling; and PAP smears for women nineteen years and over.

The Fulton-Duncan proposal would fix a coinsurance payment of 20 percent also on all benefits or covered services. There would be no coinsurance requirements for those individuals or families eligible for full federal subsidization of premium costs in the form of a certificate of entitlement for private health insurance coverage. This proposal does not set a deductible amount for the consumer to incur.

The Ullman proposal employs two approaches to cost sharing, each one associated with particular benefit packages in the two phases of its plans. In general, under the initial phase with benefits at the current Medicare level, a $60 deductible and a 20 percent coinsurance rate would be attached: to inpatient hospital care (after sixty days); to physicians' services in the home, office, clinic, or hospital; and to ambulance services, medical equipment, and prostheses. For skilled nursing-home care (after twenty days), the coinsurance rate of 20 percent only applies. The $60 deductible is a common or maximum amount applicable to all specified covered services.

In the second phase, which offers more "comprehensive" kinds of benefits, the Ullman plan relies on copayment factors for the more basic types of covered services. Generally, the range of these copayments are from $2 to $5 for hospital and extended care and for physician services. A coinsurance rate of 20 percent is, however, maintained for: diagnostic services; dental services for children (adults are not covered); eyeglasses for children (adults are not covered); and ambulance services, medical equipment, and prostheses.

The provisions for cost sharing under the Long-Ribicoff proposal are different for the federally subsidized low-income assistance plan and the program of qualified basic health insurance policies. The assistance plan asks only for a minimal copayment of $3 for a physician visit (other than for an inpatient visit), excluding visits for well-baby care and family planning. This $3 copayment is only applicable, however, for the first ten visits for physician services for an individual *or* for a family. The covered days in the hospital or in a skilled or intermediate care nursing facility is limited to sixty days under this plan, but the catastrophic coverage under a separate plan would then become effective. The current deductibles and copayments under the Medicare program would still apply except in those cases where the enrollee is also eligible for the assistance plan.

The cost sharing factors in a qualified basic private health insurance plan must meet certain specified guidelines. The deductible for inpatient hospital coverage is not to exceed $100 during a benefit year. Hospital coverage must be for sixty days and cannot have any coinsurance or copayment requirements attached to these benefits. The deductible for medical services, including physician care provided in the home, office, hospital, and other institutions, is limited to $50 for a benefit year. Coinsurance requirements on medical service benefits can be no more than 20 percent, but can be attached to all covered services under the Long-Ribicoff proposal.

Catastrophic Coverage

Only one proposal under discussion here, the Long-Ribicoff Bill, includes a specific and separate plan for universal catastrophic coverage. The Corman-Kennedy and the Young proposals—by providing for comprehensive benefits under their respective universal insurance plans and by not requiring cost sharing in any form for the consumer—meet the need for coverage against extraordinary out-of-pocket expenses by a direct approach. The Fulton-Duncan Bill, the Ullman Bill, and the Burleson-McIntyre Bill stipulate, in general, limits on the amount of direct expenditures that a family or an individual can incur under the various programs that they propose.

The federal catastrophic health insurance program under the Long-Ribicoff proposal provides for catastrophic coverage for hospital and related services and for medical services for all United States residents. At the option of their employer, employees could be covered for catastrophic costs under either a private health insurance plan or this federal program. Catastrophic coverage becomes effective after sixty days of inpatient care in a hospital or a skilled nursing home *or* after $2,000 of deductible and coinsurance expenses have been incurred by the insured. Excluded, however, from this $2,000 aggregate of deductibles and coinsurance is consumer payment for mental health services in excess of $500. Once the catastrophic benefits are available, no further coinsurance payments would be necessary on the part of the insured individual or family.

Certain provisions of this catastrophic program result in some restriction of the type and amount of coverage. First, the expenses incurred by any other family members, if less than $500, can be deemed the expenses of an individual for purposes of catastrophic benefits.[f] However, this consideration of additional expenditures can only be included in the determination of eligibility for catastrophic coverage, if the individual seeking catastrophic benefits has incurred personally at least $500 or more in the benefit period *and* if the individual had also met the deductible for a period in the preceding calendar year. With these

[f] A family member is defined to include: a spouse; a dependent; the person (or spouse of person) of whom the individual is a dependent; or a person who is a dependent of the same person of whom the individual is a dependent.

restrictions in effect, a large family could have aggregate out-ofpocket expenditures far greater than the $2,000 maximum, or a disporportionate percentage of their income.

Second, under the low-income assistance plan, if an eligible person is *not* a member of a family (or is a member of a family whose members also meet the circumstances described here) and for a continuous period *in excess* of sixty days is an inpatient in a hospital, skilled nursing home, or intermediate care facility, for each month as an inpatient, the person must pay an amount equal to his or her own cash income minus $50. This "special coinsurance" attached to long-term care institutional services suggests that the catastrophic insurance program would not alter the current financial situation, primarily with respect to the elderly in nursing homes, other than to increase their personal needs allowances in some cases. Further, this proposal sets forth the provision that no payment for extended care services would be provided during any period for which an individual is entitled to hospital insurance benefits under Medicare–Part A and offers no resolution for these kinds of circumstances.

The Fulton-Duncan Bill, which relies completely on private health insurance for national coverage under the provisions of its proposal, sets limits on the total amount of coinsurance payments that an individual or family would be burdened with before catastrophic benefits would meet all expenses for covered services. This aggregate amount would be 10 percent of the *difference* between the annual income and the "coinsurance deduction," which is graduated according to family size, *or* $1,500 for an individual and $2,000 for a family, whichever is *less.* These coinsurance deductions are given as:

Individual	$1,500
Family of two	$3,000
Family of three	$3,600
Family of four	$4,200
Family of five or more	$4,800

For example, for a family of four at an income level of $4,400, the limit on consumer expenses in the form of coinsurance payments before catastrophic coverage is effective is $20, or at an income level of $12,000, this limit is $780. The "poor" or those at and below these income levels–defined according to family size as coinsurance deduction limits–would, therefore, pay no coinsurance.

Catastrophic benefits under the Ullman Bill would also become available once out-of-pocket payments reach specified limits. These specified limits are given according to income levels based on family size and age categories. In addition, the aggregate consumer expenses are defined so as to include: (1) premium payments for a qualified private health insurance policy; (2) expenses for cost sharing, whether in the form of coinsurance, deductibles, or copayments; and (3) any expenses incurred because of the limitations placed on the amount any type of covered services.

The consumer expense limits provided for by this bill are given below for the various income classes and for two age groups, i.e., "under 65 years" and "65 years and over." The income

Income class	*Expense limits*	
	Under 65 years	*65 years and over*
1	0	0
2	$250	$125
3	$500	$250
4	$750	$375
5	10 percent of income	

classes are stipulated according to family size and these classes are the same as those employed in determining eligibility for the federally subsidized plan for coverage for the aged, poor, and medically indigent. The medically indigent groups are those persons with incomes in class 2, 3, and 4. The poor (class 1) would be

Income class	*Single individual*	*Family of 2*	*Family of 3*	*Family of 4 or more*
1	$0-2,000	$0-3,000	$0-4,500	$0- 6,000
2	2,001-3,000	3,001-4,500	4,501-6,000	6,001- 7,500
3	3,001-4,500	4,501-6,000	6,001-7,500	7,501- 9,000
4	4,501-6,000	6,001-7,500	7,501-9,000	9,001-10,500

automatically eligible for catastrophic coverage in the first phase of benefits under this proposal, since they would not be responsible for any cost sharing. The proposal requires further that all qualified policies for employee groups, the self-employed, and persons receiving unemployment insurance provide also for catastrophic coverage of the same type. However, catastrophic coverage would be extended to the aged and the medically indigent under the federally subsidized program only after three years following the implementation of this bill.

In the plan for catastrophic coverage that it proposes, the Burleson-McIntyre Bill also directly links the specified limits on the amount of out-of-pocket expenditures to the variable deductible amount, which in turn is based on income and family size. The limit in all cases on the sum of the deductible and coinsurance payments is ten times the respective deductible amount as determined for the individual or family. Since the maximum deductible attached to a qualified policy as defined under this proposal is fixed at $100, the maximum amount of consumer expenses that must be incurred before the catastrophic coverage becomes effective is $1,000. The poor and medically indigent covered under the State plan, who face reduced deductibles according to their income and family size, would, therefore, have a lower limit set for the maximum expenses, for example, as shown below:

Single individual	*Family of 2*	*Family of 3 or more*	*Deductible*	*Maximum expenses*
Less than $1,000	Less than $1,500	Less than $2,000	$10	$100
$2,000-2,500	$3,000-3,750	$4,000- 5,000	40	400
$4,500-5,000	$6,750-7,500	$9,000-10,000	90	900

Summary of the Distributional Effects of Selected Benefit Structures

Although net gains in the utilization of health services or dollar benefits would result for all income groups under the proposed plans for national health insurance, how pro-poor or regressive the actual distribution of benefits might be relative to the current inequalities in health care financing for the poor and middle income groups varies greatly. The components of the benefit structure uder proposed national health insurance legislation that could aid in eliminating the inequities in the current distribution of health care services include: eligibility criteria; the range and limits on covered services; the form and amounts of cost sharing for the consumer; and the role of catastrophic coverage. Each of these components has been discussed here in the context of the specified related provisions offered by six national health insurance proposals.

Because the Corman-Kennedy and the Young bills provide for universal coverage with all U.S. residents eligible for the same benefits, the potential for equity in the distribution of benefits is established. This is not to say, however, that by providing the right to health care by removing the initial financial barriers, all persons will have all their personal health care needs met. Additional problems regarding unmet consumer needs and associated with the availability of and access to adequate and appropriate services are generally recognized in these proposals, but dealt with through very minor provisions.

The other four bills propose national health insurance plans that specify eligibility criteria for differentiated population groups. Each of these proposals relies on private health insurance policies for coverage for the largest group, i.e., employees. The Burleson-McIntyre and the Long-Ribicoff bills ask only for the voluntary participation of employers in offering qualified policies to their employees; the Fulton-Duncan and the Ullman bills would require employers to do so. Under such a voluntary program, those employees traditionally without coverage provided directly through their employment remain at a continued financial disadvantage, since premiums for individual policies with comparable benefits are sufficiently high so as to deprive these individuals and families any, and at best poor, health insurance coverage. These types of employees are, in general, the low-income workers and include part-time employees, farm workers, and service employees, such as household help.[g]

The eligibility criteria for the poor and medically indigent groups vary considerably for the different proposed programs. The Burleson-McIntyre Bill would only include the medically indigent group in its proposed program of medical assistance on a voluntary basis. However, the categories for income eligibility are quite liberal (in the version of the bill introduced into the 94th Congress) and do take into account family size in determining the various income classes. Similar provisions are also offered by the Ullman proposal's plan for federally contracted insurance with private carriers for low-income and medically indigent groups. The aged would be automatically eligible for this program. The Fulton-Duncan proposal uses a tax credit system for federal subsidization of premiums for the poor and medically indigent. Since the tax credit is based on income tax liability, the variable family size is indirectly incorporated into the eligibility for tax credits through the role of deductions for dependents in determining income tax liability. The medical assistance plan for low-income persons under the Long-Ribicoff proposal would *not* make medically indigent groups eligible. Moreover, the income eligibility criteria, while adjusted for family size, are set for restrictively low-income levels relative to other proposals.

From among those proposals that would treat subgroups through separate programs, the Ullman Bill has the most liberal eligibility requirements for the aged population, since this proposal would make *all* persons sixty-five years and older automatically eligible for the low-income program of medical assistance. The Medicare program would be retained under the Burleson-McIntyre, Fulton-Duncan, and Long-Ribicoff proposals. For the Burleson-McIntyre and the Long-Ribicoff bills, the poor aged would also be eligible for the respective low-income plans which they propose; the Burleson-McIntyre proposal also has provisions for similar coverage for the medically indigent aged, while the Long-Ribicoff Bill does not. For the Fulton-Duncan proposal, the aged would be eligible for federal subsidies for the purpose of supplemental medical insurance policies through the tax credit program.

[g]The Fulton-Duncan Bill would require that part-time workers be included in the definition of employees under its mandatory plan. The Ullman Bill's mandatory employee plan would make eligible only those workers who currently pay social security taxes and thus would omit a number of categories of employees.

The most common services omitted from or limited in the benefit structures of the six national health insurance proposals reviewed here are: skilled and intermediate care nursing-home services; dental services for adults; outpatient and inpatient mental health services; drugs; and preventive and health-related social services. These restrictions on covered services are present even in those proposals that portend to offer comprehensive covered services for all persons, i.e., the Corman-Kennedy and Young bills, and those proposals that would phase in benefits over time to achieve a more comprehensive range of covered services, i.e., the Burleson-McIntyre and Ullman bills.

The possibility of sustaining current inequities associated with insurance benefits is simply greater when a proposal restricts its benefits to less than comprehensive range of covered services. Frequently, those services that are not covered or for which limits are attached are considered on some priority basis as "optional." It is precisely the above list of services that may represent a critical need for members of the low- and middle-income groups and/or for which they cannot afford out-of-pocket expenses, while they might have minimal coverage for other hospital and medical services.

By denying any role for consumer cost sharing and thus promoting the concept that a "catastrophic" level of expenses may exist in any financial circumstances *unrelated* to limits set on aggregate consumer expenditures by other proposals, the Corman-Kennedy and Young bills are essentially more preferable on equity grounds. By contrast, the benefit structures for the remaining four bills necessarily would have inequitable effects across income groups, depending on (1) the amount and type of cost sharing, (2) whether these factors vary according to income levels, and (3) the limits set on total consumer expenses before any catastrophic coverage would become effective.

All four bills ask for 20 percent *coinsurance* rates on most, if not all, covered services. The Burleson-McIntyre proposal would allow for reductions in coinsurance payments for the poor and medically indigent persons eligible for its proposed State plan based on adjusted gross income and family size. Therefore, some regressivity is built into this benefit structure. (There are, however, certain covered services in this proposal that have coinsurance rates of as high as 50 percent attached to them.) Cost sharing remains in effect for most of the covered services even in the second phase of the Burleson-McIntyre proposal, when the relatively broader range of benefits are offered. Minimal copayments would be in effect for the second phase of benefits under the Ullman proposal and for the program for the poor under the Long-Ribicoff Bill. Because of the fixed amount required as payment for all income classes, *copayments* deny a role for ability to pay, unless the fixed amounts are permitted to vary according to income.

Deductible amounts are also required by all these bills, except the Fulton-Duncan proposal. These *deductibles* range from \$60 under the Ullman proposal to \$150 for aggregate hospital and medical coverage under the voluntary basic private health insurance program proposed by the Long-Ribicoff Bill. The same amount of deductible payments would be necessary for individuals and families in all income classes, except under the Burleson-McIntyre proposal.

The Long-Ribicoff proposal is the only one that would structure a separate program for catastrophic benefits, recalling, of course, that there is no need for such a program under the benefit structure of the Corman-Kennedy and Young proposals. Actually, the highest level of direct consumer expenditures is required *prior* to eligibility for catastrophic benefits under this Long-Ribicoff program—after sixty days in a hospital or skilled nursing facility or $2,000, but with limitations on recognized expenses for mental health and expenses by other family members. All three other proposals provide eligibility for catastrophic coverage by criteria based on both income and family size. This latter approach necessarily incorporates pro-poor factors into the benefit structure. The Ullman proposal does set an expense limit of 10 percent of income for those not determined to be eligible as poor or medically indigent—this results in proportional effects above certain income levels depending on family size. This proposal also differentiates the expense limits for the "under sixty-five years" and "sixty-five years and over" age categories. Lower limits are given for the elderly, which reduces the distributional effects for this group. Finally, by comparison, based on the type of eligibility determination and the level of expenses to be incurred prior to catastrophic benefits, the Long-Ribicoff proposed program for catastrophic coverage would have the most pro-rich distribution of benefits for this specific type of coverage.

9 Alternative Sources of Financing National Health Insurance

The alternative means available for financing a national health insurance plan are many. There are both a number of different types of sources of financing and any combination of several of these sources to consider. The three major sources of financing discussed in this chapter are: (1) the personal income tax for funding through federal general revenues; (2) the payroll or social security tax; and (3) premiums, whether paid by the individual or family, paid by employees, or paid by employers, in whole or part, on the behalf of their employees.[a] The discussion also treats in less detail the medical deduction and tax credit approaches to financing and the various types of state taxes.

In the first part of this chapter, the evidence available on the distributional effects of the alternative types of sources of financing across family income groups is presented. With these findings as background, the various proposals for financing national health insurance according to the specific kinds of cost structures that they would establish are reviewed. The analysis emphasizes the consideration of the distributional effects in choosing among the alternative means of financing national health insurance—precisely because the question of who should pay what for health insurance and health care is generally posed in terms of the allocative effects. The most frequent example of this latter approach to choosing a means of financing is the concern with the allocation of the costs between the public and private sectors. In support of the need to also emphasize a distributional approach to analysis of the costs of national health insurance, Fein states:

> . . . Americans fail to recognize the equity consideration involved in the choice between alternative funding mechanisms, say between income and payroll taxes, view these issues as matters for technicians, and believe that fewer options exist than is the case. If so, this is regrettable. How funds are raised and the burden that thus falls upon various income groups is something that should be debated by the general public and its representatives. It should not be left to technicians.[1]

Distributional Effects of Alternative Sources of Financing

The discussion that follows presents evidence on the distributional effects across

[a]Other tax sources for federal general revenues are corporate income taxes and excise taxes.

income groups associated with the alternative means of financing national health insurance plans. The sources of financing discussed are: the payroll tax, the personal income tax, premiums, medical deductions and tax credits, and state tax revenue sources. Each of these sources is primarily reviewed independently in terms of the evidence available regarding its particular distributional effects. In addition, comparisons of the distributional effects of the payroll tax versus the personal income tax and overall comparison of the relative progressive and regressive nature of the various types of sources of financing are presented.

The Payroll Tax

Among the possible sources of financing for national health insurance, the tax institution called "the payroll tax," together with its present role in financing social security programs, is not well understood by the general public. This is true even with the increasing reliance on and prominance of this type of tax base in the financing of a variety of federal programs. In fiscal year 1975, for example, payroll or social security taxes accounted for 25 percent of federal revenues, totaling $73 billion. Further, revenues from the payroll tax, which are earmarked for the financing of federal old-age, survivors, disability, and health insurance programs (OASDHI), increased by forty-five times their level in 1949, when their share of total federal revenues was about 4 percent.[2]

When the social security tax was initiated in 1937, a 1 percent tax was levied on the first $3,000 of earnings or each wage-earner was taxed at a maximum of $30. Over the years, the tax base or the ceiling on taxable earnings was raised and the rate of taxation was increased. The result is that in 1975 the first $14,100 of earnings was taxed at the rate of 5.85 percent, and the annual maximum contribution for social security for each wage-earner was $824.85. As of January 1, 1976, the ceiling will increase again, with the limit placed on the first $15,300 to be taxed at the same rate of 5.85 percent. There is also a scheduled expansion of the maximum tax base for 1977, when the first $16,800 of earnings will be taxed and the maximum contribution will increase to about $1,000. Part of the increase in the additional taxes is linked to the levying of a payroll tax to finance the hospital insurance program for Medicare, which is set at a rate of 1.2 percent. Recent increases in the ceiling for the tax base have occurred automatically as average earnings rise, rather than by congressional approval as was necessary in the past.

The total payrolls of employers are taxed at a rate equal to that levied on the earnings of employees, but only for those payroll obligations up to the ceiling on taxable earnings. Employers are also required to pay an unemployment insurance tax. This tax rate varies from state to state, but is generally about 2 percent. The tax base is set at the first $4,200 of the worker's payroll cost in most states. Self-employed persons, included in the social security program since

1950, have their earnings taxed currently at a rate of 7 percent, but with the same ceiling on the level of taxable earnings as for employees. A schedule of the taxable ceilings and the combined employee and employer rate of taxation is given in Table 9-1.

The payroll tax is an *involuntary* tax, despite the frequent use of the term "contribution to social security," and eligibility for benefits is only loosely tied to individual contributions. Under the social security tax laws, no allowance is made for exemptions, which is one reason for the regressive nature of the payroll tax. The primary reason for the disproportionate burdens of the payroll tax across income groups is the imposition of the ceiling or maximum level of income which is taxable. This combination of characteristics–absence of provisions for exemptions, which *are* provided for under the personal income tax laws, and the placing of a ceiling on those earnings that are taxable–results "in effective payroll tax rates for the working poor that are far higher than those for upper-income groups."[3]

Table 9-1
Social Security (OASDHI) Taxable Ceiling and Rates, 1960-1976[a]

Year	*OASDHI Taxable Ceiling (Dollars)*	*OASDHI Statutory Rates (Total Percent for Both Employee and Employer)*
1960	$ 4,800	6.0%
1961	4,800	6.0
1962	4,800	6.25
1963	4,800	7.25
1964	4,800	7.25
1965	4,800	7.25
1966	6,600	8.4
1967	6,600	8.8
1968	7,800	8.8
1969	7,800	9.6
1970	7,800	9.6
1971	7,800	10.4
1972	9,000	10.4
1973	10,800	11.7
1974	12,600	11.7
1975	14,100	11.7
1976	15,300	11.7

[a]Rates do not include employer tax for unemployment insurance, since these rates vary from state to state.

Source: Social Security Administration, Office of Research and Statistics, *Reducing Social Security Contribution for Low-income Workers: Issues and Analysis,* Staff Paper No. 16 (1974), p. 48.

In addition to the regressive nature of the employees' portion of the payroll tax, there is evidence that the employers' share of the payroll tax is in fact also the ultimate burden of the employees. While studies show differences in estimates of the incidence of the payroll tax across income groups, depending on assumptions regarding the shifting of the employers' tax to employees, in all cases the payroll tax is found to be regressive *beyond* the ceiling on taxable earnings.[4]

While there is disagreement as to what proportion of the employer's tax burden is shifted to the employee, Brittain in his exhaustive study argues that the entire burden of the employer's tax is borne by the employees, since the empolyer's contribution is a tax on his total payroll and, as is the case with the employee contribution, is withheld from the workers' wages and salaries.[b] By concluding that *both* the employee and the employer contributions to the payroll tax "are, in reality, extracted from labor's real wage rate," Brittain's analysis points to" a greater regressive impact of the entire tax than is indicated by the nominal tax structure faced by employees alone."[5]

In Table 9-2, data is given on the distribution of earners, earnings, and taxes for payroll (social security) taxpayers across earnings classes for 1969, as presented by Brittain. (While income-based data would be preferable for analysis of the distribution of costs, this source is used because of the detailed evidence regarding the distributional effects of both the payroll tax and the personal income tax.) This data assumes the entire employer's tax is borne by the employee-earner, including the unemployment insurance tax. Table 9-2 also gives the cumulative percentages for earners, earnings, and taxes, in order that comparisons can be made of the relative burdens of the payroll tax. In 1969, more than 50 percent of the earners (those receiving wages and salaries) were concentrated in earnings levels of less than $4,800. This group as an aggregate, however, accounted for only about 16 percent of the total earnings, both before and after employee contributions to social security. The average tax rate declines across the earnings classes as earnings increase, with the tax rate for the "under $3,000" earnings level (9.41%) at three times the rate for the "$15,000 and over" earnings class (3.17%). The ceiling for taxable earnings was $7,800 in 1969 and, for earnings levels above this maximum, the tax rate declines by proportionately larger percentages (the ratio of tax to total earnings), reflecting the regressive nature of the payroll tax structure. The result is that more than half of the total revenues from payroll tax in 1969, for example, were the burden of those earners below the $9,000 earnings level.

Any consideration of financing national health insurance with a payroll tax must recognize the regressive incidence of the payroll tax on low-income and

---

[b]At the minimum, it is clear from analyses of the net overall impact of the payroll tax that the per capita real wage is lower with the imposition of the employer's share of the payroll tax than it would be without this tax. This is true even with any assumptions concerning the forward or backward shifting of the employer's tax and the inability to distinguish between effects in terms of money wage restraints and product price markups.

Table 9-2
Distribution of Earners, Earnings, and Tax of Social Security Taxpayers, before and after OASDHI Tax, 1969

Earnings Class ($)	*Number of Earners (Millions)*	*Total Earnings (Billions)*	*Taxable Earnings (Billions)*	*Tax (Billions)*
Under 3,000	36.44	$ 45.11	$ 45.11	$ 4.245
3,000- 3,600	5.06	16.64	16.64	1.566
3,600- 4,200	5.04	19.60	19.60	1.844
4,200- 4,800	4.77	21.41	21.41	2.015
4,800- 6,600	12.29	69.52	69.52	6.542
6,600- 7,800	6.90	49.53	49.53	4.661
7,800- 9,000	6.48	54.26	51.01	4.778
9,000-12,000	8.82	90.35	70.79	6.565
12,000-15,000	3.28	43.60	27.20	2.482
15,000 and over	3.72	92.62	33.40	2.933
Total	92.80	502.64	404.21	37.631

Table 9-2 (Cont.)

Percentage Cumulative Frequency of Earners[a]	*Percentage Cumulative Aggregate of Total Earnings*[b]	*Percentage Cumulative Aggregate of Earnings after Tax*[b]	*Tax Rate*[c] *(Percent)*	*Percentage Cumulative Tax*[d]
0.00%	0.00%	0.00%	9.41%	0.00%
39.27	8.97	8.79	9.41	11.28
44.72	12.29	12.03	9.41	15.44
50.15	16.18	15.85	9.41	20.34
55.29	20.44	20.02	9.41	25.70
68.53	34.28	33.56	9.41	43.08
75.97	44.13	43.21	8.81	55.47
82.95	54.92	53.85	7.27	68.16
92.46	72.90	71.81	5.69	85.61
95.99	81.57	80.71	3.17	92.21
			7.49	

[a] Less than percentage cumulative of earners below lower limit of class.

[b] Less than percentage cumulative aggregate of earnings accruing to earners below lower limit of class.

[c] Ratio of tax to total earnings.

[d] Percentage cumulative tax charged to those below lower limit.

Source: John Brittain, *The Payroll Tax for Social Security* (Washington, D.C.: The Brookings Institution, 1972), Table 4-3.

middle-income earners, particularly those in the poverty range. If any amount of the first dollar value of earnings were exempt from the payroll tax, then the tax burden would be redistributed, since the percentage of tax savings would be greater for the low- and middle-income groups relative to their earnings, although all contributors would actually pay less in taxes. A similar result would occur from the establishment of an exemption clause, whereby some fixed amount of earnings would be exempt from the tax for each dependent. Presently, the payroll tax structure does not take into account the extent of family financial responsibility of the earner. While some of the regressive effects of the payroll tax linked to the fixing of a ceiling on the maximum amount of taxable earnings have been mitigated by the recent increases in the ceiling, these kinds of changes in the tax structure do not solve the problem of the excessive payroll tax rates that poverty level earners face.[c]

In Figure 9-1, the historical trend in effective payroll tax rates from 1949 to 1969 is given for those earners receiving "maximum income not subject to income tax." For those families that are smaller in size, there is no benefit from the ceiling on taxable earnings, and their effective rate for the payroll tax rose from 3.6 percent in 1949 to 11.4 percent in 1969. (Discussion of all references to Brittain's analysis assumes, as is the case here, that the entire employer's tax is the burden of the employee-earner.) The rates for larger families are somewhat lower, although there was a greater increase in the respective rates for this period. Further comparisons of the relative payroll tax rates for income taxpayers is given in the discussion that follows on the personal income tax.

The Personal Income Tax

The federal personal or individual income tax is at present the largest source of revenues for general expenditures made by the federal government. This tax structure is based on the ability-to-pay principle of taxation and establishes graduated tax rates according to the levels of income for families and individuals.[d] While debates for tax reforms occur perennially, there is a more general consensus

---

[c]Brittain argues that the federal government is contradictory in its policies, since it assists those families and individuals eligible for public assistance through transfer payments on the one hand, while simultaneously levying the regressive payroll tax on employed persons below the poverty level on the other hand.

[d]A graduated income tax structure can be interpreted in terms of three different measures: (1) the marginal rate, (2) the average rate, and (3) the effective rate. The *marginal* rate is the tax rate as stated for any given income class; it applies, however, only to the range of income within the limits of successive income brackets. The *average* rate is the sum of the marginal rates across income classes divided by the actual amounts of taxable income. If the marginal rates are increasing, then the average rates will lag behind the marginal rates. The *effective* rate usually means the total tax for an individual or family divided by their respective total income.

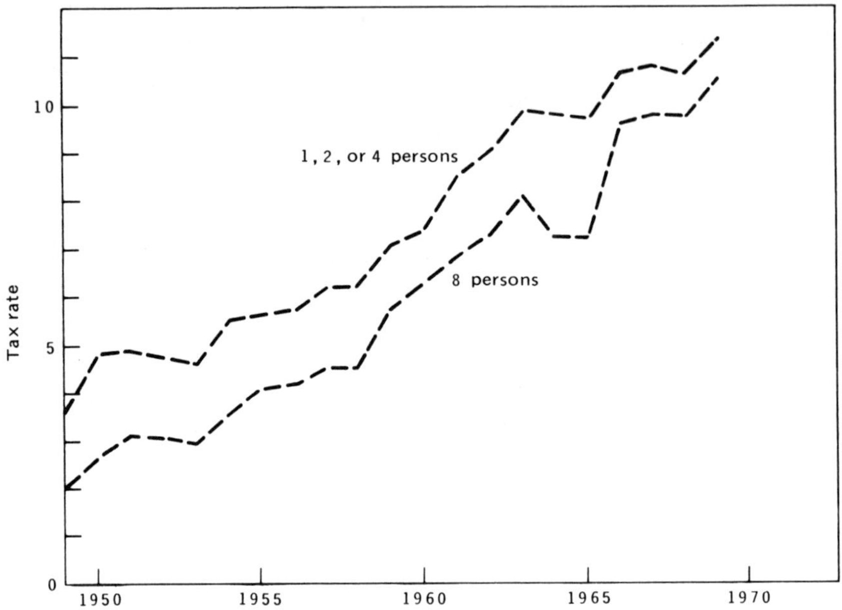

Source: John Brittain, *The Payroll Tax for Social Security* (Washington, D.C.: The Brookings Institution, 1972), Figure 4-5.

Figure 9-1. Payroll Tax Rates on Wages and Salary Income of Earners Receiving Maximum Income Not Subject to Income Tax, Various Family Sizes, 1949-1969

that the personal income tax is progressive throughout virtually the complete income scale. That is, individuals and families in the higher income classes face relatively higher personal income tax rates than do those in the lower income groups. The majority of the arguments instead concentrate on horizontal equity (equal treatment of those in the *same* income class) rather than on vertical equity, and on the numerous loopholes in the statuatory tax structure, which can be used to advantage largely by the higher-income groups. Despite the present inherent problems with the structure of the personal income tax, it is considered to be a major fiscal policy measure for reducing the inequality in the distribution of income.

The major differences in the provisions of the tax laws for the payroll tax and the personal income tax are:

1. The personal income tax is levied on *all* income, regardless of the sources from which it is derived, while the payroll tax is imposed only on wages and salaries.[e]

---

[e]Exclusions from income are made only for government transfer payments, such as social security benefits, gifts, inheritances, and income in-kind.

2. Under the personal income tax law, an exemption of $750 is allowed for *each* dependent.

3. A standard deduction of 15 percent of adjusted gross income is given under the personal income tax structure up to a limit of $2,000. A minimum deduction or low-income allowance is also available with a limit of $1,000. The standard deduction is actually another form of exemption.

4. Deductions from adjusted gross income are permitted for:

a. taxes paid to state and local governments
b. interest payments, including interest on mortgages
c. medical deductions for one-half of the cost of the premium for private health insurance coverage up to a limit of $150 and for medical expenses, if their total is greater than 3 percent of adjusted gross income
d. charitable contributions
e. casualty losses, such as losses from fire or theft
f. household and child care expenses
g. miscellaneous deductions, such as contributions to political campaigns and certain educational expenses

5. Special provisions for capital gains allowances are given under the personal income tax laws—net income gained from investment in stocks and other capital assets receives special tax treatment in terms of tax rates and deductions.

6. The personal income tax statutes provide for income-splitting on the joint returns of married couples. Basically, the total income of the husband and wife is halved, and the tax is based on this figure and multiplied by two to compute the total tax for the couple. Since the tax rate employed is the same as for the individual tax return, the progressivity of the tax structure is reduced.[6]

Calculations of the effective tax rates for the income tax and the payroll tax with respect to specific graduated income levels show the relative progressive and regressive nature of the tax rates associated with these two types of tax structures. Table 9-3 gives the estimated tax rates (calculated from statutory personal income with a standard deduction and payroll tax rates, including average state unemployment insurance rates) for the circumstances of a four-person family with one earner for 1963, 1968, and 1973. This source of evidence presents clearly the relative differences in both the actual amounts of income and payroll taxes and the respective effective tax rates for family income levels of $5,000, $10,000 and $25,000.

Figure 9-2 presents comparisons of the payroll tax rate for one and two earners with the income tax rate on wages and salaries for various family sizes for 1969 and 1973. The regressive nature of the payroll tax throughout almost the entire range of wages and salaries is depicted by the consistent decline in the effective tax rate as wages and salaries increase. The rate of decline is greater beyond the peak at the ceiling or maximum tax base and shows the realtively greater regressivity in the rates once the ceiling is reached and further earnings

Table 9-3
Federal Individual Income and Payroll Taxes for a Four-person Family with One Earner, Selected Earnings, 1963, 1968, and 1973

Earnings and Tax Items	*1963*	*1968*[a]	*1973*
$5,000 Earnings			
Income tax	$ 420	$ 308	$ 98
Payroll tax[b]	348	440	585
Total tax	768	748	683
Effective income tax rate	8.4%	6.2%	2.0%
Effective payroll tax rate[b]	7.0	8.8	11.7
Total effective tax rate	15.4	15.0	13.7
$10,000 Earnings			
Income tax	$1,372	$1,198	$ 905
Payroll tax[b]	348	686	1,170
Total tax	1,720	1,884	2,075
Effective income tax rate	13.7%	12.0%	9.0%
Effective payroll tax rate[b]	3.5	6.9	11.7
Total effective tax rate	17.2	18.8	20.8
$25,000 Earnings			
Income tax	$4,889	$4,362	$3,890
Payroll tax[b]	348	686	1,264
Total tax	5,237	5,048	5,154
Effective income tax rate	19.6%	17.4%	15.6%
Effective payroll tax rate[b]	1.4	2.7	5.0
Total effective tax rate	20.9	20.2	20.6

[a]Includes income tax surcharge.

[b]Includes both employee and employer taxes.

Source: Edward R. Fried, Alice M. Rivlin, and Nancy H. Teeters, *Setting National Priorities: The 1974 Budget* (Washington, D.C.: The Brookings Institution, 1973), Table 3-4.

are not taxable. By comparison, the effective income tax rates rise throughout the range of wages and salaries, with the relatively more progressive rates occurring at the lower scale of wages and salaries. At any wage and salary level below the point where the payroll tax and the income tax curves intersect for the respective number of earners and family sizes, the effective payroll tax rate is greater than the effective income tax rate. For example, in 1973 a four-person family with two earners faced a higher effective payroll tax rate than income tax rate for all earnings up to about $15,000.

In Figure 9-3, the effective payroll and income tax rates on wages and salaries are combined to present the total incidence of both types of taxes across the range of wages and salaries. The combined rates show a relative leveling off

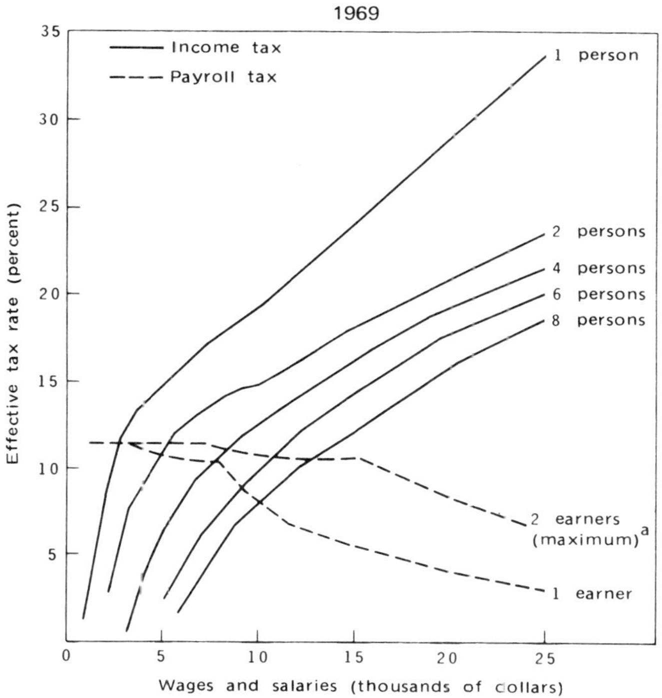

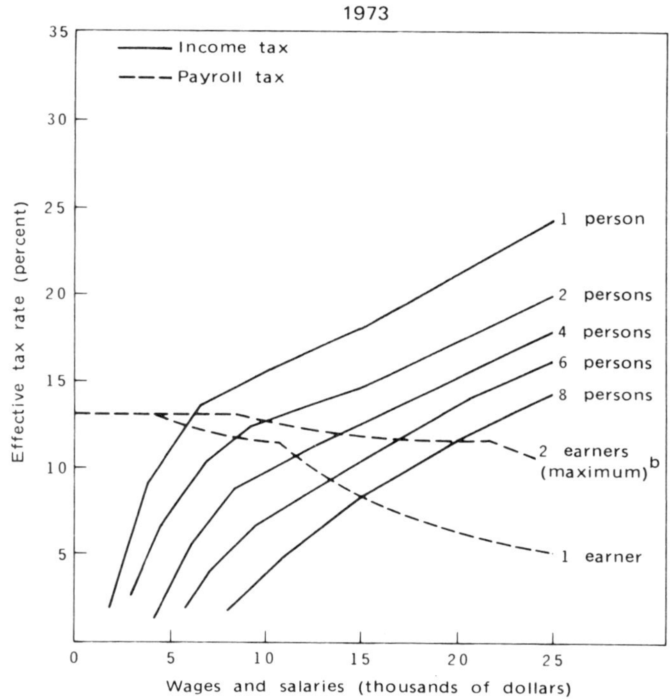

[a]Assumes two earners had equal earings.

[b]The OASDHI ceiling of $10,800 and the rate of 11 percent are used, as established in Public Law 92-336, signed July 1, 1972.

Source: John Brittain, *The Payroll Tax for Social Security* (Washington, D.C.: The Brookings Institution, 1972), Figures 4-1 and 4-2.

Figure 9-2. Payroll and Income Tax Rates on Wages and Salaries, Various Family Sizes, 1969 and 1973

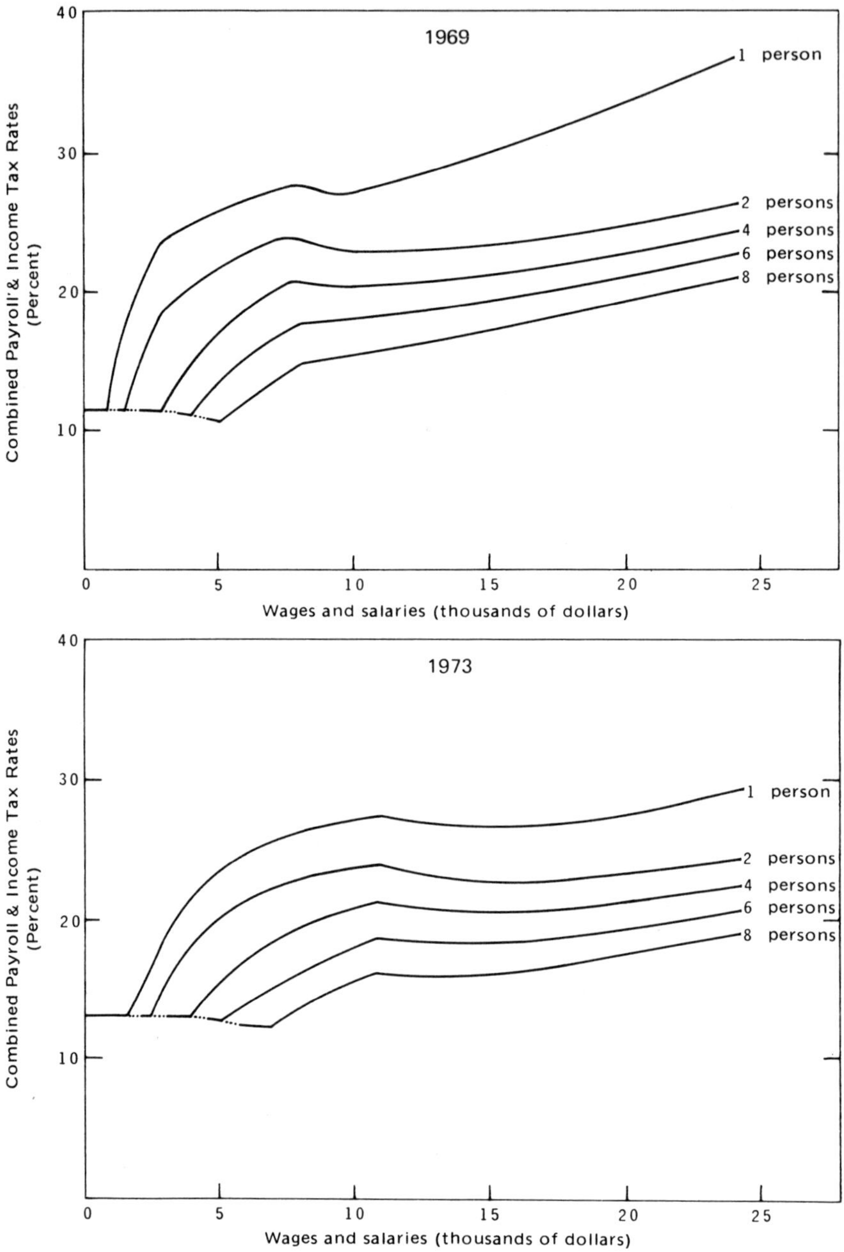

Source: John Brittain, *The Payroll Tax for Social Security* (Washington, D.C.: The Brookings Institute, 1972), Figure 4-3.

Figure 9-3. Combined Payroll and Income Tax Rates on Wages and Salaries, Various Family Sizes, One Earner, 1969 and 1973

at the higher wage and salary levels, since the progressive income tax rates are substantially mitigated by the regressive payroll tax rates. For the lower range of wages and salaries, the combined rates are substantially above the income tax rates because of the relatively higher payroll tax rates faced by the low- and middle-income earners.

Brittain, in his study of the payroll tax, estimates the effective rates for the income tax and social security tax for income tax filers below and above the poverty level of income. He finds that in 1966 the income tax rate for the "poor" was less than 1 percent, while the rate for the "nonpoor" was about 12 percent. However, the highly progressive effect of the income tax structure is largely offset by the regressive impact of the payroll tax. The estimated effective rates for the social security tax show that the tax filers below the poverty level have a significantly higher rate (8.2%) than the rate for tax filers above the poverty level (5.0%).[7] Thus, the combined rates for both types of taxes still sets the burden for the poor at an aggregate rate of about one-half of the rate for all tax filers. (See Figure 9-4 for a comparison of the historical trends in the effective payroll tax rates versus individual income tax rates on the earnings of those at the poverty level.)

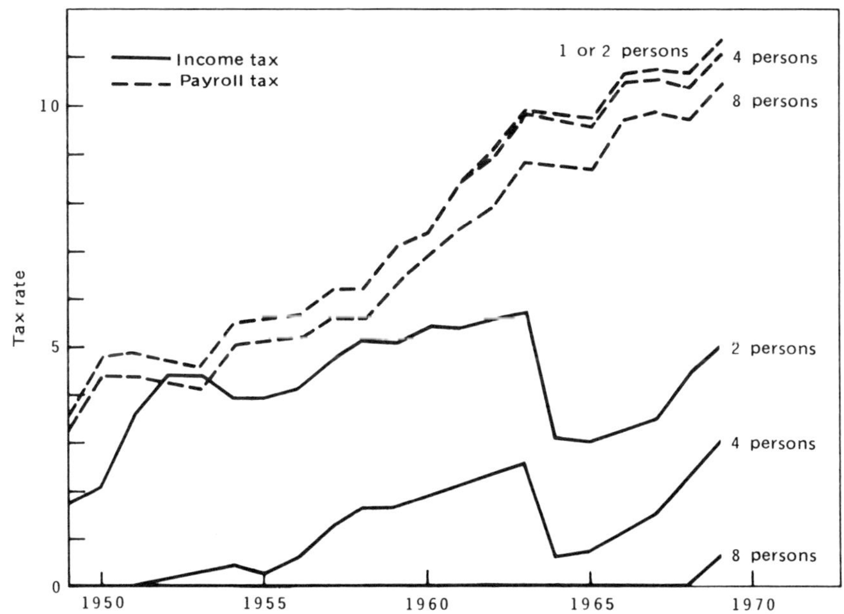

Source: John Brittain, *The Payroll Tax for Social Security* (Washington, D.C.: The Brookings Institution, 1972), Figure 4-4.

Figure 9-4. Payroll Tax Rates and Individual Income Tax Rates on Wages and Salary Income of Earners at the Poverty Line, Various Family Sizes, One Earner, 1949-1969

As evidence that the number of families who pay more in payroll taxes than in income taxes is directly related to family size, Brittain calculates equal-tax earnings levels for various family sizes. This data is given in Table 9-4. The estimated overall median wage and salary levels, by family size for one earner, are shown to be *lower* than the wages and salary level at which the income tax and payroll tax are equal, when family size increases beyond four. Because this comparison is made with respect to *median* wage and salary levels, the evidence further suggests that the number of families who pay more in payroll taxes than in income taxes is greater than one-half, when family size is larger than four and slightly less than one-half when family size is four or smaller.

Premiums

Premiums in the form of monthly or annual payments for health insurance coverage are frequently advanced by advocates as a feasible alternative source for partial or complete financing of a national health insurance plan in order to limit the federal and, possibly, state budgetary expenditures for such a plan. Premiums, however, are a very regressive type of financing, since this approach

Table 9-4
Approximate Wage and Salary Levels at which Income and Payroll Taxes Are Equal for One Earner, Amount of Tax, and Median Wage and Salary, by Family Size, 1969

Family Size	*Wage and Salary Level*[a]	*Income and Payroll Tax (Each Tax)*	*Estimated Median Wage and Salary*[b]
1	$ 2,770	$316	$2,400
2	4,890	523	6,000
4	7,707	794	8,500
6	9,088	803	8,700
10	11,754	803	8,000[c]

[a]Assumes standard deductions claimed in computing income tax.

[b]A rough estimate obtained by multiplying the estimated overall tax return wage and salary median of $6,700 by the ratio of median money income by household size to the overall median money income. "Household Income in 1969 and Selected Social and Economic Characteristics of Households," *Current Population Reports,* U.S. Bureau of the Census, Series P-60, No. 72 (1970), p. 11.

[c]Estimated median for households of seven or more persons.

Source: John Brittain, *The Payroll Tax for Social Security* (Washington, D.C.: The Brookings Institution, 1972), Table 4-2.

to private financing would require approximately the same dollar payment for each family or individual, without regard for their income levels. These regressive burdens across income groups occur regardless of whether all or part of the premium payment is made by families and individuals directly, by employees, or by employers.

Those proposals that rely on premiums as a major source of financing generally are structured around a voluntary or mandated employee-employer plan that would enroll the majority of the population. Low-income groups would, under these types of proposals, either have their entire premiums paid for by the federal government from general revenues or would be provided with some type of subsidy or assistance in meeting the costs of the premium. Under a mandatory employee-employer plan, the employer is usually required to pay the largest part of the premiums for employees, but this premium contribution is "in reality . . . the same as a tax imposed on employers."[8] Facing the circumstances of increased "taxes" or costs of labor, the employer will either lower wages or reduce the amount of wage increases. Thus, the burden of the indirect payment of the premium by the employer is no different from the burden of the direct payment of the premium by the employee or by families and individuals—the premium costs would represent a higher percentage of the income of the lower-income groups relative to the higher-income groups. Only if the employees are receiving the minimum wage is it possible that the cost of the premiums could not be shifted to these employees by the employer, although the cost could be shifted to those employees with higher wages.

When a voluntary or a mandatory employee plan is financed by premiums, it is also possible that the employer will offer an insurance policy with a more restrictive benefit package than might otherwise be the case. Since those in the higher-income groups could afford to purchase any additional supplementary coverage, while the lower-income groups would not be in the same financial circumstances, inequitable distributional effects could result with regard to the overall cost and benefit structure. This is one reason why those proposals that would use premiums to finance employee plans generally require that the policies meet certain standard benefit coverage, although significant variation can occur in the definition of a "qualified" policy with regard to covered services, limitations, and cost sharing.

The subsidy program for the low-income groups under proposals that rely on premiums as at least one source of funding can take several different forms. Several proposals would change the present personal income tax laws to allow a *full* deduction for premiums paid for private health insurance coverage. However, the premium system, which is already regressive, becomes more so with provisions for medical deductions. While tax deductions reduce tax burdens for everyone, this reduction is a function of income, and subsidies in the form of tax deductions under the present tax system are of greatest benefit to the higher-income groups.

Tax credits, by contrast, would make a premium system of financing less regressive. A tax credit system permits direct focus on the financial needs of the different income groups, and thus proposals can use tax credits to assist low-income families and individuals. There remains some question, though, as to whether either a tax deduction or a tax credit approach would have significant impact on a *voluntary* expansion of private health insurance coverage for low-income persons.

At least three additional problems could result from the premium approach to financing national health insurance. First, employers may have "a strong incentive to hire part-time workers, secondary family earners, or those who decline the insurance."[10] By including part-time workers under the employee program and by providing for a tax credit for premiums based on total family tax liability, these kinds of potential effects can largely be removed. Second, for those employers who are small in terms of the number of employees, the increased costs of employer premium contributions could result in the firm facing the possibility of either going out of business or suffering a reduction in its work force. This problem could be addressed by the use of subsidies from the federal government to such employers, with eligibility and assistance based on certain guidelines for cost increases and number of employees. Third, private insurance coverage for certain groups, such as small employee plans, self-employed individuals, and groups with a high risk factor, could result in relatively higher premium costs for comparable benefits or the same costs for a more restrictive benefit package. This possibility might be taken into account by pooling groups and individuals, with some form of federal assistance where necessary to keep all premiums with only marginal differences.

The Medical Deduction

Under the present national tax structure, there is an option available to federal taxpayers to take a medical deduction in personal income tax determinations for one-half of the amount of health insurance premiums, not to exceed $150, paid directly or as the employee's contribution through an employer plan. Deductions can also be taken for out-of-pocket expenditures for health care, including any remainder of premium expenses over $150, when the total of these kinds of expenditures exceeds 3 percent of adjusted gross income. (Expenditures for health care can *only* be claimed as a deduction if they are *not* reimbursed as health insurance benefits or by other sources of payment.) In addition, corporate income tax policy at the federal level at present does *not* require employers to make tax payments on any health insurance premium contributions that they make on behalf of their employees. Estimates made by Mitchell and Vogel show that "in 1970 the medical deduction under the personal income tax and the government's failure to tax health insurance premiums paid by employers reduced federal revenues by $3.8 billion."[11]

The purpose of this type of tax deduction is to provide incentives to improve the amount and type of private health insurance coverage contracted for by taxpayers. However, "the features of present law create an IRS (Internal Revenue Service) plan whose benefit structure consists of a deductible proportional to income and a coinsurance rate that declines with income."[12] Thus, the distributional effect of this tax benefit or subsidy across family income groups is uneven, with the nature of the income-related cost sharing resulting in average subsidies per taxpayer that increase as income increases. And, simply because of the limited effectiveness of this type of incentive in increasing the number of low-income persons who are covered by health insurance on a voluntary basis, the greatest proportion of these subsidies are received by members of the high- and middle-income groups. Further, research that links third-party payment mechanisms to the rapid inflation in the health care sector suggests that this tax policy may have had an indirect impact on the rate of increase in the prices of health care services.

The value of the subsidy or benefit to the taxpayer for purchasing health insurance or the medical deduction for premium expenses is actually the cost to the federal government measured by the rate at which the deducted income would have been taxed. This marginal tax rate for the taxpayer has been estimated for 1970 at 0.8 percent at the "less than $1,000" adjusted gross income level and at 46.6 percent at the "above $500,000" income level.[13] It is this increasing tax rate that results in a larger reduction of taxes for the higher income taxpayer, and which, therefore, results in the increased amount of subsidy as income rises. The rise in subsidies is calculated, for example, to be from 25¢ per taxpayer ($7.23 per itemizing taxpayer) for the adjusted gross income from $1,000 to $2,000 class to $40 per taxpayer (approximately the same value per itemizing taxpayer) with income of $50,000 to $100,000.[14]

In 1970, 74.3 million personal income tax returns were filed with the federal government. Medical deductions for incurred expenses were reported on 17.4 million of these returns, a figure that implies the number of families and individuals who had out-of-pocket expenditures exceeding 3 percent of their adjusted gross income. Estimates indicate also that in 1970 approximately 4 percent of all taxpayers had direct or out-of-pocket expenses that exceeded $1,000, and 400,000 taxpayers had expenses greater than $2,000 or an average of 1 taxpayer in every 200.[15]

Employing a standard of 15 percent of income as a measure of extraordinary or catastrophic medical expenses, Mitchell and Vogel find that the incidence of catastrophic expenditures declines rapidly as income increases. Their research shows that in 1970 more than half of these kinds of extraordinary expenses were borne by taxpayers with income of $7,000 or less and 75 percent by all taxpayers with income under $12,000.[16] In 1970, the total amount of expenses that were in excess of taxpayers' income was $1.7 million. The subsidy accounted for a reduction of $500,000 in this total amount, but 2.8 million taxpayers still had expenses that remained above 15 percent of their income.[17]

In addition to the total amount of health expenses that fall on the low- and middle-income groups, a larger number of families and individuals in these income groups must face the burdens of catastrophic expenditures relative to the higher-income groups. Taxpayers in the $4,000 income class who had expenses of at least 15 percent of their income numbered 8.6 percent in 1970. The percentage of taxpayers with this level of expenses then declines as the level of income increases. The respective percentages, for example, are 3.1 percent at $8,000; 1.4 percent at $12,000; and 1.0 percent at the above $15,000 income level.[18]

The Tax Credit

The tax credit approach to financing national health insurance—in combination with premiums paid to private health insurance carriers—would make available to taxpayers a credit against their federal personal income tax liability as a means of subsidizing the premium costs through general revenues.[f] A tax credit plan usually provides for a graduated schedule of credits with the relatively low-income groups receiving the largest credits and those with higher incomes, smaller credits. Cash recipients or those with little or no tax liability would receive vouchers for the purchase of a health insurance policy, which would be acceptable as payment for coverage by private health insurance organizations.

Differences in proposals that employ a tax credit approach might include the following:

1. The extent to which the tax credits are graduated across the different income groups
2. Whether eligibility for the tax credit is based on adjusted gross income or on income tax liability
3. Whether the tax credit plan is "open-ended" and gives some credit to *all* income levels or no tax credit is available for taxpayers with income above a specified amount
4. Whether a voucher is received for the purchase of private health insurance, if there is a 100 percent tax credit for the lowest income grup, or if there is insufficient tax liability
5. Whether all taxpayers, e.g., including the elderly (persons sixty-five years and over), are eligible for the tax credit plan

---

[f]Other tax credits allowed under the present income tax statutes include: (1) the retirement income credit—for equal treatment of retired persons living on private pensions but not receiving tax-exempt social security benefits; (2) the credit against foreign income tax payments; and (3) the investment tax credit.

6. Whether the provisions for the medical deductions under the present personal income tax statutes are repealed or altered

The gross cost to the federal government of a tax credit plan is the total tax revenues foregone plus the expenditures for any credit vouchers. The loss of tax revenues depends on the number of tax returns eligible for a specified amount of credit for each of the gross income or tax liability classes.[19] Possible savings to the federal government would result from the recovery of tax revenues, if the medical deduction option is removed from federal tax law, and from a reduction in expenditures under the present Medicaid program if the tax credit plan replaces Medicaid.

In evaluating tax credits provisions in national health insurance proposals, three areas of concern regarding distributional effects are: the role of the medical deduction, the "notch problem" in defining income classes, and the eligibility of elderly persons covered by the Medicare program.

Frequently, a proposal for tax credits as a means of subsidizing private health insurance coverage will ask that the medical deduction be abolished as it exists in the present federal income tax statutes. However, the amount of the tax credit depends only on the costs of the premium for purchase of a qualified plan and does not take into account the range of services covered and whether these services are subject to coinsurance and deductibles. If the tax credit plan does not also allow for deductions for those expenses for health services *not* covered, or imposed coinsurance and deductibles so that the full cost of covered services is not met by the qualified type of benefit package, it is estimated that as much as 30 percent of the average family medical expenses would not be reimbursed (with large variations across the different income groups). Particularly, if the proposal gives only small amounts of credit to certain income groups, it may not be appropriate to eliminate the medical deduction, since the value of the deduction to taxpayers could be greater than the value of the credit.

Some of the problems of the treatment of the middle- and high-income classes are alleviated under a tax credit plan, if the tax liability rather than the adjusted gross income is used to determine eligibility. The tax liability approach allows a role for other factors—such as exemptions, deductions, and other tax situations—that members of middle- and high-income classes can more usually take advantage of in making their tax returns. For those proposals that significantly limit eligibility for the tax credit, one possible solution to mitigating the distributional effects would be to allow the medical deduction only for those not eligible for the tax credit. However, problems would still remain because persons with health insurance and eligible for the tax credit might incur relatively large out-of-pocket expenditures, again because certain types of health care services are not covered or only partially covered by the qualified policy.

It appears that complete elimination of the medical deduction would only be appropriate under a proposal providing a tax credit for virtually *all* taxpayers and even then recognizing that large consumer expenditures would not be reimbursed. Otherwise, deductions would be eliminated for many families and individuals who would not benefit, or would incur relatively higher costs, as is probably the case for the middle-income groups, under the tax credit plan than under alternative proposals. In order for a tax credit approach to fully take into account the level and distribution of the costs of health care in the financing of a national health insurance proposal, consideration must be given to maintaining the medical deduction—in some revised format—for a more equitable plan for subsidization of the costs of health care.

A problem common to most national health insurance proposals that do not provide for universal eligibility across income groups is the "notch problem." When income classes are established as criteria for determining eligibility for a tax credit or for the amount of the credit, some taxpayers whose income is only slightly below or above an income class limit will either gain or lose a relatively large amount of credit with only a marginal difference in income. For example, a taxpayer with taxable income of $7,999 may receive a tax credit of $400 on his income tax of $600 for a net tax liability of $200, while a taxpayer with income of $8,001 would receive a tax credit of only $300 against income taxes of $600 for a net tax liability of $300. This "notch problem" results in unequal treatment of families and individuals with substantially the same income.

One basic solution to this problem is to employ smaller income class intervals for the determination of eligibility for the different amounts of credit, the latter varying by relatively small increments. While this approach does not completely remove the inequities that might otherwise be present between taxpayers, it does significantly lessen them. The alternative solution, which does completely rectify this problem, is to eliminate all categories of income classes and base the tax credit directly on the adjusted gross income.[20] Using this approach, the amount of tax credit would be gradually reduced by x dollars for every y dollar of additional gross income. Moreover, this approach indirectly resolves the problem of use of gross income versus income tax liability. It permits a more particular definition of those low-income groups that might be eligible for a 100 percent credit and accommodates *any* reduction factor depending on how liberal a plan of tax credits is desired.

Since a tax credit proposal relies on the private sector for provision of health insurance coverage, usually the Medicare program for the elderly is maintained under the proposal. In this case, it is necessary for the tax credit plan also to incorporate mechanisms whereby the Medicare eligibles would receive tax credits for the purchase of supplementary or additional private health insurance coverage. Because not all services are covered under Medicare, or services have coinsurance and deductibles attached to them, about half of the elderly population currently has private insurance to supplement Medicare coverage.[g] In addition, premiums are paid by the elderly for coverage under the optional medical insurance program available under Medicare–Part B. Total out-of-pocket expenditures by the aged for premiums for this Medicare supplemental medical insurance and certain types of additional private health insurance coverage could be several hundred dollars annually. Whatever the amount of these premiums, a tax credit should also be made available for those persons sixty-five years and over without regard to income, since the majority of these persons are concentrated in the lower-income groups anyway. (Further discussion of the Medicare program is presented in Chapter 10.)

State Taxes

State general revenues are an alternative source of financing national health insurance incorporated into a limited number of proposals. Their use for funding some portion of a national health insurance plan is primarily to reduce the role of federal financing (and possibly private sector financing through premiums), but in most cases they would be associated with those programs proposed for the poor and medically indigent. This association of state financing of health care for the low-income groups is linked to the present financial participation of states in the Medicaid program, although traditionally states and municipalities have been the financier of last resort for health care services. Those proposals that do not include a role for state financing presumably were influenced by the experience of the Medicaid program, whose original intent was to have the wealthier states receive less federal funding for this program, than the poorer states—an indirect form of subsidization. It resulted, in general, in the reverse type of transfer of federal monies.

State general revenues, which are the source of state financing under several proposed national health insurance plans (usually in combination with financing by federal general revenues), are derived largely from state sales taxes, property and excise taxes, and, for some states, personal income taxes.[h] Sales and excise taxes fall hardest on those in the lowest-income brackets. The sales tax, for example, is regressive throughout the entire income range, with a tax rate estimated to be six times as large for the under $2,000 income class and three

[g]Blue Cross-Blue Shield (through their Medex programs) and private health insurance companies offer policies with benefits for those services not covered by Medicare, such as intermediate nursing-home care, private-duty nursing and prescription drugs. Policies that pay the coinsurance and deductibles for additional hospital days and some outpatient services, and policies that provide both types of coverage.

[h]Other sources of state revenues are: corporate business taxes, tobacco and alcoholic beverage taxes, inheritance and gift taxes, and non-tax receipts, such as licenses.

times as large for the $8,000-$10,000 class, as for the $50,000 or more income class. Further, a large family with income comparable to a single individual could pay as much as 50 percent more in sales taxes annually.[21] How regressive the sales tax is depends on which goods and services are subject to the tax—the exemption of food and clothing, for example, would make the sales tax less regressive. In addition, the burden of sales taxes are greater for those living on fixed income transfers, such as social security benefits and public welfare cash assistance. The property tax is also regressive over a wide range of income, although there is some variation in the relative effective rates, and this tax does not always fall equally on families and individuals with equal incomes.

National health insurance proposals have been introduced that would maintain the current Medicaid program and, therefore, state financing would continue to have a major role. Other proposals would phase out this state funding over a period of time. However, it should be recognized that even if the Medicaid program is eliminated under proposed national health insurance legislation, to the extent that the range of covered services is limited, the states would by mandate or by necessity assume the financing of those services not covered under a national health insurance program for some of their constituents.

Summary of Evidence Regarding Distributional Effects

In the discussion above, evidence of the distributional effects associated with alternative sources of financing for national health insurance plans was presented. This evidence indicates that, depending on particular choices among types of financing, the costs of a plan would place varying financial burdens on individuals and families in different income groups. In general, most proposals employ more than one source of financing to cover the costs of specified insurance programs, and usually the net distributional effects for *particular* income groups are difficult to assess. However, it is clear that major trade-offs in terms of distributional effects can occur by combining two or more sources of financing. For example, if federal general revenues, which are largely based on the personal income tax and therefore a very progressive source of financing for individuals and families, is complemented by partial financing by payroll tax revenues—a very regressive type of financing—inequitable burdens across income groups could still result. Davis finds that, under the Kennedy-Mills proposal (legislation introduced in the 93rd Congress), which provided for financing by federal and state general revenues and a payroll tax, the costs of coverage would be a greater burden for "families with incomes between $5,000 and $20,000" than for families with either lower or higher incomes.[22]

Premiums and payroll taxes are the most regressive types of financing, since each of these sources would have those in the lower-income groups assuming costs for insurance coverage that are a higher percentage of their income than for those in the higher-income groups. The personal income tax, by comparison, is progressive throughout the range of income—that is, as income increases, the effective tax rate increases.

One approach to mitigating the regressive burdens of the payroll tax is to allow for exemptions. Increasing the ceiling or the maximum taxable earnings base does not relieve the burdens of the payroll tax for the low- and middle-income groups. Since all earnings are taxed at the same rate, those with earnings below the proposed ceiling would still contribute a substantially higher percentage of their earnings toward the cost of national health insurance than would those with earnings above this ceiling. The customary provision offered by proposals to relieve the regressive effects of costs in terms of premium payments is to either allow for medical deductions on personal income tax returns for premiums or structure a tax credit system to provide for some subsidization of the purchase of private health insurance. The evidence is that medical deductions under the present tax laws do not relieve the regressive burdens of a premium-financing system and, in fact, benefit most those in the higher-income groups. Further, under a voluntary program, medical deductions are not sufficient incentive to expand the amount and type of coverage, although this was the original intention of the law.

In contrast with medical deductions for premiums, the use of tax credits to subsidize the costs of private insurance coverage can be directed specifically at the distributional effects of the cost of premiums across income groups. The extent to which a tax credit system effectively compensates for the regressive burdens of premiums depends on a number of characteristics of this type of assistance program, including: the use of tax liabilities rather than income levels to define eligibility; the amount of the tax credit for given eligibility categories; and the treatment of those individuals and families who have no tax liability.

The role of state revenues as an alternative source of financing is less prominent in terms of the number of proposals that provide for their use and the amount of state revenues that would be required. The use of state revenues for financing a national health insurance plan would increase the burdens for the lower-income groups and for larger family units. Most sources of state revenues are regressive and primary sources, such as the sales tax and property tax. These taxes, in particular, have higher effective rates for both low- and middle-income groups.

Some proposals would alter certain provisions of the basic financing sources reviewed here. For example, the medical deduction laws would be changed to allow *full* premium cost as a deduction; or a higher employer premium contribution would be required; or differential rates for the payroll tax for employers versus employees would be required. However, evidence supports the conclusion that many of these changes would not be effective as means of redistributing the costs more equitably.

The Distributional Effects of Selected Cost Structures

This section presents a review of the cost structures proposed under six national health insurance bills introduced in the 94th Congress. The most obvious differences in the cost structures of these selected national health insurance proposals are the allocation of public versus private sources of financing. Two proposals—the Corman-Kennedy bill and the Young bill—basically rely only on tax revenues to fund their universal insurance programs. Three other proposals—the Fulton-Duncan (AMA) bill, the Burleson-McIntyre (HIAA) bill, and the Ullman (AHA) bill—would be financed primarily by premiums. The Long-Ribicoff proposal, as introduced in the 94th Congress, illustrates a cost approach that combines both public and private financing.

The less obvious differences in these cost structures are related to the distributional effects of the various sources of financing that they propose. None of these proposals is progressive in its primary overall approach to financing, and only one, the Young bill, employs cost provisions that guarantee at least proportional burdens in the distribution of costs across income groups. The particular cost structures of each of the six bills is presented below, followed by a summary comparison of the proposed cost structures reviewed here in terms of their predicted relative distributional effects.

Corman-Kennedy Bill

The total cost of the national health insurance plan proposed by the Corman-Kennedy Bill (the Health Security Act) would be financed by a combination of payroll tax revenues and contributions from federal general revenues. The share of the costs assumed by each of these two sources would be set at equal amounts or half of the total costs. The payroll tax would be levied at different rates for three tax bases: (1) at 1.0 percent on wages and salaries; (2) at 3.5 percent on employers' total payrolls; and (3) at 2.5 percent on self-employment and unearned income. Federal, state, and local government employees' earnings would also be subject to the tax under this proposal, although state and local governments would not pay the employers' tax. Members of the uniformed services would *not* be taxed on their earnings. For all employers, their entire payroll account would be subject to the new employers' payroll tax. In those cases where an employer's current obligations for health insurance benefits for their employees exceed the amount of the 3.5 percent tax payment, the employer must also absorb the employees' tax contribution up to the amount of the current dollar obligations.

The provisions of this bill would raise the ceiling on the total amount of wages, unearned income, and self-employment income, which would be taxed to the first $21,150 annually. (As of January 1, 1976, all other social security or payroll taxes will be levied on the first $15,300 of earnings for each individual earner.) For taxpayers over sixty years of age, the first $5,000 of earned and unearned income would be exempt from the additional new payroll tax. Since this bill would eliminate the Medicare program, the current social security tax earmarked for the hospital insurance plan (Part A) would be repealed.

Under the Corman-Kennedy Bill, "health security unearned income" has a specific definition. Unearned income is defined as that amount of adjusted gross income, not to exceed the total health security contribution base of $21,150 for a taxable year, and reduced by: taxable wages; taxable self-employment income; any payments excluded from taxable wages; remuneration for service in certain federal government positions or as a member of the uniformed services on active duty; remuneration for service performed by an alien employed by a foreign government, any agency of a foreign government, or an international organization; and any other income not exceeding $5,000 for taxpayers sixty years and older.[i] The proposal requires that every individual residing in the United States who has health security unearned income of $400 or more must file a return for purposes of this unearned income tax. Basically, the effect of these provisions of the bill regarding unearned income imposes a tax on all income of up to $21,150 whether earned or unearned. This means that if an individual earns more than $21,150 from employment, he or she would not be required to pay the new tax on unearned income imposed by this bill. However, if an individual earns, for example, $15,000 in wages, this amount would be taxed at 1.0 percent, and any amount, say $3,000, in unearned income would be taxed at 2.5 percent, up to the combined maximum of $21,150 of the health security contribution base.

Contributions from federal general revenues would, according to the financing structure established by this bill, be equal to the total receipts from the payroll tax for the universal health insurance plan. No direct contributions from state general revenues would be required under this proposal, but Medicaid programs would remain optional for the individual states to provide for coverage of certain services not covered in the benefit package offered by the Corman-Kennedy Bill. Any such services provided by state Medicaid programs would be partially reimbursed by the use of federal general revenues. Under the provisions of the Corman-Kennedy Bill, medical deductions would be permitted on federal income tax returns only for expenditures for services *not* covered under the Health Security Act. No deductions would be allowed for the cost of medical care covered by the Act.[j]

---

[i]The remuneration for federal government service include services performed as President, Vice-President, or a Member, Delegate, or Resident Commissioner of the Congress.

[j]Those services not covered under the Health Security Act include: skilled nursing-home care (after the limit of 120 days has expired), intermediate nursing-home care, certain types of prescription drugs, dental care for adults, and psychiatric services when they exceed the duration of benefits available under the Corman-Kennedy Bill.

The funds for the Health Security program would be held in a trust with three accounts: (1) a health services account to pay benefit costs; (2) an account for administrative costs; and (3) a health resources development fund account. The present hospital and medical insurance trust funds of the Medicare program would be transferred to the new trust fund under the specified provisions of this bill.

Young Bill

The Young Bill is the only proposal for a national health insurance plan that would be financed almost entirely by a payroll tax. In addition, federal general revenues are indirectly used to cover a substantial portion of the costs of this plan, since federal income tax credits, a form of foregone federal revenues, would also be available to all contributors (payroll taxpayers) to the program.

The new payroll tax imposed by the provisions of this bill would levy different tax rates on three bases: (1) a 2.0 percent tax on employees' wages and salaries; (2) a 5.0 percent tax on unearned income and self-employment earnings; and (3) a 6.0 percent tax on employers' total payroll. However, there is no ceiling or maximum placed on the amount of earned or unearned income that is taxable, as in the case of the current social security tax or, for example, as in the Corman-Kennedy Bill. Therefore, since the tax rate is the same for all levels of earned and unearned income, this type of payroll tax is proportional. An individual or family with earnings of $10,000 would pay $200 in taxes, one with earnings of $20,000 would pay $400–the percentage of payroll taxes to total earnings is the same for all earnings levels.

Provisions of the Young Bill define "unearned income" as the amount of adjusted gross income for the taxable year, *including payments for AFDC and SSI,* reduced by any such income (whether from wages or any other source) that is already taxed for purposes of financing the cost of this plan.[k] Aged and disabled persons, and persons under eighteen years would not have their unearned income subject to this payroll tax.[l]

The federal income tax credit plan under the Young proposal would allow for a tax credit of up to one-half of *all* health-insurance-related taxes, with maximum credits of $250 per individual, $500 per joint tax return, and $750 for an

[k]For purposes of determining unearned income, adjusted gross income is also reduced by remunerations for services performed as a member of a uniformed service on active duty outside the United States and for services performed by an alien in the employ of a foreign government, or an instrumentality of a foreign government, or an international organization.

[l]The tax imposed on benefit payments under aid to families with dependent children or supplemental security income would be treated as a tax on wages and collected by the state agency making such payments or by the federal agency paying such benefits through deductions and tax withholding with respect to the benefit payments.

employer per contribution for each employee. For families and individuals, the effect of this tax credit approach is to reduce the payroll tax to a rate of 1.0 percent until the level of earnings is reached where the maximum credit applies. Thus, the proportionality of the tax structure is maintained across earnings groups. In the case of an individual, for example, only after the maximum credit is attained at $25,000 or when the 1.0 percent tax payment equals $250 does this type of tax become thereafter a progressive tax.

The current social security tax for the hospital insurance program under Medicare (Part A) would be repealed, since this proposal provides for universal coverage and the Medicare program would be eliminated. The Young Bill would establish a new independent Social Security Administration to administer the proposed national health insurance plan, together with the current social security programs and the supplemental security income program.

Fulton-Duncan Bill

The Fulton-Duncan proposal would primarily be financed by premiums, together with federal general revenues under a premium subsidy plan and payroll tax revenues for the continuation of the Medicare program. In addition, a substantial role is proposed for consumer out-of-pocket payments in the form of coinsurance to help defray the costs of coverage under this proposal.

The mandated employee program requires employers to pay at least 65 percent of the premium for qualified private health insurance coverage for each employee, with the employee paying the balance of the premium costs. The program for the poor and medically indigent–directed at the unemployed and the self-employed–would be partially financed by premiums and partially by federal general revenues through the system of premium subsidies.[m] Federal assistance under this proposal in the form of premium subsidics would be provided by two mechanisms: (1) by the granting of tax credits that would result in a reduction of federal income tax receipts and (2) through a voucher system whereby "certificates of entitlement" acceptable by private insurance carriers toward premium payments would be redeemed from federal general revenues through a special trust fund created for this purpose. Employed persons covered under the employee plan would also be eligible for a certificate of entitlement or a credit against income taxes, but only if the employee's share of the premium under the group plan exceeds the amount of premium that would be paid under the program for the poor and medically indigent. Premiums for supplemental

[m]Individual states can make arrangements whereby insurance carriers would participate in the pooling of individuals and small groups to increase the availability of coverage for all persons, at a premium cost of not more than 125 percent of the premium for enrollees in large employee groups in the same state.

insurance for the elderly to cover services not offered as benefits under the Medicare program would be paid by the federal general revenues.

The amount of the tax credit for an individual or a family is based on taxable income and measured by their income tax liability. For qualified plans, the amount of credit is equal to the full premium cost for persons with no tax liability and slowly decreases for each $10 increase in tax liability, with a credit of 10 percent of the premium cost available to those with taxes of $891 or more. The schedule of tax credits is as follows:[n]

Amount of Tax Liability	*Amount of Adjusted Gross Income*[o]	*Amount of Tax Credit*[p]
$ 0	$4,300 or less	100%
$100	$5,000	90%
$300	$6,350	70%
$500	$7,600	50%
$700	$8,750	30%
$900	$9,950	10%

Individuals or families with no tax liability would receive a voucher certification that would be accepted by a carrier for the premium of a qualified insurance policy. Those with a tax liability less than the amount of the credit could also receive a certificate or claim the additional credit like an overpayment of taxes. Taypayers who elect a tax credit cannot claim the premium as a medical expense deduction for income tax purposes. An employee, covered under an employee-employer plan, can count 80 percent of the employer's contribution to a qualified plan, in addition to the employee's own premium contribution, in computing the amount against which a tax credit can be taken on a personal income tax return. Employers would receive cash subsidy payments from the federal government or be entitled to credits against income taxes, if their obligations to provide for qualified private health insurance coverage for their employees results in a total payroll cost of more than 3 percent.

[n]This schedule for determining the amount of tax credit applies to all types of returns, including individual and joint returns of married couples. The tax liability of a husband and wife filing separate returns would be combined and the taxes of dependents are included, even though the dependent files an individual return.

[o]Equivalent adjusted gross income is for a family of four with the standard deduction.

[p]This is the percentage of premium cost.

Burleson-McIntyre Bill

The Burleson-McIntyre proposal utilizes premiums primarily and also federal and state general revenues. It relies on the payroll tax only for the financing of the continuation of the Medicare program. The employee-employer plan would be financed entirely by premiums, as is also the case for the separate program whereby individuals would enroll in qualified private plans. The State health insurance plan for the poor and medically indigent would be partially financed by premiums, and the balance of the program costs would be covered by federal and state general revenues.

At the option of the employer, employees may be required to contribute a share of the premiums for enrollment in an employee plan. However, the amount of the employee's premium contribution is limited, under the provisions of this bill, to 10 percent of monthly wages over the following amounts of average monthly income:

Individual	$167
Family, with 1 dependent	$250
Family, with 2 or more dependents	$333

In annual terms, these "cutoff" income levels are: $2,000, $3,000 and $4,000, respectively.

Under the State plan, the poor or low-income persons would not pay premiums. This group is defined as being at income levels below $2,000 for an individual, $3,000 for a family of two members, and $4,000 for a family with three or more members. The medically indigent would pay premiums established at rates of 10 percent of income over the the same specified income levels on an annual basis *only*. For the medically indigent eligible for the State plan on a monthly basis (2 months), premium rates are set at 20 percent of monthly income above the given limits. Under either the employee plan or the State plan for the medically indigent, if annual income is $2,400, $3,600 or $4,800, respectively, or each family type, as given above, is at a level of income at 120 percent of the limits, then an individual would pay $3.33 per month or $50 per year as a premium contribution, a family with one dependent would pay $5.00 per month or $60 per year, and a family with two or more dependents would pay $80 per year. Uninsurables under the State plan and individual policyholders under the employee plan would pay the entire premium as determined by the administering carrier.

The cost of the State plan not covered by premiums would be met by federal and state general revenues. The federal share would be from 70 to 90 percent and would vary according to the per capita income of the particular state, with the remainder of the balance of costs paid by state general revenues.

Further, foregone federal general revenues are accounted for by the provision that employees and individuals who itemize their deductions on personal income tax returns could take their entire premium cost as a deduction. Employers can also take their entire premium contribution as a normal business deduction under present law, but contributions to nonqualified plans would not be deductible.

Ullman Bill

This proposal relies on four sources of financing, i.e., premiums, federal general revenues, the payroll tax, and medical deductions.

The mandated employee-employer plan in this proposal would be financed by premiums. An employer would be required to incur at least 75 percent of the premium costs, with the employee paying the balance of the premium. Employers would receive subsidy payments from the federal government, if their share of the premium payments exceed 4 percent of the average total wages paid to their employees. This subsidy, paid from federal general revenues, would be equal to the amount of the excess of employer premium costs above the 4 percent of total wages, but for a maximum of ten employees.

The premium for health insurance coverage for persons receiving unemployment compensation would be entirely financed by federal general revenues as part of the employee-employer plan. If an employed person is also eligible for the federally financed plan according to the income requirements proposed under this bill and the employee's share of the premium contribution is larger than it would be through the federal plan, a subsidy from the federal government equal to the difference would be granted. A 10 percent subsidy would also be available for the self-employed and other persons for their group premium if: (1) the family or individual is enrolled in a health care corporation or (2) the family or individual is enrolled in another organization providing comprehensive services for a defined population group through open enrollment and approved by HEW.[q]

The plan for coverage of the aged, low-income, and medically indigent persons proposed by the Ullman bill would be financed by the present Medicare payroll tax, federal general revenues, and premium contributions from the medically indigent group. The aged and low-income individuals and families under the federal plan would not pay any premium for coverage. The medically indigent would pay an annual premium according to their income class and based on whether enrollment is for an individual or a family. The income classes for the medically indigent, which also differentiate income levels according to family

[q]By subscribing to an approved plan, individuals and families can take their premium contribution as a deduction on their federal personal income tax return.

size, are the same income grouping employed for determining the eligibility for the medically indigent. These three classes are:

Income class	*Individual*	*Family of 2*	*Family of 3*	*Family of 4 or more*
2	$2,001-3,000	$3,001-4,500	$4,501-6,000	$6,001-7,500
3	$3,001-4,500	$4,501-6,000	$6,001-7,500	$7,501-9,000
4	$4,501-6,000	$6,001-7,500	$7,501-9,000	$9,000-10,500

The amount of the premium for the individual or family based on the medically indigent income classes are:[r]

Class	*Individual*	*Family*
2	$ 50	$125
3	100	250
4	150	375

The payroll tax levied to finance the benefits of the present Medicare program would continue and would be the initial source of funding for this federal plan. All additional costs of the plan would be appropriated from federal general revenues. The total amount of general revenues would also include: the subsidy payments under the employee plan, the foregone revenues because of medical deductions on personal income tax returns, the administrative costs of the various programs, and sufficient funds to establish a 5 percent reserve. The Medicare trust funds would be retained and would receive the revenues from the Medicare payroll tax and those general revenues applicable to insurance for the aged, except for the specified costs of their catastrophic coverage. All other costs would be paid from general revenues directly.

Long-Ribicoff Bill

The Long-Ribicoff Bill relies on several funding mechanisms for the financing of the three separate programs that it would establish. The catastrophic insurance program would be financed through an additional payroll tax on employers' total payrolls and on self-employment income, which both are currently subject to the payroll or social security tax. The medical assistance plan for low-income persons would be financed by federal and state general revenues. Premiums paid

[r]The amount of premium contribution by the medically indigent would be raised under the provisions of this bill if the consumer price index rises by 3 percent or more in a year and at the same rate as the rise in this index.

by employers would be the source of financing for the certified private health insurance program for employees and the self-employed. In addition, since the Medicare program would be maintained, the payroll tax for the financing of the hospital insurance plan (Part A) would remain in effect.

The payroll tax rate for the financing of the catastrophic program is set at 1.0 percent on employers' total payrolls—accounted for by wage and salary obligations up to the current ceiling on earnings ($15,300) for social security taxes. The same rate of 1.0 percent would be placed on self-employment income up to the ceiling imposed for purposes of social security taxes. There are no provisions in the proposed legislation to alter the ceiling or maximum amount of taxable payrolls and self-employment income.

Under the financing of the plan for low-income persons by federal and state general revenues, the share that any given state would assume is dependent on the state's present expenditures under the Medicaid program and would thus vary from state to state. The given amount of the state's share is equal to the total of the present payments under Medicaid by the state for those types of services also covered under the proposed medical assistance plan. For those states that have eligibility requirements under their Medicaid program that are less liberal than the criteria for income eligibility set forth by the proposed plan, the state's contribution would also include an amount equal to one-half of the payments that it would have made under Medicaid *if* its eligibility requirements for all services were the same as provided for by the new Long-Ribicoff proposal. The state's contribution would be *reduced* by an amount equal to one-half of the expenditures it makes for the types of services not covered by the new plan, but which are eligible for federal matching monies under the present Medicaid statutes. For all states, the contributions are fixed amounts that would not increase in future program years and are based on the respective expenditures made in the year before the new medical assistance program is implemented. The balance of the costs of the program for low-income persons would be financed by federal general revenues. All general revenues for use in financing the medical assistance plan, both federal and state, would be held in a newly formed special medical coverage trust fund.

The provisions of this bill also call for the initial use of federal general revenues for the implementation phase of the catastrophic insurance program. For the first three years, appropriations from federal general revenues would provide for an operating fund and a contingency reserve. These appropriations, together with the revenues from the additional special payroll tax, would be held in a separate health insurance trust fund for the administration of program receipts and expenditures. The amount of the general revenue appropriations during each of the initial three years of the implementation of the catastrophic plan would be equal to one-third of the estimated expenditures for the program. These appropriations would be repayable to the U.S. Treasury *without* interest.

Summary of the Distributional Effects of Selected Cost Structures

The most obvious differences in the cost structures of the six selected national health insurance proposals reviewed here are the allocations of public versus private financing. Two proposals, the Corman-Kennedy Bill and the Young Bill, rely only on tax revenues to fund their universal insurance plans. Three other proposals—the Fulton-Duncan Bill (AMA), the Burleson-McIntyre Bill (HIAA), and the Ullman Bill (AHA)—are primarily financed by premiums. The Long-Ribicoff Bill, as introduced in the 94th Congress, actually illustrates a cost approach that combines both public and private financing sources. The less obvious, but significant, differences in these cost structures are related to the distributional effects of the various sources of financing which they propose.

The Young Proposal would use payroll taxes as a major source of financing. However, a relatively large portion of the total costs of this plan would also be paid from federal general revenues, because of the tax credit system that it proposes. Employers' total payrolls would be taxed at a rate of 6 percent, while employees' wages and salaries would be taxed at 2 percent. As is also the case with the Corman-Kennedy proposal, unearned income, in addition to self-employment income, would also be subject to the payroll tax. The Young Bill proposes a 5.0 percent tax on unearned income and on self-employment income. This proposal would eliminate the hospital insurance program under Medicare (Part A), together with the voluntary medical insurance plan under Part B, and the present social security tax associated with this program would be repealed. This action would remove one regressive tax structure from the present sources of federal financing of health care.

By completely removing the ceiling on the taxable earnings and by taxing all earnings of employees at the same rate, a *proportional* structure of cost burdens is built into the payroll tax. This proportional structure also results for the payroll tax on employers' total payrolls, and on self-employment and unearned income. Through the tax credit system, which this proposal incorporates into its approach to financing national health insurance, some progressivity ultimately occurs in the distribution of the cost burdens. However, these progressive effects are found only at relatively high income levels, for example, above $25,000 for individuals, since the *maximum* tax credit for health-insurance-related tax payments that is effective in altering the proportionality of the tax structure is associated with the high earnings classes only.

The most surprising provision of the Young Bill is that AFDC and SSI benefit payments would be taxed under the definition of unearned income specified by this proposal. Not only are there arguments against this type of taxation from an efficiency prospective, since the federal government would be using its own transfers as a tax base, but also the distributional effects of this type of tax are regressive.

The Corman-Kennedy proposal would have half of the total costs of its universal insurance plan financed by federal general revenues and half by payroll tax revenues. For all three bases for the payroll tax, i.e., wages and salaries, employers' total payrolls, and self-employment and unearned income, the tax rates are lower under this proposal than those proposed by the Young Bill, because of the heavier reliance on the use of federal general revenues. Most importantly, the payroll tax is a very regressive form for financing a national health insurance plan. While the Corman-Kennedy Bill does increase the ceiling on taxable earnings and self-employment income (or the total contribution base including unearned income) to $21,150, the distributional effects of the payroll tax across earnings levels remain proportional until the ceiling or maximum earnings base is attained, after which the effects are regressive.

Estimates of the distribution of the burdens of this kind of combination of tax sources for financing suggest that the overall cost structure of this proposal could be regressive. Higher combined effective tax rates for both the payroll tax and the personal income tax could occur for those income groups within the vicinity of the poverty level and up to the new proposed ceiling on taxable earnings for the payroll tax relative to those combined effective rates for the higher income groups.[s]

The Corman-Kennedy Bill would repeal the current social security tax imposed for the financing of Medicare-Part A, which would be eliminated. An additional regressive element of the current structure of financing, the medical deduction, would also be removed by the provisions of this proposal, except in those cases where expenditures are made for services not covered in the Health Security Act benefit package. Marginal state revenues would be required under the Corman-Kennedy proposal, if a state chooses to maintain a health care financing program for the poor and medically indigent to cover those services not covered by the proposed universal plan. The use of any state revenues would increase the regressive effects of the overall cost structure, by imposing higher costs on the low- and middle-income groups through the various state taxes.

Those proposals that rely on premiums as a major source of financing have the most regressive distributional effects. Three premium-based private health insurance proposals are reviewed in the discussion above—the Fulton-Duncan Bill, the Burleson-McIntyre Bill, and the Ullman Bill. The Fulton-Duncan proposal would use federal general revenues, in addition to premium revenues, for a tax credit program to subsidize the cost of premiums, and payroll tax revenues for the continuation of the hospital insurance program under the current Medicare program.

[s]Much of the income of those below the poverty level is the result of government transfers which are not taxable under either the personal income tax or the payroll tax provisions.

The tax credit approach to assistance for premium payments under the Fulton-Duncan proposal is relatively effective in easing the burdens of the cost of insurance for the low- and middle-income groups. It is the case, however, that those individuals and families who have income tax liabilities marginally above the defined eligibility category are affected by the "notch problem" under the tax credit system provided by this proposal. The effects of the Medicare payroll tax, currently at a rate of 2.0 percent of a total combined payroll tax rate of 11.7 percent, would add further to the inequities in cost burdens imposed by this premium approach to financing national health insurance.

The Burleson-McIntyre proposal would rely primarily on premiums to finance its employee-employer plan, although the employee's premium contribution would be limited to 10 percent of monthly wages above fixed amounts of monthly total earnings, which in effect acts as an exemption would for a tax revenue base. However, as the evidence presented here indicates, some, if not all, premium contributions by employers on behalf of their employees can be assumed to be the ultimate burden of the workers, in the last analysis, either in the form of lower wages than might otherwise be gained or in the form of higher prices for the products and services that they produce. Employees and other individual policyholders could take their *entire* premium cost as a deduction against personal income taxes. This could offer some relief from the regressive effects of the cost burdens of the premium approach, since deductions might represent a larger percentage of total tax liability for low- and middle-income groups than for high-income groups.

The State plan under the Burleson-McIntyre proposal would be largely financed by federal general revenues (70 to 90 percent), which builds in a progressive financing component. However, these federal funds would be complemented by state general revenues, which are generally considered to have regressive distributional effects. The overall effects of the financing of this State plan would, therefore, vary based on an allocation process linked to respective per capita state income levels.

The plan proposed under the Ullman Bill uses an approach similar to that offered by the Burleson-McIntyre proposal. The mandated employee-employer plan would have the employer pay 75 percent of the premium cost and the basic arguments regarding the shifting of the ultimate cost burdens to the employees hold true. This plan would retain the Medicare program and thus the regressive effects of the payroll tax imposed for Medicare financing would remain, as is also the case for the Burleson-McIntyre proposal. In addition, the regressive premium payment is also required of the medically indigent under the proposed plan for the poor. However, only federal general revenues are used to subsidize the program for the poor and medically indigent—no state general revenues would be involved.

The Long-Ribiciff Bill incorporates three sources of financing—a new payroll tax, premiums, and federal and state general revenues. By combining the use of the payroll tax for the financing of the catastrophic plan and the use of premiums for the employee plans, this proposal would rely on two very regressive types of financing sources to cover the major costs of the overall plan. The plan for medical assistance for low-income persons would be funded jointly by federal and state general revenues. The federal and state contributions would vary from state to state, but are linked to the costs for the states under the current Medicaid program. This latter provision offers the strong possibility that the maldistribution of the costs of the Medicaid program across the rich and poor states would persist under this proposal.

Notes

1. Rashi Fein, "Impact of National Health Insurance Plans on Financing," in *National Health Insurance: Proceedings of the Conference on National Health Insurance,* planned and edited by Robert D. Eilers and Sue S. Moyerman (Homewood, Ill.: Richard D. Irwin, Inc., 1971), p. 78.

2. John A. Brittain, *The Payroll Tax for Social Security* (Washington, D.C.: The Brookings Institution, 1972), p. 1.

3. Ibid., p. 2.

4. See ibid., Chapter 4, especially pp. 108-114; and Joseph A. Pechman and Benjamin A. Okner, *Who Bears the Tax Burden* (Washington, D.C.: The Brookings Institution, 1974), p. 58

5. Brittain, op. cit., p. 82.

6. For a complete discussion of certain income tax policies, such as personal deductions, exemptions, and income splitting, see Harold M. Groves, *Federal Tax Treatment of the Family* (Washington, D.C.: The Brookings Institution, 1963).

7. These effective tax rates are based on "ordinary income" defined as adjusted gross income less realized capital gains. Brittain also estimates the social security tax plus the unemployment insurance effective rate to be 10.1 percent for income tax filers below the poverty level, or almost double the combined effective rate for those above the poverty level of 5.8 percent. See Brittain, op. cit., Table 4-1 and p. 95.

8. Karen Davis, *National Health Insurance: Benefits, Costs, and Consequences* (Washington, D.C.: The Brookings Institution, 1975), p. 29.

9. Ibid.

10. Ibid., p. 70.

11. Bridger M. Mitchell and Ronald J. Vogel, *Health and Taxes: An Assessment of the Medical Deduction,* prepared for the Office of Economic Opportunity (Santa Monica, Calif: Rand Corporation, 1973), p. v.

12. Ibid.

13. Ibid., p. 9.

14. Ibid., Table 2.

15. Ibid., p. 24.

16. Ibid., pp. 25 and 27.

17. Ibid., p. 24.

18. Ibid., p. 27.

19. For example, Waldman finds that under the AMA proposal introduced in Congress in 1969, 45.8 million returns, or 68 percent of all returns for persons under age sixty-five years, would be eligible for the proposed tax credit under this bill. The other 21.8 million returns indicate tax liabilities greater than the amount of the credit allowable. See U.S. Department of Health, Education and Welfare, Social Security Administration, Office of Research and Statistics, *Tax Credits for Private Health Insurance: Estimates of Eligibility and Cost under Five Alternative Proposals,* by Saul Waldman, Staff Paper No. 3 (October, 1969), p. 32.

20. Ibid., p. 48.

21. See Horst Claus Recktenwald, *Tax Incidence and Income Redistribution: An Introduction* (Detroit: Wayne State University Press, 1971), p. 171.

22. Davis, op. cit., p. 150.

10 The Distributional Effects of the Medicare and Medicaid Programs

The experience of the federal government with the Medicare and Medicaid programs offers useful insights into the possible distributional effects of a national health insurance plan. This is true not only because these programs for the elderly and the "poor" may be maintained as components of proposed legislation, but perhaps more important because these programs rely on cost and benefit structures similar in several cases to those provided for by the more general national health insurance proposals. The Medicaid program, in this regard, is of particular relevance, because it fixes an income criterion, among others, for determining a recipient eligibility. The Medicare program offers the opportunity to review and analyze an insurance plan that stipulates cost sharing in the form of deductibles and coinsurance payments on the use of health services.

Medicare

With the 1965 Medicare amendments to the Social Security Act, two separate but related health insurance plans were established for those persons sixty-five years and over who were eligible for benefits under the social security program. The first plan, Part A, is a basic compulsory program of hospital insurance (HI), and the second plan, Part B, is a voluntary program of supplementary medical insurance (SMI) for which the enrollee must pay a monthly premium. Benefits were initiated in July 1966, except as they relate to posthospital extended care services in skilled nursing facilities, which were not covered until January 1967.

By 1967, 99 percent of all persons sixty-five years and older, or more than 19 million elderly, were already enrolled in the compulsory Medicare hospital insurance plan, while about 92 percent were enrolled voluntarily in the optional medical insurance plan.[a] By 1968, this latter group of enrollees had increased to about 95 percent.[1] Currently, Medicare beneficiaries number more than 24 million, and as many as 97 percent of those eligible for the hospital insurance plan have also enrolled in the medical insurance plan.

[a]All persons sixty-five years and older who are eligible for social security benefits are also eligible for the Medicare program. Persons who are sixty-five years or older who are not eligible for social security benefits, but who have enrolled in the voluntary Medicare medical insurance plan, can also enroll in the Medicare hospital insurance plan on a voluntary basis by paying a monthly premium. Effective July 1, 1976, this monthly premium for the voluntary hospital insurance plan will increase to $45 per month.

The Medicare program is administered by the Department of Health, Education and Welfare and the direct locus of responsibility for administrative control and program policy is with the Bureau of Health Insurance of the Social Security Administration. The actual day-to-day operations of the Medicare program, such as reviewing recipient benefit claims and making reimbursement payments to health providers, is assumed by 132 commercial insurance companies and Blue Cross-Blue Shield plans who are contracted with to act as fiscal intermediaries for the hospital insurance plan and carriers for the medical insurance plan.

Benefits

Covered services under Part A, the hospital insurance plan, include benefits for the following services for a limit of *ninety days* for a hospital stay and *one-hundred days* for care in a skilled nursing home during a benefit period:

1. semiprivate room rates
2. regular nursing services
3. costs of intensive care units
4. drugs administered during an inpatient stay
5. laboratory tests, X rays, and other radiological services and therapy, if included in the hospital billing
6. medical supplies, such as casts, surgical dressings, and splints, and the use of wheelchairs
7. operating and recovery room costs
8. rehabilitative services, such as physical therapy, occupational therapy, and speech therapy

Services not covered by Part A are: private duty nursing; extra charges for a private room; the first three pints of blood; and personal coveniences, such as telephone, radio, or television.

Under Medicare's hospital insurance plan, *lifetime* hospital reserve days are set at sixty days. These covered days can automatically be applied for any hospital stay of greater than ninety days. However, these extra benefits are not renewable once the reserve days have been exhausted. A "benefit period" under Part A begins with the day of admission to a hospital and ends sixty days after the day of discharge from the hospital.[b] There is no limit, however, to the number of benefit periods which an enrollee in the hospital insurance plan can have.

---

[b]Usually Medicare covers hospital care only if the patient is in a hospital that participates in the Medicare program. In some cases, the hospital insurance can cover care in a qualified nonparticipating hospital, if the patient is admitted for emergency treatment, and the hospital is the nearest one geographically to provide such emergency care.

Care in a psychiatric hospital is limited to no more than 190 days of *life-time* benefits. Further, if the enrollee was a patient in a psychiatric hospital within 150 days immediately prior to eligibility for the Medicare coverage, these days of hospitalization must be subtracted from the 190 days of lifetime total benefits for psychiatric inpatient care.

Medicare's hospital insurance plan will also help to pay for inpatient care in a participating skilled nursing home, when certain conditions are met: (1) the patient has been in a hospital at least three consecutive days before the transfer to a skilled nursing facility; (2) the transfer to the facility is necessary because of the condition that required the patient's care in the hospital; (3) a physician certifies the need for skilled nursing or rehabilitative services on a daily basis; and (4) the facility's utilization review committee approves the patient's stay.[2]

Home health care benefits are also offered under Medicare that cover part-time skilled nursing care; physical therapy; and speech therapy. If the patient needs any of these three, Medicare can also pay for: occupational therapy; part-time services of home health aides; medical social services; and medical supplies and equipment provided by the agency. Not covered are: full-time nursing care at home; drugs and biologicals; and homemaker services. Home health care services can be paid for under either the hospital or medical insurance plans, depending on which conditions are met. Hospital insurance could pay for up to 100 home health visits during the twelve months after discharge from a hospital or participating skilled nursing facility. Medical insurance could pay, if a physician certifies the need for these services and sets up a plan for home health care and the agency providing the services participates in the Medicare program.

Medicare-Part B covered services include:

1. medical and surgical services provided by a physician in office or patient's home, in hospital, emergency room, or outpatient clinic
2. diagnostic tests and procedures that are part of treatment
3. other services ordinarily provided in a physician's office and included in billing: X rays; nursing services in the physician's office; drugs and biologicals administered by the physician or nurse; medical supplies; physical therapy; and speech therapy
4. radiology and pathology services provided by a physician
5. outpatient mental health services provided by a physician (limited to no more than $250 in any one benefit year)
6. podiatrists' services, except for routine foot care
7. dental care, only if it involves surgery of the jaw or related structures or the setting of fractures
8. certain necessary ambulance services

Services not covered are: routine physical examinations; routine foot care; eye or hearing examinations for prescribing or fitting eyeglasses or hearing aids;

immunizations (routine); and cosmetic surgery, unless required because of accident or injury or to improve body-function.

Costs

Cost sharing on the part of the enrollee is required under *both* the hospital and medical insurance plans of Medicare. Medicare–Part A has deductibles attached to the coverage for inhospital services *and* a daily coinsurance payment for hospital stays of greater than sixty days. As of January 1976, the deductible is $104, and the respective coinsurance for hospital stays from the sixty-first day to the end of the ninety days is $26 and after ninety days, under the lifetime reserve, is $52 daily. Coverage for extended care facilities also has a daily coinsurance payment of $13 after the first twenty days of the patient's stay. Chart 1 presents cost sharing under Medicare–Part A.

Chart 1

	Inpatient hospital deductible	*Inpatient hospital daily coinsurance*		*Extended care facility daily coinsurance after 20 days*
		After 60 days	*After 90 days*	
July 1966	$ 40	$10		
January 1970	52	13	$22	$ 6.50
January 1976	104	26	52	13

Under Medicare–Part B, medical insurance benefits require a $20 deductible and a 20 percent coinsurance rate of payment for the enrollee for outpatient hospital diagnostic services. All benefits under the coverage for supplemental medical services require an annual deductible of $60 and also a coinsurance payment of 20 percent. The monthly premium to be paid by the enrollee for this voluntary Medicare medical insurance coverage will increase from $6.70 to $7.20, effective as of July 1, 1976. This premium is matched by federal funds from general revenues. Chart 2 presents cost sharing and premiums under Medicare–Part B.

Medicaid

The Medicaid program, established in 1965 under Title XIX of the Social Security Act, is a joint federal and state government program to provide public

Chart 2

	Outpatient hospital diagnostic services		*Supplemental medical*		
	Deductible	*Coinsurance*	*Annual deductible*	*Coinsurance*	*Monthly premium*
July 1966	$20	20%	$50	20%	$3.00
January 1970	$20	20%	$50	20%	$5.30*
January 1976	$20	20%	$60	20%	$7.20*

*Effective July 1970 and July 1976, respectively.

financial assistance for medical care for the poor. Federal participation is in the form of federal matching funds financed from general revenues and also in the structure of certain standards and guidelines regarding benefit levels and provider reimbursement.[c] In addition to those persons eligible for Medicaid benefits under the categorical assistance programs (old-age assistance, aid to the blind, aid to the disabled, aid to families with dependent children), at each state's option, medically indigent groups can also be covered under the Medicaid program.[d] Generally, medical indigence is defined as a level of income not to exceed 133 1/3 percent of the maximum cash payments for families of the same size under the AFDC program. Eligibility for Medicaid coverage for medically indigent persons can also be implemented by "spend down" provisions—persons and families can qualify for medical assistance by disregarding all income that had been spent for medical care in determining their qualifications for eligibility.

In 1969, three years after the establishment of the Medicaid program, only 11 states had not adopted Title XIX programs. By January 1970, the deadline after which federal financial participation would no longer be possible, only two states, Arizona and Alaska, had not instituted a state plan for

[c]Federal financial participation is also available for 50 percent matching of certain administrative costs of the program and for 75 percent matching of the costs of professional medical personnel, such as inspectors for the periodic medical review of patients.

[d]Frequently included in discussion of and data on recipients under the Medicaid program are those covered under general assistance or general relief, which also provides for some medical coverage in certain circumstances, but which is completely funded by state monies. These general relief recipients and the respective "medically needy" group are adults between the ages of twenty-one to sixty-five years who do not qualify for categorical assistance and usually are single individuals, childless couples, and unemployed males who are heads of households.

Medicaid. Twenty-four states and the District of Columbia currently have extended the optional coverage to the medically indigent.[e]

Federal guidelines initially mandated five basic services to be offered as minimum benefits under state Medicaid plans: inpatient hospital services; outpatient hospital services; skilled nursing-home services; physician services; and other laboratory and X-ray services. In 1967, early periodic screening, diagnosis and treatment services (EPSDT) for eligible children under twenty-one years of age were included in this minimum level of service benefits, together with home health services for those who would need nursing-home care otherwise.

Optional covered services which also qualify for federal matching funds under either the benefits for cash recipients or medically indigent are quite comprehensive, but the range of services vary from state to state. These optional benefits include: clinic services; private duty nursing; dental services and dentures; prescribed drugs; eyeglasses; prosthetic devices; physical therapy and related services; preventive and rehabilitative services; inpatient hospital and skilled nursing home services in an institution for tuberculosis or mental disease (for those persons 65 years and over); and any other type of medical or remedial care recognized under state law. In 1971, an amendment to Title XIX also made available intermediate nursing home services to both cash receipients and the medically indigent at the option of the state.

Under Medicaid, cost sharing for any covered services on the part of cash recipient eligibles is not permitted in any form. However, states do have the option to require copayments for the services covered for the medically indigent, given the level of cost sharing is related to their income. In 1970, only New York State had introduced such a system of income-related copayments for the medically indigent group. In addition, through "buy in" agreements with the federal government, state Medicaid programs can pay the premiums, deductibles, and copayments under Medicare, if persons are eligible for benefits under both Medicaid and Medicare. Some states use fiscal agents to assist in the processing of claims and the reimbursement of providers, as is the case for the Medicare program. No incentives are directly built into either the Medicare or Medicaid structure or guidelines to promote changes in the existing health care system.

Federal financial participation rates range from 50 to 83 percent, with the high income states receiving 50 percent federal matching funds. Federal matching funds are *either* determined on a base amount, a uniform percentage of federal funds under categorical assistance programs, plus additional amounts based on an income-related formula *or* solely on the states' ability to pay—states with lower per capita income should receive a higher percentage of federal

---

[e]Included also in the group that has extended coverage to the medically indigent are: the Virgin Islands, Guam, and Puerto Rico. Eighteen states or U.S. possessions limit the income criteria for eligibility for the medically indigent to less than the maximum of 133 1/3 percent of cash assistance payments.

matching funds and vice-versa. However, the level of federal financial participation also varies from state to state, because the matching arrangements are dependent on the type of medical assistance program, eligibility requirements, and overall benefit levels.

Through federal financial participation, the Medicaid program was to encourage the poorer states to allocate more of their own funds for medical care with the incentive of receiving relatively higher rates of federal funding than the high-income states. Since the federal government would also assume a greater proportion of the additional costs of medical assistance, this increased federal financing would shift the burden of the Medicaid program to those states with the higher per capita income levels. Thereby, income would be redistributed from the high income states to states with low per capita income levels, because federal funding is through general revenues, which are largely collected from progressive tax bases, i.e., personal and corporate income. In fact, during fiscal year 1969, for example, more than 40 percent of *all* federal Medicaid funds were received by two states, New York and California. For this same period, these two states were responsible for only about 23 percent of the total costs of the program.[3]

The Medicare and Medicaid Experience

The emphasis of the present system of federal programs for financing personal health care, primarily Medicare and Medicaid, is largely placed on the needs of the elderly. In 1970, for example, 67 percent of the estimated expenditures for personal health care for those persons sixty-five years and older was met by public monies, including state and local government funds. The remainder of the total expenditures of $15.7 billion for 1970 was paid through private sources, such as out-of-pocket expenses, private health insurance benefits, and philanthropy. By contrast, the $9.3 billion total expenditures for children (those persons under nineteen years of age) in 1970 are substantially represented by private financing (73%), while only 27 percent was apportioned to the public sector. For those persons in the age category of 19-64 years, as little as 22 percent of their total expenditures for personal health care was met by public sources of financing. (See Figure 10-1.)

Estimates for 1973 of the distribution of public financing of personal health care show modest increases in the percentage of public sources for the 0 to 19 years population (29%) and the 19 to 64 years population (27%), with a marginal decline to 64 percent in public funding of health care for the elderly.[4]

Since 1967, the first full year of the program, the overall expenditures under Medicare have accelerated greatly. In fact, most of the political reaction to the effects of the Medicare program has focused on the extent to which the costs incurred by the federal government for this insurance program for the aged population exceeded the original estimated expenditures.

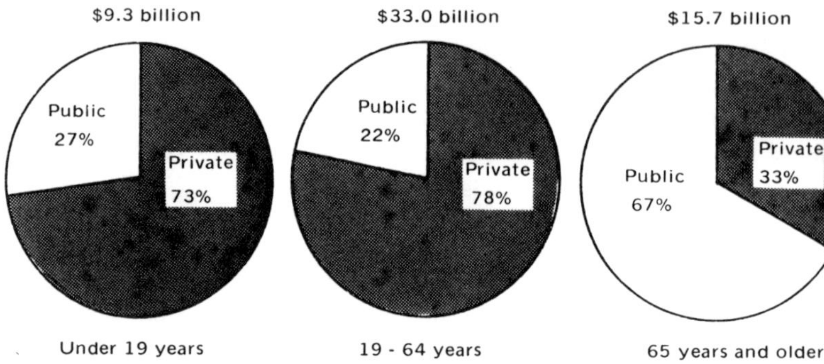

Source: Barbara S. Cooper and Mary F. McGee "Medical Care Outlays for Three Age Groups, Young, Intermediate and Aged," *Social Security Bulletin,* Vol. 33, No. 5 (May, 1971), Table 1.

Figure 10-1. Estimated Personal Health Care Expenditures for Three Age Groups by Source of Funds, 1970

In fiscal year 1967, the cost of the combined hospital and medical insurance plans was about $3.4 billion. The majority of these expenditures were for benefit payments, with about 3 percent of the total expenses related to administration of the program. By far the largest portion of this total cost to the federal government was as a result of the hospital insurance coverage, with related expenditures of $2.6 billion in 1967. On a per capita basis, $131 was expended for each enrollee for hospital benefits in 1967, while medical service benefits under Part B were only $37 per enrollee.

For fiscal year 1974, estimates of the total Medicare expenditures for the federal government are set at $11.3 billion. This level of expenditures indicates a more than tripling of total costs for the combined insurance plans over about an eight-year period. Since the implementation of the Medicare program, benefits paid by the federal government per enrollee have also increased by almost the same percentage to a level of about $460. This rise in per capita expenditures reflects the increased utilization of services that occurred with the establishment of the Medicare program, but it also reflects the rapid inflation in the prices of hospital care and medical services, which, in turn, is partially a result of the program. It can be assumed that most of the increase in utilization reflects the unmet health care needs of the elderly, which surfaced with the availability of federal financing through insurance.[f]

---

[f]There may also have been some overutilization of services generated by the increased availability of insurance benefits for the aged, as is frequently argued by critics of the program.

However, the fact that Medicare pays less than half of the average annual health bill for the aged person remains the case. Because of a number of factors, most importantly the cost sharing requirements under Medicare and again the inflation in the costs of hospital care and medical services, out-of-pocket expenses incurred by the elderly also doubled on a per capita basis. Premium payments by enrollees, included here in the total for federal expenditures, alone accounted for more than 10 percent of the estimated $11.3 billion in 1974.

In Table 10-1, estimates are given for the percentage distribution of total expenditures for Medicare according to the various sources of financing for fiscal years 1970 to 1974. As is shown by the data for 1974, almost 96 percent

Table 10-1
Estimated Source of Funds for Medicare Expenditures for Fiscal Years 1970-1974

Source of Funds[a]	*1970*	*1971*	*1972*	*1973*	*1974*
Total Medicare Expenditures (in Millions)	$7,149	$7,875	$8,819	$9,478	$11,322
Percent from					
Payroll tax	61.2%	59.2%	61.8%	70.0%	71.5%[b]
Premiums paid by enrollees	13.8[c]	13.6	14.2	11.7	10.4
Premiums paid by Medicaid		1.6	1.6	1.4	1.0
General revenues	24.9	25.6	22.6	17.0	17.0
Hospital Insurance Expenditures (in Millions)	$4,953	$5,592	$6,276	$6,841	$ 8,044
Percent from					
Payroll tax	88.4%	84.9%	90.5%	94.7%	95.5%[b]
General revenues	11.6	15.1	9.5	5.3	4.5
Medical Insurance Expenditures (in Millions)	$2,196	$2,282	$2,543	$2,637	$ 3,278
Percent from					
Premiums paid by enrollees	45.0%[c]	44.9%	44.4%	44.7%	41.5%
Premiums paid by Medicaid		5.3	5.1	5.2	4.2
General revenues	55.0	49.8	50.5	50.1	54.4

[a]Excludes small amounts transferred from the railroad retirement account and from interest on investments.

[b]Includes small amounts paid in premiums for the hospital insurance plan by persons previously uninsured who are 65 years and older and who are eligible for voluntary coverage since 1973.

[c]Includes premium payments by enrollees and by the Medicaid program.

Source: Barbara S. Cooper and Nancy L. Worthington, "National Health Expenditures, 1929-72," *Social Security Bulletin,* Vol. 35, No. 1 (January, 1973), p. 8; Barbara S. Cooper, Nancy L. Worthington, and Paula A. Piro, "National Health Expenditures, 1929-73," *Social Security Bulletin,* Vol. 36, No. 3 (March, 1974), p. 6; and Nancy L. Worthington, "National Health Expenditures, 1929-74," *Social Security Bulletin,* Vol. 37, No. 2 (February, 1975), p. 7.

of the expenditures under the hospital insurance plan were funded through a payroll tax, with as little as the remaining 5 percent allocated from federal general revenues. In 1974, 42 percent of the costs of the medical insurance plan was financed by premiums paid by enrollees for this optional coverage. The remainder of the expenditures under Medicare–Part B was funded through federal general revenues.

When the financing of the hospital and medical insurance plans are analyzed as combined expenditures, 72 percent of all Medicare expenditures in 1974 were financed by the regressive payroll tax, about 17 percent by federal general revenues, and more than 11 percent through premiums paid almost entirely by the enrollees. The proportion of total Medicare expenditures funded by general revenues, a progressive type of financing, in fact declined by about 8 percent from its level in 1970, indicating the movement toward increased regressivity in the financing of the Medicare program by the heavier reliance on payroll tax revenues and premiums.

Data on the initial impact of the Medicare program *across income groups* for persons sixty-five years and over is presented in Table 10–2. By comparing charges per person for medical services (defined broadly as those services covered under Part B) prior to and after the implementation of the Medicare program, together with the percentage distribution of the sources of financing of these services, the role of the medical insurance plan in meeting the needs of the elderly in the various income classes can be analyzed.

Prior to the initiation of Medicare–Part B, by far the largest portion (74 to 91 percent, depending on income level and family size) of expenditures for medical services was met through direct patient payments, listed in Table 10–2 as out-of-pocket payments. Of primary interest is the fact that out-of-pocket expenditures by the aged were only cut in half by the impact of the Medicare program on medical service coverage. Medicare's medical insurance plan, of course, has many restrictions on the types of services covered as benefits and, in addition, has substantial cost sharing factors requiring enrollees to incur personal expenses. Therefore, the percentage of charges per person that remained to be paid either directly by the elderly or by Medicaid for low-income eligibles is consistently in the 40 to 50 percent range. At all levels of income and for various family sizes, as little as 9 to 25 percent of charges for medical services in 1965 was met by private health insurance benefits. While private health insurance benefits were cut by the impact of the Medicare program, 5 to 10 percent of expenditures for medical services in 1967 still reflected some role for this type of private coverage.

Higher charges were incurred by those in the relatively higher-income groups, suggesting that the lack of adequate insurance coverage and other financial means for payment hindered the elderly in the lower-income classes from receiving health care sufficient to meet their needs prior to the availability of Medicare coverage. Charges incurred by persons across income groups are more closely aligned in the data presented for 1967, although the highest charges per person continue to be associated with the higher-income classes.

Table 10-2
Charges per Person 65 Years and over for Medical Services, by Source of Payment and Family Income, 1965 and 1967[a]

1965

Family Income ($)	Charges per Person	Percentage Distribution: Total	Private Insurance	Out of Pocket
All persons	$66	100.0	19.4	80.6
One-person family	64	100.0	17.5	82.5
Under 1,000	44	100.0	8.7	91.3
1,000-1,999	46	100.0	17.5	82.5
2,000-2,999	86	100.0	21.0	79.0
3,000 or more	97	100.0	17.5	82.5
Two-person family	67	100.0	20.9	79.1
Under 2,000	47	100.0	11.6	88.4
2,000-2,999	55	100.0	21.8	78.2
3,000-3,999	71	100.0	19.7	80.3
4,000 or more	91	100.0	25.7	74.3
Families of three or more[b]	69	100.0	18.5	81.5

1967

Family Income ($)	Charges per Person	Percentage Distribution: Total	Medicare	Private Insurance	Out of Pocket
All persons	$ 95	100.0	45.1	7.8	47.1
One-person family	98	100.0	48.1	7.2	44.7
Under 1,000	87	100.0	56.0	5.2	38.8
1,000-1,999	91	100.0	49.1	4.3	46.6
2,000-2,999	86	100.0	39.9	8.7	51.4
3,000 or more	108	100.0	47.4	10.3	42.3
Two-person family	94	100.0	43.6	8.5	47.9
Under 2,000	70	100.0	42.9	4.6	52.5
2,000-2,999	78	100.0	44.8	8.5	46.7
3,000-3,999	93	100.0	41.9	6.2	51.9
4,000 or more	121	100.0	44.4	11.3	44.3
Families of three or more[b]	93	100.0	44.8	6.6	48.6

[a] Medical services are defined as both ambulatory medical services and inhospital surgical and medical services, including physicians' visits in the home or office, visits to a clinic, emergency room, or health center, and visits to a private laboratory. Charges classified as "out of pocket" are direct outlays made by the enrollee and include deductible and coinsurance amounts, unfiled claims, and disallowed charges and premium payments that are not matched by general revenues.

[b] Data by income are omitted because figures generally do not meet standards of reliability for precision.

Source: Regina Loewenstein, "Early Effects of Medicare on the Health Care of the Aged," *Social Security Bulletin,* Vol. 33, No. 4 (April, 1971), Table 10.

The distribution of the percentages of out-of-pocket expenditures across family income groups prior to Medicare is closely correlated with the distribution of Medicare expenditures in 1967. In general, those persons with relatively higher out-of-pocket expenditures for medical services in 1965 had a marginally higher proportion of their charges paid under the Medicare program. There is, however, no consistent pattern to show that the benefits of the Medicare program increase in percentage terms as the level of income increases. The variation in the portion of charges per person is less across income classes for two-person families than for one-person families.

Recent data on expenditures for the Medicaid program are not as readily available as for the Medicare program. Presumably, this is because of the joint federal-state structure and the many variations in the State plans. However, published data do indicate the general nature of the distribution of expenditures.

For fiscal year 1974, the estimate of total expenditures under the Medicaid program by both federal and state and local governments is more than $11 billion, an amount approximately equal to total federal expenditures under Medicare for the same year. The accelerated growth of Medicaid expenditures is reflected in the annual increases from a level of $1.4 billion in fiscal year 1966 for total government vendor payments prior to Medicaid. Together, Medicaid and Medicare currently represent about 60 percent of all national health expenditures by the public sector.

In fiscal year 1973, the number of Medicaid recipients (eligibles) totaled 23.5 million, of which more than 15 million were eligible as recipients of cash assistance.[5] The rapid increases in the number of recipients in past years of the Medicaid program have moderated somewhat, and a substantial portion of the recent increases in expenditures actually represents the effect of inflation in the prices of hospital care and medical services, coupled with increased utilization rates for recipients.

Estimates of the distribution of Medicaid expenditures by type of service are: 40 percent for inpatient hospital services; 30 percent for nursing-home services; 10 percent for physician services; and about 20 percent for drugs, laboratory services, X rays, and other covered services. The fastest growing benefit-service group is nursing-home care. In fiscal year 1970, Medicaid spent $1.3 billion for skilled nursing-home care, when Medicare spent $365 million on extended care services, and the cash assistance programs spent an additional $300 million for intermediate care services.[6] By 1974, a total of $7.5 billion was expended on all nursing-home services by all sources of financing, with more than half ($3.9 billion) of these expenditures incurred by the public sector, primarily because of the expanded coverage for intermediate care facilities.[7]

This distribution of Medicaid expenditures by type of service largely reflects the number and distribution of recipients according to the categorical asssistance programs and the health care needs of the various age groups in this population. In general, two-fifths of all Medicaid benefits are received by the aged, persons sixty-five years and over who are eligible for Medicare coverage, but usually require long-term nursing-home services.[8] The remaining 60 percent of Medicaid expenditures for benefits is distributed almost equally among three recipient groups—the blind and disabled, adults under the AFDC program, and children under twenty-one years, primarily through AFDC.[9]

The specific approaches to financing health care employed in Medicare and Medicaid, and the consequent limitations of these kinds of programs, offer lessons for the structure of a national health insurance plan. Despite the significant impact of the Medicare and Medicaid programs toward improving acess to health care for the elderly and the poor, certain groups within the population, including those eligible for Medicare and Medicaid, incur high personal expenses and remain with unmet needs. These situations can be verified by a variety of evidence on cost burdens and benefit levels.

The restrictions placed on public expenditures by the less-than-comprehensive benefit structure under the Medicare program, coupled with the burdens of substantial cost sharing for the enrollee, result in large private payments for health care services by the elderly. Table 10-3 presents data on per capita personal health care expenditures for persons sixty-five years and older for fiscal year 1966 (the period immediately before full implementation of both Medicare and Medicaid) and for fiscal year 1973 by type of service. Only 64 percent of all expenditures on a per capita basis by the elderly were met by public financing in 1973. While there has been a dramatic shift in the percentage distribution of health expenditures from the private sector to the public sector, the average aged person still is directly responsible for almost half of the expenditures for nonhospital services (about 90 percent for drugs), even when considering *both* Medicaid and Medicare coverage.

This responsibility either is met through direct out-of-pocket expenses or through the purchase of supplementary private health insurance policies. For many elderly persons just above income eligibility requirements for Medicaid, and without qualifications for categorical assistance, limited personal incomes are strained or adequate health care is denied for financial reasons. Estimates show that, in order to seek coverage for those services not included as Medicare benefits and primarily to assist in paying for coinsurance and deductibles required under Medicare, about half of the elderly population or about 11 million aged persons have one or more private health insurance policies, i.e., Medicare supplements.[10] In 1975, older Americans paid more than $500 million for a variety of such types of policies.[g]

[g]Four broad categories of such policies are available: hospital indemnity policies; major medical policies; enrollment in health maintenance organizations (HMOs); and Medicare supplements. The latter type of policy is the most commonly owned. For all types of policies, the benefits vary, and so annual premiums can range from $50 to $300 or more.

Table 10-3
Per Capita Personal Health Care Expenditures for Persons 65 Years and Older and Percentage Distribution by Source of Payment and by Type of Service, Fiscal Years 1966 and 1973

	1966		*1973*	
All services	$445	100.0%	$1,052	100.0%
Public	133	29.9	678	64.4
Private	312[a]	70.1	374	35.6
Hospital services	$179	100.0%	$ 509	100.0%
Public	86	48.0	415	81.5
Private	93	52.0	94	18.5
Physician services	$ 71	100.0%	$ 186	100.0%
Public	5	7.0	106	57.0
Private	66[a]	93.0	80	43.0
Nursing-home services	$ 68	100.0%	$ 149	100.0%
Public	28	41.2	84	56.4
Private	40	58.8	65	43.6
Drugs	$ 63	100.0%	$ 97	100.0%
Public	5	7.9	12	12.4
Private	58	92.1	85	87.6
All other services	$ 65	100.0%	$ 111	100.0%
Public	10	15.4	61	55.0
Private	55	84.6	50	45.0

[a]Monthly premiums paid by enrollees for Medicare supplementary medical insurance are included in the public sector expenditures.

Source: Barbara S. Cooper and Mary F. McGee, "Medical Care Outlays for Three Age Groups: Young, Intermediate, and Aged," *Social Security Bulletin,* Vol. 34, No. 5 (May, 1971), Table 6; and Barbara S. Cooper and Paula A. Piro, "Age Differences in Medical Care Spending, Fiscal Year 1973," *Social Security Bulletin,* Vol. 37, No. 5 (May, 1974), Table 2.

Different, but equally severe, limitations are associated with the Medicaid program, primarily because of the requirements for income eligibility. Secondly, because the Medicaid program does little to improve direct access to the health care system beyond its financing function, certain well-defined groups remain with levels of health expenditures (including both public and private financing sources) well below those for comparable population groups. In Table 10-4, the mean health expenditures are compared for three such groups having the lowest per capita expenditures and other groups by characteristics of race, geographic area, and income.

For example, nonwhites have lower mean expenditures for health care than whites, according to survey data from 1970. Their consistently lower level of average expenditures is indicated for hospital care, physician services, dental services, and drugs. For all types of services, whites, on the average, have health

Table 10-4
Comparison of Those Groups with Lowest Mean Health Care Expenditures with Other Groups in the Population, 1970

	Type of Service				
Low Expenditure Group	*Hospital*	*Physician*	*Dental*	*Drugs*	*All Services*
Nonwhites	$ 86	$37	$15	$24	$173
Whites	111	65	30	30	259
Rural children with family income of less than $6,000	10	16	6	9	46
Other children	47	36	23	13	127
Middle income ($6,000-$10,999) people under 65 in central cities	64	53	24	20	176
Others under 65	99	58	30	28	233

Source: *Expenditures for Personal Health Services: National Trends and Variations, 1953-1970,* Ronald Andersen, Study Director, Department of Health, Education and Welfare, Health Resources Administration (October, 1973), Table 14.

expenditures half again as large as the estimated expenditures for nonwhites. The most critical differentials in mean expenditures are shown in Table 10-4 for rural children in families with incomes less than $6,000, compared with expenditures for all other children. It can readily be assumed that because of the low ceiling placed on income requirements in rural, generally poorer, states that many families are not eligible for medical assistance. The lack of alternative means of financing and poor geographic access to sources of health services complicate their circumstances further. Mean expenditures for all other children are three times as large as for rural children whose families have incomes of less than $6,000. The gap in the current system of financing health care is also shown by the comparison of expenditures for the adult population under sixty-five years of age with middle incomes ($6,000-$10,999) who reside in urban centers or core cities. In this case, Medicaid and Medicare assistance is not available, and the extent of coverage by private health insurance is largely dependent on limited financial means.

An important measure for evaluating any federal program is the geographic distribution of benefits to eligible recipients. Under the Medicare program for the elderly, the distribution of benefits is very closely aligned with the geographic distribution of the number of elderly persons. In Table 10-5, data on the regional distribution of Medicare benefits for 1970 indicate that the largest discrepancy in the proportion of total benefits, relative to the number of elderly persons, resulted in the South. The percentage of Medicare payments is only 25.7 percent, while the number of elderly with residence in the Southern

Table 10-5
Regional Distribution of Medicare and Medicaid Benefits under Current Programs and Recipient Groups, 1970

	Medicare		Medicaid	
Region	*Number of Elderly*	*Medicare Payments*	*Number of Poor*	*Federal Medicaid Payments*
	Millions			
All regions	20	$7,494	27	$2,930
	Percentage Distribution			
Northeast	25.9%	28.6%	17.8%	39.6%
North Central	28.5	27.7	21.9	19.2
South	30.1	25.7	45.7	16.7
West	15.4	18.0	14.6	24.5
Total	100.0	100.0	100.0	100.0

Source: Edward R. Fried, Alice M. Rivlin, and Nancy H. Teeters, *Setting National Priorities: The 1974 Budget* (Washington, D.C.: The Brookings Institution, 1973), Table 4-3. Population data are from U.S. Bureau of the Census, *Statistical Abstract of the United States, 1972* (1972), Tables 36 and 542. Payments distribution are from U.S. Social Security Administration, Office of Research and Statistics, *Health Insurance Statistics,* HI-41, "Health Insurance for the Aged: Monthly Reimbursements per Person by State, 1970," (1973), Table 1; and U.S. Department of Health, Education, and Welfare, National Center for Social Statistics, "Numbers of Recipients and Amounts of Payments under Medicaid and Other Medical Programs Financed from Public Assistance Funds, 1970," NCSS B-4 (CY 70) (1972; processed), Table 1.

regional states is more than 30 percent of the total aged population. Relatively higher proportions of Medicare payments are linked also with lower percentages of elderly persons for both the Northeast and West regions.

By comparison with this distribution of Medicare benefits, significantly larger distortions occurred in the geographic distribution of Medicaid benefits relative to the number of poor in 1970. (See Table 10-5.) Since the Medicaid program differs from state to state in terms of eligibility requirements and covered services under the federal-state focus, the North Central and South regions have lower percentages of benefit payments, compared with their respective percentages of the poor. The South, which accounted for almost half of the total population at the poverty level in 1970, received only about 17 percent of all Medicaid payments by the federal government. By far the largest regional payments (40%) were made on behalf of the poor in the Northeast region, while this region's poor population represented only about 18 percent of the total number of poor nationally. A similar discrepancy occurred for the West region, with 10 percent more federal Medicaid payments going to states in this region than would be expected based on the number of poor. Only the North Central region is without any significant variance in their regional payments for federal benefits relative to the estimated number of eligibles under the Medicaid program.

Cooper and Worthington analyze the cost and benefit incidence of the various government medical care programs—including Medicaid and Medicare—on a state-by-state basis.[11] With respect to the Medicaid program and federal funding, they find that in 1969 almost 90 percent of those states with per capita cost incidence above the national average also had higher than average per capita income. By contrast, their estimates of cost burdens for state and local program funding show less than average incidence for about 60 percent of the higher-income states.[12] By spending more of their own state funds for medical assistance, high income states were able to receive more federal funds. Thus, by 1969 only twelve states that had per capita incomes *less* than the national average had estimated benefit-cost ratios greater than one. Twenty-two states were at a disadvantage as a result of the funding pattern of Medicaid—in 1969 they experienced benefit-cost ratios of less than one, even though their per capita income levels were less than the national average.[13] Estimates also indicate that in 1969 under the cost structure of Medicare, six industrial states (New York, California, Pennsylvania, Illinois, Ohio, and Michigan) were burdened with almost half of the total costs of the Medicare program.[14] However, because the distribution of benefits is linked directly to the number of aged in the state population, twenty-three states with an aged population less than the national average had benefit-cost ratios of less than one, or Medicare benefits were less than the costs incurred. The cost and benefit structures of Medicare worked to the advantage of twenty states that had larger elderly populations than the national average, but that contributed less to the program than they received in benefits.[15]

A major detailed study of the distributional effects of the Medicare and Medicaid programs on a national basis was undertaken by Stuart and Bair.[16] Their findings regarding the disribution of the costs and benefits under these two programs for fiscal years 1967 and 1968 are presented here in summary form. In Table 10-6, estimates of the effective tax (cost) and benefit rates for the Medicare program across income classes as calculated by Stuart and Bair are given; similar results for the Medicaid program are given in Table 10-7. Discussion is also presented for the combined impact of Medicare and Medicaid in terms of their redistributive effects.

The revenue or cost base for expenditures under the combined hospital and medical insurance plans of Medicare depends on payroll taxes (specifically earmarked for Medicare), contributions from federal general revenues, and premiums paid by enrollees. After allocating the burdens of these cost factors to recipient and nonrecipient households for each income class and determining the respective base rates, the contribution rates for each base were aggregated to provide the estimates for each income class.

Table 10-6
Effective Tax and Benefit Rates for Medicare in Fiscal Years 1967 and 1968[a]

	Costs		*Benefits*	
Income Class ($)	*1967*	*1968*	*1967*	*1968*
0- 2,999	0.018	0.021	0.104	0.132
3,000- 4,999	0.010	0.012	0.020	0.027
5,000- 9,999	0.008	0.010	0.004	0.006
10,000-14,999	0.008	0.010	0.003	0.003
15,000+	0.006	0.007	0.001	0.002
Total	0.008	0.009	0.008	0.009

[a]See Tables 6–A, 6–B and Appendix Tables A–1 and A–2 in the source for additional details.

Source: Bruce C. Stuart and Lee A. Bair, *Health Care and Income: The Distributional Effects of Medicaid and Medicare Nationally and in the State of Michigan,* 2d ed. (Lansing, Mich.: Michigan Department of Social Services, 1971), Table 6–C.

Table 10-7
Effective Tax and Benefit Rates for Medicaid in Fiscal Years 1967 and 1968[a]

	Costs		*Benefits*	
Income Class ($)	*1967*	*1968*	*1967*	*1968*
0- 2,999	0.004	0.006	0.076	0.130
3,000- 4,999	0.004	0.006	0.008	0.014
5,000- 9,999	0.003	0.005	0.001	0.002
10,000-14,999	0.004	0.006		
15,000+	0.005	0.007		
Total	0.004	0.006	0.004	0.006

[a]See Tables 6–D, 6–E and Appendix Tables A–1 and A–2 in the source for additional details.

Source: Bruce C. Stuart and Lee A. Bair, *Health Care and Income: The Distributional Effects of Medicaid and Medicare Nationally and in the State of Michigan,* 2d ed. (Lansing, Mich.: Michigan Department of Social Services, 1971), Table 6–C.

According to these estimates, for both 1967 and 1968 the structure of costs for Medicare in terms of program-related contributions is, in fact, regressive. That is, the lower-income classes contributed a higher percentage of their disposable income towards the costs of Medicare than did the higher-income recipients. These estimates do indicate some leveling off of the effective tax (cost) rates in the middle-income range. However, this proportionality gives way to regressive rates again for the highest-income class of $15,000 or more. These results confirm the expectation that a program financed primarily through a payroll tax yields regressive burdens for the poor and middle-income groups.

In the Stuart and Bair study, the distribution of benefits under the Medicare program is found to be skewed decidedly in favor of the poor elderly population.

Assuming that the distribution of benefits under both the hospital and medical insurance plans varies only according to the number of elderly in each income class, almost half of the benefits–measured by dollar expenditures to medical vendors–were received by the lowest-income recipients (under $3,000) both in 1967 and 1968.[h] The estimates of the effective benefit rates, defined as the increase in per household disposable income due to Medicare expenditures, are given in Table 10-6 also. For example, in fiscal year 1968, the dollar value of Medicare benefits for the elderly in the "less than $3,000" disposable income class represented more than 13 percent of disposable income. The benefits for those in the $10,000-14,999 class represented only about 2 percent of after-tax income.[17] Because of the inequities in the utilization of health services for the elderly in different income groups prior to 1966, the study concludes that, based on its findings, expenditures for benefits under the Medicare program have a redistributive impact across the income groups that clearly is "an equalizing force" within the federal government's role in the financing of health care.

The *net* distributional effects of the cost and benefit structures of the Medicare program can be measured in several ways. By using a benefit-cost ratio, Stuart and Bair show that the low-income elderly–for each dollar they contributed to the program–received far more benefits than those in the high-income groups. The "pro-poor" benefit structure far outweighs the effects of the regressive cost structure. However, by comparing the net Medicare benefits and the net costs for households in different income classes for 1967 versus 1968, the study shows an increase in "what the poor gained" that is not completely offset by "what the rich lost."[18] Thus, the middle-income classes are the group that was burdened with the inequities of the Medicare program, due to net costs that were a greater percentage of their income than the cost percentages for the highest-income class.

The allocation of cost burdens under Medicaid by income class was determined by the same process as for the costs under Medicare, except that the calculated number of potential recipient households (adjusted for family size) is divided into the actual number of recipients to determine an enrollment rate. Since half of the expenditures under the Medicaid program are financed through federal general revenues and half through state and local funds, the Stuart and Bair study divided all Medicaid vendor payments into three sources: (1) federal general revenues, (2) state general revenues, and (3) revenues from local property taxes. The estimates of these dollar value cost burdens for respective income

[h] Stuart and Bair assume that Medicare benefits are distributed largely according to the number of aged persons based on information available on utilization rates across income groups for the different types of services. With regard to Part A benefits, they conclude that the longer hospital stays associated with low income elderly is sufficiently balanced by the fact that they have fewer hospital admissions than do high income elderly. With regard to Part B coverage, it is assumed that the availability of Medicaid coverage for the low income elderly accounts for almost equal utilization rates across income groups.

classes increase as income increases, with the highest burden placed on those in the $15,000 and over class. However, when the cost estimates are translated into effective tax rates, given in Table 10-7, the results show, in general, a proportional tax structure. On the average, the effective tax rate for each household increased by 0.4 percent of disposable income to meet the costs of Medicaid.

Benefits under the Medicaid program also were allocated in the study according to the number of enrolled households in each income class. As is the case for Medicare, the distribution of benefits under the Medicaid program is overwhelmingly propoor, as would be expected. For both 1967 and 1968, this regressive distribution—whereby the low-income classes have higher effective benefit rates than the high-income classes—is clearly shown in the schedule of effective benefit rates given in Table 10-7. From 1967 to 1968, the effective benefit rates doubled for all income classes due to the increase in the total value of benefits distributed.

Since the benefits of the Medicaid program are directed specifically at the poor, and the cost structure is basically proportional, the *net* distributional impacts of Medicaid are: (1) very favorable to the poor; (2) decidedly less so for the near-poor; and (3) progressive for those with income above $5,000. Stuart and Bair's study also concludes, however, that the distribution of net benefits under the Medicaid program can result in redistributive impacts on a *regional* basis that, in fact, sustain certain program-related inequities across income groups, even among the poor and near-poor.

Figure 10-2 plots the average net gains and losses per household for Medicare and Medicaid in 1968 versus the distribution of households by income deciles. The total area under a curve represents the value of funds redistributed by each program. The slope of the curve indicates the rate of program-related income redistribution—the greater the slope, the higher the rate.

The study found that the Medicare and Medicaid programs resulted in the redistribution of a combined total of $8.6 billion in 1968, an amount that represented about 1.5 percent of national disposable income. Persons with incomes of less than $5,000 received benefits estimated at more than 75 percent of this total expenditure. In this same year, the poor and near-poor group contributed only about 14 percent toward the expenditures under Medicare and Medicaid.[19]

By summing the effective cost and benefit rates for Medicare and Medicaid, as is shown in Table 10-8, the combined distributional effects of these two programs are obtained. Since both programs are directed at the needs of the lower-income households, the combined effective benefit rates are *regressive* over the entire income range—that is, as income *increases,* benefits as a percentage of income *decline*. In addition, the aggregate of these benefit rates for each income class increased from 1967 to 1968, except for the upper middle-income group. However, the combined redistributional impacts of the cost structures of Medicare and Medicaid are also *regressive* (as income *increases,* costs as a percentage of income also *decrease*) for the complete range of incomes for 1967 and 1968,

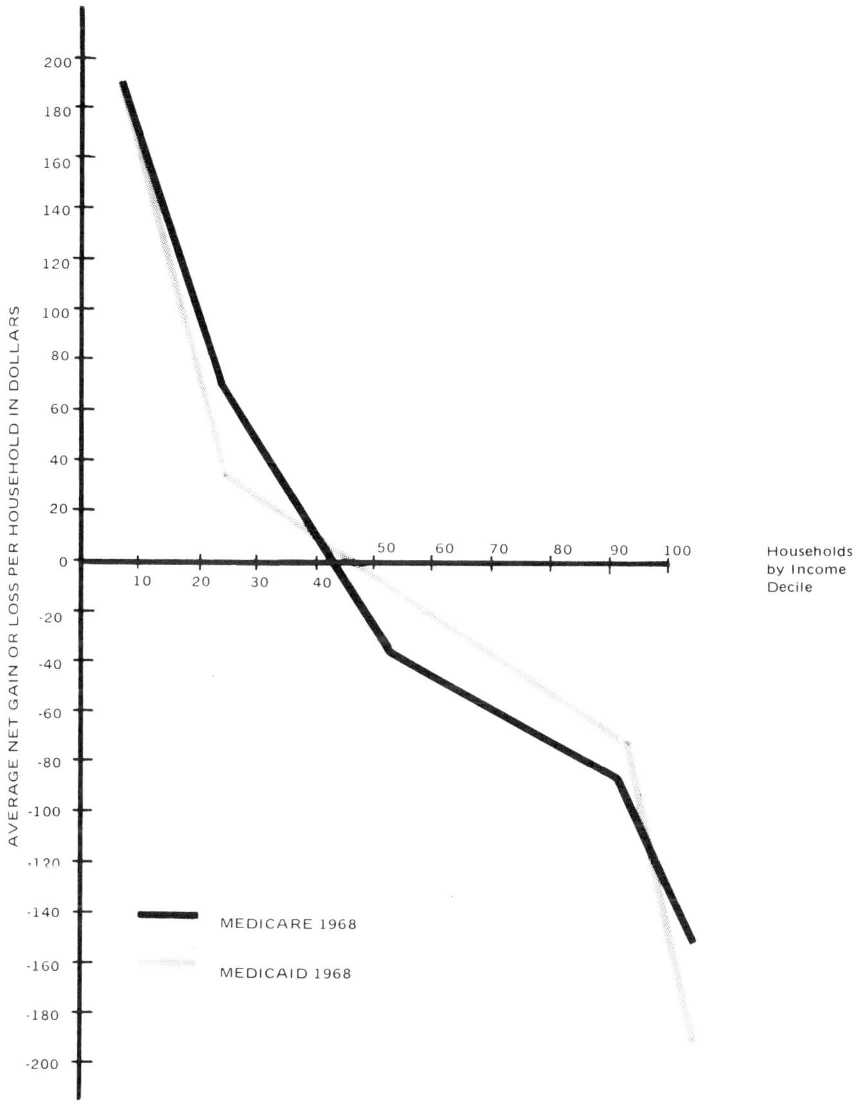

Source: Bruce C. Stuart and Lee A. Bair, *Health Care and Income: The Distributional Effects of Medicaid and Medicare Nationally and in the State of Michigan*. 2d ed. (Lansing, Mich.: Michigan Department of Social Services, 1971), Figure 6-A.

Figure 10-2. Redistribution of Household Income due to Medicare and Medicaid Programs, Fiscal Year 1968

Table 10-8
Combined Effective Tax and Benefit Rates for Medicare and Medicaid in Fiscal Years 1967 and 1968

	Costs		*Benefits*	
Income Class ($)	*1967*	*1968*	*1967*	*1968*
0- 2,999	0.022	0.027	0.180	0.262
3,000- 4,999	0.013	0.017	0.028	0.042
5,000- 9,999	0.012	0.015	0.006	0.008
10,000-14,999	0.012	0.015	0.003	0.003
15,000+	0.010	0.014	0.001	0.002
Total	0.012	0.015	0.012	0.015

Source: Bruce C. Stuart and Lee A. Bair, *Health Care and Income: The Distributional Effects of Medicaid and Medicare Nationally and in the State of Michigan,* 2d ed. (Lansing, Mich.: Michigan Department of Social Services, 1971), Table 6-M.

although they are more nearly proportional for the nonpoor groups. While the effective cost rates increased for all income classes from 1967 to 1968, the combined impact suggests a trend toward greater, rather than less, inequality in the cost structures of Medicare and Medicaid.

Data is also available from another source that permits a combined analysis of the benefit structures under the Medicare and Medicaid programs with the third national program more indirectly involved in the financing of health care, i.e., federal subsidies in the form of medical deductions under the personal income tax laws. The distribution of the dollar benefits of these three programs across family income groups is given in Table 10-9. Medicare payments, which represent the largest program in terms of total federal benefits in 1970, show a *regressive* distribution, with those elderly persons in the "under $5,000" income class receiving more than half of these benefits. Payments under the Medicaid program, measured by federal matching funds only, indicate an even greater regressivity in the distribution of benefits, with as much as 67 percent of all Medicaid payments made on behalf of those persons in the lowest (under $5,000) family income class. Although this program is directed at the poor and medically indigent, families with income greater than $10,000 are estimated to have received about 10 percent of Medicaid federal benefit payments in 1970, presumably under circumstances of catastrophic illness with eligibility determined by spend-down provisions under certain state plans.

As was shown in earlier discussion in Chapter 9, the distribution of federal subsidies for premium costs for private health insurance coverage and for out-of-pocket expenditures that represent more than 3 percent of adjusted gross income under the personal income tax is quite *progressive.* More than half of these types of subsidies were received by families with income of $10,000 or more in 1970. Of further interest is the finding that, under the medical deduction sys-

Table 10-9
Distribution of Federal Medical Care Benefits under Medicare, Medicaid, and Income Tax Subsidies by Family Income and Age, 1970

		Program			Age	
Family Income Class ($)	*Total Federal Benefits*	*Medicare Payments*	*Medicaid Payments*	*Federal Individual Income Tax Subsidies*	*Under 65*	*65 and over*
			Millions of Dollars			
All classes	$14,224	$7,494	$2,930	$3,800	$4.994	$9,230
			Percentage Distribution			
Under 5,000	46%	54%	67%	13%	29%	55%
5,000- 9,999	27	26	24	31	26	27
10,000-14,999	16	14	5	26	23	12
15,000 and over	12	7	4	30	22	7
Total	100	100	100	100	100	100

Source: Edward R. Fried, Alice M. Rivlin, and Nancy H. Teeters, *Setting National Priorities: The 1974 Budget* (Washington, D.C.: The Brookings Institution, 1973), Table 4-2. Total Medicare and Medicaid payments are from U.S. Social Security Administration, Office of Research and Statistics, *Compendium of National Health Expenditures Data,* (SSA) 73-11903 (1973), p. 73; the distribution is derived from unpublished estimates of payments by family income. The amount of tax subsidy is from Bridger M. Mitchell and Ronald J. Vogel, "Health and Taxes: An Assessment of the Medical Deduction," (1973); processed, pp. 21 and 31; the distribution is based on data in this source p. 34 and in Martin S. Feldstein and Elizabeth Allison, "Tax Subsidies of Private Health Insurance: Distribution, Revenue Loss and Effects," Discussion Paper 237 (Harvard Institute of Economic Research, Harvard University, April, 1972; processed), p. 5. Medicaid payments for persons over 65 years are distributed as 67 percent to the "under $5,000" class and 33 percent to the "$5,000-$9,999" class. All Medicare payments are distributed to the group 65 and over. Tax subsidies for ages over and under 65 years are estimated from the Brookings file of 1970 individual income tax returns.

tem, subsidies in the form of foregone tax liability totaled $3.8 billion in 1970, while the federal participation in the Medicaid program amounted to only $2.9 billion in this same year. Because of the progressive nature of the distributional effects of the benefit structure under the medical deduction program and the sizeable amount of subsidies involved, the distribution of the *total* federal benefits across family income groups under these three programs is *less regressive* than the distribution of benefits under either the Medicare or Medicaid programs.

When the distribution of benefits is examined for the age categories "under sixty-five years" and "sixty-five years and over," quite different results occur. The over sixty-five years age group shows much the same distribution of total benefits as are given for Medicare payments, as might be expected. However, for persons under sixty-five years, the distribution of total benefits indicates only a very slight regressivity across the given income groups. Moreover, as much as 45 percent of the total benefits for this age group was received by persons with income of $10,000 or greater and 22 percent by families with income of $15,000 or more, primarily because of the beneficial effects of the tax subsidy for the higher-income groups.

Summary

The major effect of the Medicare program in financing health care services for the elderly has been the shift of a substantial portion of those expenses formerly incurred by persons 65 years and over to the public sector. However, only half of the average health care bill for an aged person is covered as Medicare benefits—a much higher proportion of their expenses is met by public financing for those low-income elderly also eligible for state Medicaid benefits.

The emphasis of the Medicare program is largely on hospital care. A larger number of elderly persons have been hospitalized since the establishment of Medicare, although the rate of hospitalizations per person 65 years and over has remained relatively constant and the average length of stay has declined. There appears not to have been a significant increase in the rate of use of physician services with implementation of the Medicare program. Rather, outpatient services shifted from clinic and home visits to office visits.

The Medicare program has increased the number of elderly receiving health care services and the benefits of this health insurance program have been an equalizing force in the distribution of health services. This conclusion is supported by Stuart and Bair's study of the distribution of benefits of Medicare across income groups. However, other studies suggest that the provision for coinsurance and deductible payments under Medicare has been some deterrent to the use of health services by the poor elderly. In addition, while the Medicare program provides for uniform benefits and automatic eligibility, large variations in Medicare benefits occur by region. Twenty states, shown to have larger elderly populations than the national average, in fact contributed less to the program than they received in benefits.

The Medicare program is financed primarily by earmarked funds from a payroll tax, premiums for the medical insurance plan (Part B), and limited federal general revenues. The payroll tax and premiums are regressive forms of financing—the relatively greater burdens of the cost of Medicare are borne by the low- and middle-income groups.

Covered services under Medicare are quite restrictive and thus substantial out-of-pocket payments are necessary for services such as dental care and drugs. Moreover, all covered services have coinsurance and/or deductible payments attached to them. The limited benefits under Medicare have initiated a role for supplemental private health insurance plans for the elderly to assist them in meeting the expenses of uncovered or limited services and coinsurance and deductible expenses. Increasing numbers of elderly persons have purchased these types of private insurance policies at an additional cost of as much as several hundred dollars annually.

At least two further problems associated with the overall structure of Medicare are: (1) the related increases in charges for hospital and physician services and (2) the inadequate coverage for catastrophic expenditures. The employment of coinsurance and deductibles, while impeding at times financial access to services, and the provisions for provider cost-reimbursement have not been sufficient to control the cost increases related to a major health insurance program.

The most immediate problem with the overall structure of the Medicaid program is the large variations that exist regarding income eligibility requirements and range of covered services for the poor and medically indigent persons. Although the basic intent of Medicaid was to redistribute federal funds from the high-income states to the low-income states, substantially greater proportions of federal Medicaid monies have in fact flowed to the high-income states because of these kinds of variations. This type of maldistribution is also reflected in regional data—the North Central and South regions have a lower percentage of benefit payments relative to their percentage of the poor. Moreover, the matching formulas for federal financial participation allow high-income states to spend more of their own funds for medical assistance and thereby receive greater federal matching funds.

The overall benefits of the Medicaid program has been to provide financial access to health care services primarily to the poor, but also in some states to medically indigent persons. However, many of the low-income groups are excluded from Medicaid coverage because of the restrictive eligibility requirements generally in the states with low per capita income. Thus, many poor and near poor remain without adequate health care—it is one author's claim that in some states as many as 90 percent of the poor are not covered by Medicaid.[20] In addition, many inequities exist across the various state Medicaid plans in terms of the range of covered services that are "optional" beyond the basic covered services required for state participation in Medicaid.

The growth in both federal and state Medicaid expenditures in the last decade has been substantial. This growth has primarily been due to the large increases in the number of cash assistance eligibles, but also because of the increases in the rate of utilization of services. While the expansion in the number of eligibles appears to be subsiding, Medicaid in general lacks sufficient controls over the utilization of services which in turn contributes to increases in the costs of health services. The current crises in both federal and state budgets and the ever increasing cost of medical care require immediate consideration of alternatives to the Medicaid approach to financing health care for the poor. A broader-based national health insurance plan would over the long term solve the many of the problems of eligibility, covered serivces and cost increases associated with the Medicaid experience.

Notes

1. Bruce C. Stuart and Lee A. Bair, *Health Care and Income: The Distributional Effects of Medicaid and Medicare Nationally and in the State of Michigan,* 2d ed. (Lansing, Mich.: Michigan Department of Social Services, 1971), p. 109.
2. U.S. Department of Health, Education and Welfare, Social Security Administration, *Your Medicaid Handbook* (January, 1975), p. 17.
3. Barbara S. Cooper and Nancy Worthington, "Comparison of Cost and Benefit Incidence of Government Medical Care Programs, Fiscal Years 1966 and 1969," Social Security Administration, Office of Research and Statistics, Staff Paper No. 18 (September, 1974), p. 17.
4. Barbara S. Cooper and Paula A. Piro, "Age Differences in Medical Care Spending, Fiscal Year 1973," *Social Security Bulletin,* Vol. 36, No. 5 (May, 1974), p. 5.
5. Karen Davis, *National Health Insurance: Benefits, Costs and Consequences* (Washington, D.C.: The Brookings Institution, 1975), Table 3-9.
6. Howard N. Newman, "Medicare and Medicaid," *The Annals of the American Academy of Political and Social Sciences,* Vol. 399, 114-124, 1972, reprinted in *Medicaid: Lessons for National Health Insurance,* Allen D. Spiegel and Simon Podair, eds. (Rockville, Md.: Aspen Systems Corporation, 1975), p. 321.
7. Nancy L. Worthington, "National Health Expenditures, 1929-74," *Social Security Bulletin,* Vol. 37, No. 2 (February, 1975), p. 4.
8. John Holahan, *Financing Health Care for the Poor: The Medicaid Experience* (Lexington, Mass.: D.C. Health & Company, 1975), p. 9.
9. Ibid., p. 10.
10. "Health Insurance for Older People: Filling the Gaps in Medicare," *Consumer Reports* (Mount Vernon, N.Y.: Consumers Union of United States, Inc., January, 1976), p. 27.

11. See Cooper and Worthington, op. cit. Their study also includes analysis of: disability insurance, workmen's compensation, maternal and child health, school health, and other government health programs.

12. Ibid., p. 15.

13. Ibid., p. 21.

14. Ibid., p. 6.

15. Ibid., p. 9.

16. Stuart and Bair, op. cit.

17. Ibid., p. 111.

18. Ibid., p. 115.

19. Ibid., p. 127.

20. Holahan, op. cit., p. 110.

11 National Health Insurance and Income Distribution: Findings, Conclusions, and Recommendations

If an appropriate priority is to be given to the impact of a national health insurance plan on the families and individuals at various income levels, then the form and content of the benefit and cost structures of any proposal for such a plan must be based on their personal health care needs and their ability to pay. In general, the primary emphasis of discussions of national health insurance proposals has focused on the allocation between (1) public versus private funding and (2) federally administered programs (usually associated with proposed universal-coverage plans) versus plans that would rely on the current fragmented approach to financing with a major role for the private health insurance industry. The sophistication of the debates surrounding the form and content of the benefit structure has substantially, although certainly not completely, pacified issues concerning: the range of benefits offered as covered services; the role of cost sharing; and the need for catastrophic coverage that would set limits on the amount of out-of-pocket expenditures by consumers. The variety of alternative sources offered by the cost structures of the current proposals, i.e., federal general revenues, the payroll tax, premiums, etc., largely defines the political debate at hand. Further, estimates of the *overall* costs of implementation of a national health insurance plan suggest that only marginal differences would occur from among bills whose provisions structure a number of combinations of sources to finance personal health care on a national basis.[1] The most neglected area of decisionmaking has been the distribution of the benefits and costs of a national health insurance program across income classes. It is this component of public concern that has been the major focus of the discussion here.

This chapter initially summarizes the available evidence regarding the potential distributional effects of both the benefits and costs of proposed national health insurance plans. Conclusions are offered by establishing a ranking of the six selected national health insurance proposals according to their respective *gross* (total) redistributional effects. Recommendations are made as to what kinds of provisions would be necessary in order for a national health insurance plan to adequately address the problem of equity in the distribution of benefits and costs.

Findings

The current patterns of income distribution indicate that significant inequalities are present in the distribution of income for both families and unrelated individuals. The percentage share of aggregate money income received by the lowest fifth (20%) of all families was only about 5 percent in 1972. The highest fifth of all families, ranked by income levels by comparison received more than 40 percent of aggregate money income in 1972. Even more severe inequalities are present in the distribution of income for unrelated individuals—a group that includes many elderly persons—based on 1972 data. The highest fifth received more than 50 percent of aggregate money income for unrelated individuals, as compared with only 3.3 percent received by the lowest fifth. The number of "poor," those with incomes at or below the poverty level of income, defined at $4,275 for a family of four, was almost 25 million in 1972.

Expenditures for personal health care totaled more than $90 billion in fiscal year 1974. The public sector—expenditures by federal, state, and local governments—represented 38 percent of this total, with more than half of public funding accounted for by the financing of the Medicare and Medicaid programs. For 1974, almost an equal amount, 35 percent or about $31 billion, was actually direct out-of-pocket payments made by consumers. This latter proportion is a decided decline for the 68 percent of total personal health expenditures represented by direct consumer expenses in 1950. Only about half of this long-term decrease in direct consumer payments is due to the increasing role for private health insurance coverage. While the proportion of benefit payments by the health insurance industry tripled over the last twenty-five years, insurance benefits remain at only 26 percent of total personal health expenditures. The remainder of the decline in the need for direct consumer payments is due to increased expenditures under the Medicare insurance program for the elderly and the Medicaid program of medical assistance for low-income and medically indigent groups.

The most important findings regarding the aggregate distribution of personal health care expenditures by source of funds is, first, the relatively large proportion currently met by direct consumer payments (35%) and, second, the relatively constant proportion of expenditures met by health insurance benefits (25%) and by state and local governments (12%) during the last decade.

The distribution of personal health care expenditures by type of service and by source of funds indicate clearly the misplaced priorities under the current fragmented systems of financing health care. Hospital care expenditures—the single largest expenditure group and the most expensive type of care—are currently met almost totally by public funds and private health insurance benefit payments. Only about 11 percent of total hospital expenditures are accounted for by direct consumer payments. Private payments, however, represented as much as 76 percent of total expenditures for physician services, with almost an equal proportion met by direct consumer out-of-pocket payments (39%) and private insurance benefits (37%). All other types of services, including dental services, prescriptions and drugs, etc., are almost completely paid for by direct consumer payments. The only other type of service that is supported by any significant contribution of public monies is nursing-home care, although direct consumer payments remain substantial also. Private insurance benefits currently pay for only *5 percent* of nonhospital and nonphysician services.

For 1974, the level of per capita expenditures is estimated at $420, with the largest proportion by source of financing represented by direct consumer out-of-pocket payments, that is, $148. On the average, each person incurred about $170 of expenses for hospital care in 1973, with only about 10 percent of these expenses requiring out-of-pocket consumer payments. About $80 per person was spent on physician services in 1973, but the consumer paid directly for about *half* of these types of expenditures.

The percentage increase in per capita expenditures over the period from 1967 to 1974 was not as great as the percentage increase in total personal health care expenditures, since population increases accounted for about 11 percent of the $49 billion increase in total expenditures for this period. Inflation in the prices of health care services accounted for more than 50 percent of the rise in total personal health care expenditures over this eight-year period. Thus, those personal health care services purchased in 1974 with a per capita expenditure of $420 would only have required an expenditure of almost $140 less, or $279, at 1967 health care prices. The residual 39 percent of the increase in total personal health care expenditures since 1967 is the combined result of increased utilization of health services and the use of more advanced medical technological improvements.

An important indicator of the need for national health insurance is the current status of private health insurance coverage. Recent trends in enrollment in private health insurance plans show continued annual growth in the number of persons with some type of coverage. However, as recently as 1972, only 77 percent of the total population was enrolled in a hospital insurance plan (several types of policies providing for very limited benefits) and about 74 percent in medical insurance plans (generally policies which cover inpatient physician visits and surgical costs only). These enrollment rates are slightly higher when considering only the "under sixty-five years" age group, since most of the elderly rely primarily on Medicare coverage. Only about half of the population had any coverage for prescription drugs and private-duty nursing. An even lower proportion is covered by health insurance for outpatient physician visits and nursing-home care, and as little as 9 percent for dental services.

Data on the extent of health insurance coverage for family income groups show the significantly lower rates of enrollment for the low- and middle-income groups, while the rates for the higher-income groups are in the 90 percent range. More importantly, these rates appear to have stabilized somewhat, and, when increases in enrollment have occurred, these are generally concentrated in the enrollment for the upper middle- and high-income classes. According to surveys of persons queried as to why they do not have health insurance, the most common response from the low- and middle-income groups is that "they cannot afford it."

Of particular interest is the finding that *children* in low- and middle-income groups are frequently without health insurance coverage. In 1968, for example, less than half of the children in the $3,000–$4,999 family income class had hospital coverage. The significance of this finding is further substantiated by the data presented in Chapter 6 regarding the utilization of services by children in low- and moderate-income groups, where it was also shown that these children are frequently members of large families. The needs that these circumstances present are further complicated by the poorer health status of low-income persons and, particularly, poor children.

A typical plan of insurance with broad benefits for both hospital and medical coverage has an annual premium cost for a family of four in the range of $500 to $600. In addition, cost sharing factors are attached to the benefits, usually in the form of deductibles and coinsurance payments. These additional amounts of out-of-pocket expenses for the consumer, together with payments for services *not* covered, can increase the overall direct payments by several hundred dollars.

Most employees are covered by some type of health insurance through their place of employment. Those traditionally not covered under group employee plans are greatest in certain industries, i.e., in argriculture, construction, and trade and service industries, and are most likely to be low-wage earners, i.e., self-employed, women, and nonwhites. The largest proportion (47%) of covered workers share the premium cost of the insurance plan with their employer. About 20 percent pay the entire premium themselves and the remainder (33%) have the premium paid by their employer. The largest proportion of employees who do have health insurance through their employer do *not* have comprehensive types of coverage.

Chapter 6 presented an analysis of data on the utilization of personal health services for different income classes. Arguments are frequently made that Medicare and Medicaid have impacted sufficiently on the use of health services by the elderly and low-income persons so as to equalize utilization rates across income groups. The evidence on recent utilization patterns across income classes suggests that, while some gains have been made toward achieving this goal of removing financial barriers to health care, inequalities in the utilization of health services remain. The latter finding evolves when consideration is also given to the particular measures of utilization over time for different types of services and the role of other intervening factors, such as age, in addition to the relationship between use of services and family income. A most significant finding, which is only one critical example of the very basic inequities that result under the current system of financing health care, is that utilization differentials show that children in low-income groups have physician-visit rates well below those for children in all other income classes.

The major findings regarding the present pattern of health expenditures across income groups point directly to the need for a national health insurance plan that would redistribute more equitably benefits in the form of covered services. First, aggregate family outlays or direct consumer out-of-pocket payments are a *larger* percentage of family income, as family income *decreases.* Second, as many as 70 percent of those in the lowest-income groups had *no free* health care in 1970, and as little as 30 percent of the mean total expenditures represented "free" services for families below the poverty level. Third, the percentage of the average expenditures for a family that is covered by insurance benefits is *directly* related to the level of family income. Fourth, children in large families, especially those in low- and moderate-income classes, are less likely to receive adequate health care because of financial circumstances. This results from the finding that family size has a strong influence on the level and distribution of expenditures across family income groups with respect to all sources of payment except insurance benefits.

The major findings with respect to the sources of financing of expenditures for the different types of health services reinforce the necessity for a national health insurance plan that provides for a more equitable distribution of benefits in two ways. First, for all types of services, with the exception of hospital care, out-of-pocket expenditures are greater than Medicaid and other welfare sources for low-income groups. Actually, it was found that private insurance benefits paid for a larger portion of hospital expenditures for low-income families than did Medicaid. Second, according to the level of expenditures for different types of services for the various income groups, the "mix" of health services utilized by families in different income classes reflects very unsimilar patterns. For example, low-income groups show a larger expenditure for drugs met by out-of-pocket payments than do high-income groups. Also high-income families spend more for dental care—the kind of health service that is more directly related to the ability-to-pay as reflected in income level and possibly also covered under an expensive private insurance plan.

Because of the inequities verified in the current patterns of utilization of, and expenditures for, personal health care services, the benefit structures of proposed national health insurance plans must be critically examined in terms of provisions for: eligibility, covered services, cost sharing factors, and the role of catastrophic coverage. Eligibility criteria that focus on enrollment of subgroups of the population in separate programs or plans are generally inadequate in providing for equitable treatment of all persons. The requirements for eligibility are frequently quite arbitrary, as in the case of the definition of a part-time worker for enrollment in an employee plan or the use of the poverty income level for enrollment in a plan for low-income persons.[a]

[a]One of the major problems in establishing eligibility for any social program directed at individuals and families in need is the selection and definition of specific criteria, such as measures of income level or socioeconomic status. The arbitrary poverty level designation is really an inadequate policy measure for reaching those families and individuals in need of some, if not complete, financial assistance for health care services. The more equitable plan would provide for preferential treatment for those at least below the median income level for determining eligibility, benefits, and costs.

With respect to the possible distributional effects of the range of and limits on covered services, any proposal that provides for less than full and complete comprehensive benefits for all persons poses the problem of deciding which groups would, in fact, be deprived of equitable treatment in terms of benefits. Most proposals place restrictions or limitations on nursing-home care, dental care for adults, drugs, and mental health serivces. These types of services are apparently considered for unknown reasons to be optional services, when for low- and moderate-income groups they may be necessities, but commonly not utilized because of financial circumstances. The spectrum of covered services, of course, defines the extent to which redistributional effects could occur when less than comprehensive benefits are proposed.[b]

It is interesting to note that the choice of whether to include cost sharing factors in proposals for national health insurance has become an either-or situation. Either the proposal does not require any cost sharing, or the cost sharing takes the form of a minimal deductible amount (usually more than $50, but less than $150 annually) and coinsurance factors (with a arbitrary rate usually set at 20 percent). Because imposition of deductibles and coinsurance factors requires the same amount of out-of-pocket payments *regardless* of income level, cost sharing will always result in severe regressive distributional effects, unless it is directly linked to income or some other measure of ability to pay.[c]

The role of catastrophic coverage is a significant one in terms of addressing the relative needs for national health insurance coverage for families and individuals at different levels of income. Those proposals with provisions for universal coverage and *no* requirements for cost sharing would automatically include catastrophic benefits also. However, unless the benefit package is completely comprehensive and covers *all* types of services, distributional effects that could be regressive would occur in particular situations when those services not covered result in catastrophic levels of expenses.

Those proposals that have special provisions or separate programs or plans for catastrophic coverage will *always* have regressive distributional impacts across income groups, *if* they fix a limit on the amount of total expenses that must be incurred before catastrophic benefits are effective and *if* it is the *same* limit for consumers at all levels of income. Proportional effects result if the limit on expenses is set at the same *percentage* of income, as is sometimes proposed. In

---

[b]These redistributional effects associated with covered services are further complicated by: limits placed on the number of covered days or services; restrictions on the type of providers reimbursed under the plan, including nonphysician personnel; and the role of cost sharing in limiting the use of particular types of services.

[c]Copayments are also a regressive form of cost sharing, since the same amount of consumer payment is required of all users regardless of income level, e.g., $5 per physician visit. However, because coinsurance payments are directly affected by the inflation in the prices of health services, they are an even more undesirable form of cost sharing than copayments where the dollar amount of payment is fixed.

order to eliminate these kinds of additional cost burdens and, in fact, have the distribution of catastrophic benefits be propoor, it is necessary to gradually increase limits on total expenses, defined as percentages of expenses to income, by x percentage points for every y amount of additional income.

Each type of financing source employed in alternative cost structures has impact directly on the distribution of income, according to the regressive, proportional, or progressive burdens that families and individuals would face. Premiums are the most regressive form of financing. Premium costs would require the same amount of payment regardless of the level of income, and thus they represent a greater percentage of income for the poor and moderate-income classes than for the higher-income groups. Even when premiums are paid in whole or part by the employer, the cost burdens can ultimately be shifted to the employee. This shifting of employers' contributions or costs to the employees occurs either in the form of lower wages than would otherwise be the case or in higher prices for the products that workers produce and buy as consumers. Generally, those proposals that rely on premiums as a major source of financing also incorporate a medical deduction or a tax credit system into their cost structure.

The use of the medical deduction or tax credits, actually foregone federal revenues, is an attempt to compensate for the regressive effects associated with premium financing, and also to shift a portion of the program costs from the private to the public sector. A tax credit system can be effective in mitigating the regressive burdens of a premium (or a payroll tax) approach to financing, *if* the amount of tax credit is based on tax liabilities (as opposed to income), and the credit gradually decreases as tax liability increases. The medical deduction, by comparison, as it currently exists under personal income tax law is not an effective approach to relieving the regressive impacts of premium costs or expenses associated with covered or uncovered services. Evidence shows that the federal subsidies in the form of a medical deduction actually are distributed more in favor of the higher-income classes than low- and middle-income groups.

The payroll or social security tax is also a very regressive form of financing. Because the payroll tax generally is imposed on earnings or self-employment income up to a ceiling or maximum taxable base level *and* at the same tax rate, the burdens of this type of taxation are greater for those in the low- and middle-income groups than in the high-income groups. In addition, the payroll tax does not allow for exemptions, as is the case for the personal income tax, unless specified by particular provisions. It is important to recognize that a payroll tax on employers' payroll costs also represents program cost burdens, which are again passed on to employees resulting in additional regressive distributional effects. (Some proposals for national health insurance would place a payroll tax on unearned income; in this case, the distributional effects are dependent on the definition of unearned income also.)

One source for progressive financing of national health insurance is a graduated personal income tax, employed directly through revenues earmarked for this purpose or indirectly through the use of federal general revenues. This approach to financing places the cost burdens on families and individuals according to their ability to pay—the higher the level of income, the larger the percentage of income paid in taxes. An additional source for progressive financing is graduated corporate income taxes, which currently represent only about 16 percent of taxed federal general revenues.[d]

By contrast, state general revenues are found to be a regressive source of financing. Higher effective tax rates for low- and middle-income groups than for high-income groups are associated with the sales tax and the property tax, which are the primary revenue bases for most states.

Evidence concerning the fiscal incidence of the Medicare and Medicaid programs is consistent in finding that the benefit structure is propoor for both programs. The poor elderly receive far more benefits relative to what they pay into Medicare, and the middle-income aged are probably most burdened by the inequities due to the structure of costs and benefits under Medicare. These overall distributional effects result from the use of regressive financing sources for Medicare: a payroll tax with revenues earmarked for the hospital insurance plan; premiums required for enrollment in the voluntary medical insurance plan; and cost sharing for the consumer in the form of deductibles and coinsurance. The gross distributional effects due to the combined cost and benefit structures of the Medicaid program are: (1) very favorable to the poor; (2) less beneficial for the near-poor; and (3) progressive above $5,000, with these income groups paying more in program costs than they receive in benefits. Findings indicate that there are significant geographic inequalities associated with the distribution of benefits and costs under Medicaid. Certain high per capita income states receive far greater federal benefit payments than they incur in program costs.

Conclusions: Ranking of Proposals

Because national health insurance plans are primarily directed at the financing and utilization of personal health care services, income can be redistributed (1) through the cost structure in terms of "who should pay for what," and (2) through the benefit structure in terms of "who should receive what benefits." National health insurance proposals can, therefore, be classified according to the progressive or regressive effects of their cost and benefit structures—the percentage of total costs incurred by families and individuals increases or decreases as the level of income rises and, similarly, the percentage of total benefits received by families and individuals increases or declines as the level of income rises. By assuming that a more equitable distribution of income is an important and

---

[d]In fiscal year 1975, 42 percent of federal general revenues were accounted for by personal income taxes and 28 percent by social security taxes.

relevant objective, a higher ranking would be given to the national health insurance plan that provides for a more equitable distribution of costs and benefits across income classes based on certain criteria. The equity criterion for the distribution of benefits requires relative gains in access to personal health care services for those in income groups that currently face inequalities, compared with other income groups. The equity criterion for the distribution of cost burdens is the ability-to-pay principle of vertical equity, which requires a progressive source of financing.

Each of the six bills reviewed here would establish provisions within their proposed cost and benefit structures that would have some favorable redistributional effects across income classes. In order to integrate conclusions regarding the relative degree to which progressive, proportional, and regressive provisions would have impact on the distribution of income, rankings of the six selected proposals are presented.

Initially, these proposals are ranked according to the redistribution of income that would result due to the structure of benefits. Because direct measures are not available for the specific distributional effects, the priority ranking is based on more general findings of Chapter 8 regarding: the eligibility criteria for the various plans or programs proposed; the range of and limits on covered services; the form and amount of cost sharing; and the plan for catastrophic coverage.

Ranking of Proposed Benefit Structures According to Certain Distributional Effects

1. The Young Bill is almost completely analagous to the Corman-Kennedy Bill in that it provides for *universal* coverage under one national plan and does *not* require cost sharing. It does offer the most comprehensive range of covered services, although some limitations for certain types of services are in effect.

2. The Corman-Kennedy Bill ranks as one of the proposed plans with the *most* equitable approach to the structure of benefits, by providing *universal* eligibility and coverage, together with no cost sharing requirements. However, it does restrict the amount of covered services for psychiatric inpatient and outpatient service, skilled nursing-home care, adult dental services, drugs, medical appliances and devices, and other personal health-related social services.

3. The Ullman Bill calls for *mandatory* private health insurance coverage for all employees. It makes *aged* persons automatically eligible for state plan for low-income and medically indigent groups. It has very liberal eligibility requirements for a State plan based on *both* income and family size. It *phases in* benefits in two stages, and the second phase is fairly comprehensive. A coinsurance rate of 20 percent is attached to benefits in the first phase, and it replaces some coinsurance with *copayments* in the second phase. Relatively lower deductible is required by this proposal. Catastrophic benefits are included when total expenses

(including premium costs) limits are reached. These limits are *graduated* for the poor and medically indigent and *proportional* for all higher income groups. Limits also vary by *age*.

4. The Burleson-McIntyre Bill proposes a *voluntary* program to provide private health insurance coverage for employees and other individuals not eligible for a State plan for the poor and medically indigent. *Liberal* income requirements are set according to *family size* for the State plan. It maintains the Medicare programs for aged, with premiums for Part B paid for through state general revenues for those aged who are eligible for the State plan. Benefits are *phased in* over two periods, and the range of covered services in the second phase is fairly comprehensive. *Coinsurance* of 20 percent is proposed (for some services a higher rate) for both phases of benefits, with several exceptions. It allows for reduction in $100 deductible and coinsurance payments for the poor and medically indigent, based on ability to pay, which is measured by income and family size and also for limits on expenses for catastrophic benefits.

5. The Fulton-Duncan Bill calls for *mandatory* employee coverage through private health insurance plans. It provides for *federal subsidies* in the form of tax credits against personal income tax liabilities (or a certificate of entitlement for private health insurance) for the premium costs. The Medicare program is retained for elderly. Covered services are limited significantly in the range of services, but are limited in amount only for skilled nursing-home services and dental care. *All* services have a 20 percent *coinsurance* factor attached for all persons, including the medically indigent. *No* deductible is required. However, *catastrophic benefits* are available based on a schedule of income and insurance deductions.

6. The Long-Ribicoff Bill would provide for three separate programs and also would maintain *Medicare* for aged. It calls for a *voluntary* program for basic coverage for employees, and medical assistance plan for the poor (eligibility requirements at poverty level) only, excluding medically indigent groups. The *poor elderly* covered under Medicare would have the cost of the Part B premium paid under this medical assistance plan. All private health insurance plans offer only the same covered services as under Medicare. The bill would also allow for a 20 percent coinsurance factor and deductible for both hospital and medical services coverage. *Catastrophic* benefits would be dependent of the same limits of expenses for all persons, regardless of income. Catastrophic coverage for hospital expenses would be available *only* after sixty days of inpatient care. Restrictions are included on amounts of expenses recognized for mental health benefits and for other family members. Only *copayments* are required for a limited number of outpatient physician visits for the poor, and so catastrophic benefits would be effective once limited visits are exceeded or after sixty days of hospitalization.

A ranking of the six national health insurance plans is presented for the respective cost structures that are proposed. This priority ranking is based on evidence offered in chapter 9 regarding the regressive and progressive characteristics of the various sources of financing. The ranking considers also the projected contribution of each component of the cost structure when more than one financing source is used in combination.

Ranking of Proposed Cost Structures According to Certain Distributional Effects

1. The Young Bill calls for a *proportional* payroll tax structure by removing the ceiling on taxable bases. It would, however, tax AFDC and SSI benefit payments under the definition of unearned income. The tax credit system cuts the tax rate on earnings to 1.0 percent for earnings levels up to $25,000 and builds in some progressivity, *but* this is only after the $25,000 earnings level is reached.

2. The Corman-Kennedy Bill requires half of the total costs to be financed from *progressive* source, i.e. federal general revenues, but half also from *regressive* payroll taxes. Evidence suggests that the overall distributional cost effects could be at least *slightly* progressive.

3. The Burleson-McIntyre Bill is primarily financed by premiums, with federal and state general revenues financing for a plan for low-income and medically indigent groups. The premium cost structure is *proportional*, since the premium payment is based on fixed percentage of income. Federal contributions would vary from 70 to 90 percent; the state contribution would depend on per capita income. Medicare payroll tax would remain in effect.

4. The Fulton-Duncan Bill calls for *premiums* as the major source of financing. Some federal general revenues would be used for a *tax credit* program for poor and medically indigent groups. Decreasing tax credits would be available for premium costs, according to increasing amounts of income tax liabilities—this incorporates some *progressivity* into cost structure. The *Medicare* program is maintained, and its payroll tax remains in effect. Tax credits would also be available to eligible *aged* persons for premiums for Medicare supplemental insurance policies from private carriers.

5. The Ullman Bill is primarily financed by *premiums*. For the State plan for low-income and medically indigent groups, premium payments (and deductibles) are graduated, based on income level and family size (which builds in some *progressivity*). The aged are automatically covered under the State plan *without* premium payments, but the Medicare payroll tax is retained. Some *federal subsidies* would be granted to employers and the self-employed.

6. The Long-Ribicoff Bill basically relies primarily on *regressive* source of financing, with the exception of federal general revenue contributions to a medical assistance plan for the poor. A *regressive* payroll tax on only employees' payroll and self-employment income would be used to fund a program for catastrophic coverage. Also *premiums* would be required under a voluntary program for qualified basic private health insurance coverage. The payroll tax also would remain in effect for Medicare hospital insurance plan. State general revenue con-

tributions (a regressive source) would be dependent on current state Medicaid expenditure levels.

A final ranking would combine the potential impacts of the respective cost and benefit structures for each proposed plans in judging the gross, or total, redistributional effects.

Ranking According to Benefit Structures

1. Young Bill
2. Corman-Kennedy Bill
3. Ullman Bill
4. Burleson-McIntyre Bill
5. Fulton-Duncan Bill
6. Long-Ribicoff Bill

Ranking According to Cost Structure

1. Young Bill
2. Corman-Kennedy Bill
3. Burleson-McIntyre Bill
4. Fulton-Duncan Bill
5. Ullman Bill
6. Long-Ribicoff Bill

Of interest is the conclusion that the rankings given here for the six selected bills do not vary significantly according to the characteristics and provisions of both the benefit and cost structures, particularly in the case of those proposals that do not provide for universal coverage under one plan or comprehensive benefit package. It is for this reason that the choice of the sources of financing, empolyed for all six proposals in some combination of sources, were judged to have the overriding impact on the distributional effects of their proposed national health insurance plans. Therefore, a ranking of the six proposals shows the same rank preferences for the proposed plans based on the overall distributional effects as concluded from the ranking according to the structure of costs. However, no one proposal is

Ranking According to Both Benefit and Cost Structures

1. Young Bill
2. Corman-Kennedy Bill
3. Burleson-McIntyre Bill
4. Fulton-Duncan Bill
5. Ullman Bill
6. Long-Ribicoff Bill

acceptable, given the criterion of elimination of the current inequities in the financing of personal health care, since none of these six selected proposals provides for a truly progressive approach to financing the costs of a national health insurance plan.

Recommendations

The following recommendations present specific provisions that must be included in any proposal for national health insurance that would eliminate any possibility of potential distributional effects due to the cost and benefit structures of the proposed plan (or significantly mediate any such effects). These recommendations are listed below in an ordering of priority, as suggested by the fact that alternative kinds of provisions would result in possible redistributional effects in terms of regressive cost burdens or progressive or nonregressive benefits.

1. A progressive cost structure should be established for the financing of the plan, whether through a *graduated* tax on personal income, on corporate or business income, and on estates and gifts, or in combination.
2. The plan should provide for universal coverage with all persons eligible for the same benefits or covered services.
3. There should be no requirement for cost sharing by the consumer in the form of deductibles, coinsurance payments, or copayments. If it is determined that some role for cost sharing is necesssary to assist in defraying the costs of the program, deductible and copayments should be utilized, rather than coinsurance factors. All costs sharing should be according to ability to pay.
4. Included in the complete range of comprehensive benefits should be: all covered services, without limitations or cost sharing for intermediate long-term nursing-home care, mental health services, adult dental care, all preventive and rehabilitative services, health-related social services transportation, and child care.
5. All services should be covered when provided by nonphysician personnel.
6. If priorities with respect to the extent of coverage must be set during an implementation period, due, for example, to substantiated concerns regarding the total costs of the plan or the possible inflationary impact, then any phase in of benefits should make all children under seventeen years and all aged persons initially eligible for a comprehensive program of benefits.
7. Under circumstances of a less-than-comprehensive benefit package and/or a role for cost sharing, catastrophic benefits should be given a priority. Catastrophic coverage should become effective in those circumstances when total out-of-pocket expenses for the consumer exceed a certain proportion of the family or individual's disposable income, with the designated proportions set according to increasing limits as income levels rise.
8. Medicare (and its payroll tax) and Medicaid programs should be eliminated, together with the present medical deduction under current personal income tax laws.

Notes

1. Most estimates of total program costs (transferred costs and induced costs) are given for earlier proposed legislation and more current versions of proposals by the same sponsors have a number of modified provisions regarding costs and benefits. See, however, the House Ways and Means study for the 93rd Congress: "Estimated Health Expenditures under Selected National Health Insurance Proposals, A Report to the Congress" in *National Health Insurance Hearings,* Vol. 2, since the comparisons of total costs are for several bills that use very different approaches to national health insurance, including the Kennedy-Griffiths Bill.

Selected Bibliography

Andersen, Ronald, and Anderson, Odin W. *A Decade of Health Services: Social Survey Trends in Use and Expenditures.* Chicago: The University of Chicago Press, 1967.

Andersen, Ronald; Kravits, Joanna; and Anderson, Odin W. *Equity in Health Services: Empirical Analyses in Social Policy.* Cambridge, Mass.: Ballinger Publishing Co., 1976.

Andersen, Ronald, and Riedel, Donald C. *People and Their Hospital Insurance.* Chicago: Center for Health Administration Studies, University of Chicago, Research Series 23, 1967.

Arrow, Kenneth. *Optimal Insurance and Generalized Deductibles.* Santa Monica, Calif.: Rand Corporation, 1973.

Bach, G. L., and Ando, Albert K. "The Redistributional Effects of Inflation," *Review of Economics and Statistics,* 39, No. 1 (February, 1957), 1-13.

Berki, Sylvester E. "Economic Effects of National Health Insurance," *Inquiry,* 8, No. 2 (June, 1971), 37-55.

Bice, Thomas W.; Eichhorn, Robert L.; and Fox, Peter D. "Socio-Economic Status and Use of Physician Services: A Reconsideration." *Medical Care,* 10, No. 3 (May-June, 1972), 261-271.

Blechman, Barry M.; Gramlich, Edward M.; and Hartman, Robert W. *Setting National Priorities: The 1975 Budget.* Washington, D.C.: The Brookings Institution, 1974.

Boulding, Kenneth E., and Pfaff, Martin, eds. *Redistribution to the Rich and the Poor: The Grants Economics of Income Distribution.* Belmont, Calif.: Wadsworth Publishing Company, 1972.

Brittain, John. *The Payroll Tax for Social Security.* Washington, D.C.: The Brookings Institution, 1972.

Bronfenbrenner, Martin. *Income Distribution Theory.* Chicago: Aldine-Atherton, Inc., 1971.

Campbell, Rita Ricardo. *Economics of Health and Public Policy.* Washington, D.C.: American Enterprise Institute, 1971.

The Cost of a National Health Security Program and Their Financing, prepared for the Committee for National Health Insurance by I. S. Falk, Chairman, Technical Subcommittee (September, 1971), mimeo.

Crew, Michael. "Co-insurance and the Welfare Economics of Medical Care," *American Economic Review,* 54, No. 5 (December, 1969), 406-408.

Davis, Karen. *National Health Insurance – Benefits, Costs, and Consequences.* Washington, D.C.: The Brookings Institution, 1975.

Ehrenreich, Barbara and Ehrenreich, John. *The American Health Empire: Power, Profits, and Politics.* New York: Random House, Inc., 1970.

Feldstein, Martin. "The Welfare Loss of Excess Health Insurance," *Journal of Political Economy,* 81, No. 2 (March-April, 1973), 257-280.

——; Friedman, Bernard; and Luft, Harold. *Distributional Aspects of National Health Insurance Benefits and Finance.* Harvard University Center for Community Health and Medical Care, Health Care Policy Discussion Paper Series No. 13, (October, 1972).

Fisher, Peter. *Prescription for National Health Insurance: A Proposal for the U.S. Based on Canadian Experience.* Croton-on-Hudson, N.Y.: North River Press, 1972.

Fried, Edward R.; Rivlin, Alice M.; Schultze, Charles L.; and Teeters, Nancy H. *Setting National Priorities: The 1974 Budget.* Washington, D.C.: The Brookings Institution, 1973.

Garvy, George. "Inequality of Income: Causes and Measurement," *Studies in Income and Wealth.* New York: National Bureau of Economic Research, 15 (1952), 25-48.

Gillespie, W. Irwin. "Effects of Public Expenditures on the Distribution of Income," *Essays in Fiscal Federalism,* Richard A. Musgrave, ed. Washington, D.C.: The Brookings Institution, 1965.

Ginsburg, Paul B., and Manheim, Larry M. "Insurance, Copayment, and Health Services: A Critical Review," *Journal of Economics and Business.* 25, No. 3 (Spring-Summer, 1973), 142-153.

Grossman, Michael. *The Demand for Health: A Theoretical and Empirical Investigation,* (NBER Occasional Paper 119). New York: Columbia University Press, 1972.

Groves, Harold M. *Federal Tax Treatment of the Family.* Washington, D.C.: The Brookings Institution, 1963.

Hester, James, and Leveson, Irving. "The Health Insurance Study: A Critical Appraisal," *Inquiry,* 11 (March, 1974), 53-60.

Holahan, John. *Financing Health Care for the Poor.* Lexington, Mass.: Lexington Books, 1975.

Jones, Donald D., and Follman, J. F., Jr. *Health Insurance and Prescription Drugs.* New York: Health Insurance Association of America, 1971.

Joseph, Hyman. "Empirical Research on the Demand for Health Care," *Inquiry,* 8 (March, 1971), 61-71.

Kelly, Terence, and Schieber, George. *Factors Affecting Medical Services Utilization: A Behavioral Approach.* Washington, D.C.: The Urban Institute, 1972.

Krizay, John, and Wilson, Andrew. *The Patient as Consumer: Health Care Financing in the United States.* Lexington, Mass.: Lexington Books, 1974.

Marmor, Theodore R. *The Politics of Medicare.* Chicago: Aldine Publishing Company, 1970.

Mitchell, Bridger, and Phelps, Charles. *Employer-Paid Group Health Insurance and the Costs of Mandated National Coverage.* Santa Monica, Calif.: Rand Corporation, 1974.

_____, and Vogel, Ronald J. *Health and Taxes: An Assessment of the Medical Deduction.* Santa Monica, Calif.: Rand Corporation, 1973.

Morgan, James; Katona, G.; Lininger, C. A.; and Mueller, E. *1961 Survey of Consumer Finances.* Ann Arbor, Mich.: University of Michigan Survey Research Center, 1962.

Newhouse, Joseph P. *A Design for a Health Insurance Experiment.* Santa Monica, Calif.: Rand Corporation, 1972.

_____; Phelps, Charles E.; and Schwartz, William B. "Policy Options and the Impact of National Health Insurance," *The New England Journal of Medicine,* 290, No. 24 (June 13, 1974), 1345-1359.

Pauly, Mark V. "A Measure of the Welfare Cost of Health Insurance," *Health Services Research* (Winter, 1969), 281-292.

_____. "Efficiency, Incentives and Reimbursement for Health Care," *Inquiry,* 7, No. 1 (March, 1970), 114-131.

_____. *Medical Care at Public Expense: A Study of Applied Welfare Economics.* New York: Praeger Publishers, 1972.

_____. *National Health Insurance: An Analysis.* Washington, D.C.: American Enterprise Institute, 1972.

Pechman, Joseph A., and Okner, Benjamin A. *Who Bears the Tax Burden.* Washington, D.C.: The Brookings Institution, 1974.

Phelps, Charles. *Demand for Health Insurance: A Theoretical and Empirical Investigation.* Santa Monica, Calif.: Rand Corporation, 1973.

_____, and Newhouse, Joseph P. *Coinsurance and the Demand for Medical Services.* Santa Monica, Calif.: Rand Corporation, 1973.

_____. *The Effects of Coinsurance on Demand for Physician Services.* Santa Monica, Calif.: Rand Corporation, 1972.

Recktenwald, Horst Claus. *Tax Incidence and Income Distribution: An Introduction.* Translated by Martha V. Stolper. Detroit: Wayne State University Press, 1971.

Rosett, Richard, and Huang, Lien-Fu. "The Effect of Health Insurance on the Demand for Health Care," *Journal of Political Economy,* 81, No. 2 (March-April, 1973), 281-305.

Smith, James D. "The Concentration of Personal Wealth in America, 1969," *The Review of Income and Wealth,* Series 20, No. 2 (June, 1974), 143-180.

Somers, Herman, and Somers, Anne. *Doctors, Patients, and Health Insurance.* Washington, D.C.: The Brookings Institution, 1961.

_____. *Medicare and the Hospitals: Issues and Prospects.* Washington, D.C.: The Brookings Institution, 1967.

Spiegel, Allen D. and Podair, Simon, eds. *Medicaid–Lessons for National Health Insurance.* Rockville, Md.: Aspen Systems Corporation, 1975.

Stuart, Bruce C. "National Health Insurance and the Poor," *American Journal of Public Health,* 62, No. 9 (September, 1972), 1252-1259.

_____, and Bair, Lee A. *Health Care and Income: The Distributional Effects of*

Medicaid and Medicare Nationally and in the State of Michigan. 2d ed. Lansing, Mich.: Michigan Department of Social Services, 1971.

———, and Stockton, Ronald. "Control over the Utilization of Medical Services," *Milbank Memorial Fund Quarterly* (Summer, 1973), 341-394.

Tax Burdens and Benefits of Government Expenditures by Income Class, 1961 and 1965. New York: Tax Foundation, Inc., 1967.

U.S. Congress. House. Committee on Ways and Means. "Estimated Health Expenditures under Selected National Health Insurance Proposals, A Report to the Congress," *National Health Insurance Hearings,* Vol. 2, 93rd Congress (1974).

U.S. Congress. House. Committee on Ways and Means. *National Health Insurance Resource Book.* Prepared by the Staff of the Committee on Ways and Means for the Use of the Committee. Washington, D.C.: Government Printing Office, 1974.

U.S. Department of Commerce. Bureau of the Census. "Money Income in 1972 of Families and Persons in the United States," *Current Population Reports,* Series P-60, No. 90 (December, 1973).

U.S. Department of Health, Education and Welfare. Health Resources Administration. *Expenditures for Personal Health Services–National Trends and Variations, 1953-1970,* Ronald Andersen, Study Director, (October, 1973).

U.S. Department of Health, Education and Welfare. Health Services and Mental Health Administration. *Health Services Use: National Trends and Variations, 1953-1971,* Ronald Andersen, Study Director, (October, 1972).

U.S. Department of Health, Education and Welfare. Public Health Service. "Age Patterns in Medical Care, Illness and Disability, United States, 1968-69," *Vital and Health Statistics,* Series 10, No. 70.

———. "Cost and Acquisition of Prescribed and Non-Prescribed Medicines, United States, July 1964-June 1965," *Vital and Health Statistics,* Series 10, No. 33.

———. "Health Insurance Coverage, United States, July 1962-June 1963," *Vital and Health Statistics,* Series 10, No. 11.

———. "Hospital and Surgical Insurance Coverage—1968." *Vital and Health Statistics,* Series 10, No. 66.

———. "Limitation of Activity Due to Chronic Conditions, United States, 1969 and 1970," *Vital and Health Statistics,* Series 10, No. 80.

———. "Medical Care, Health Status and Family Income, United States," *Vital and Health Statistics,* Series 10, No. 9.

———. "Persons Hospitalized by Number of Hospital Episodes and Days in a Year, 1968," *Vital and Health Statistics,* Series 10, No. 64.

———. "Volume of Physician Visits, United States, July 1966-June 1967," *Vital and Health Statistics,* Series 10, No. 49.

U.S. Department of Health, Education and Welfare. Social Security Administration. "Age Differences in Medical Care Spending, Fiscal Year 1973," *Social Security Bulletin,* 37, No. 5 (May, 1974), 3-14.

———. "Counting the Poor: Another Look at the Poverty Profile," *Social Security Bulletin,* 28, No. 1 (January, 1965), 3-29.

———. "Early Effects of Medicare on the Health Care of the Aged," *Social Security Bulletin,* 33, No. 4 (April, 1971), 3-18.

———. "Effect of Coinsurance on Use of Physician Services." *Social Security Bulletin,* 34, No. 6 (June, 1972), 3-19.

———. "The European Experience in Social Health Insurance." *Social Security Bulletin,* 35, No. 7 (July, 1973), 21-30.

———. "Five Years of Medicare—A Statistical Review." *Social Security Bulletin,* 33, No. 12 (December, 1971), 17-27.

———. "Group Health Insurance Coverage of Full-Time Employees, 1972," *Social Security Bulletin,* 36, No. 4 (April, 1974), 17-35.

———. "Medical Care Outlays for Three Age Groups: Young, Intermediate and Aged," *Social Security Bulletin,* 33, No. 5 (May, 1971), 3-14.

———. "Medical Care Price Changes under the Economic Stabilization Program," *Social Security Bulletin,* 35, No. 6 (June, 1973), 28-32.

———. "National Health Expenditures, 1929-74," *Social Security Bulletin,* 37, No. 2 (February, 1975), 3-20.

———. "Private Health Insurance in 1972: Health Care Services, Enrollment and Finances," *Social Security Bulletin,* 36, No. 3 (March, 1974), 21-40.

———. "Two Decades of Employee-Benefit Plans," *Social Security Bulletin,* 34, No. 4 (April, 1972), 3-18.

U.S. Department of Health, Education and Welfare. Social Security Administration. Office of Research and Statistics. *Comparison of Cost and Benefit Incidence of Government Medical Care Programs, Fiscal Years 1966 and 1969,* Staff Paper No. 18 (September, 1974).

———. *Compendium of National Health Expenditures Data.* Compiled by Barbara Cooper, Nancy Worthington, and Mary F. McGee, 1973.

———. *Health Insurance Plans Other Than Blue Cross or Blue Shield or Insurance Companies,* Research Report No. 35 (1971).

———. *National Health Insurance Proposals—Provisions of Bills Introduced in th 93rd Congress as of July, 1974.* Compiled by Saul Waldman. Washington, D.C.: Government Printing Office, 1974.

———. *Private Health Insurance Organizations as Intermediaries or Fiscal Agents under Government Health Programs,* Staff Paper No. 7 (January, 1971).

———. *Projections of National Health Expenditures, 1975 and 1980,* Note No. 18 (October 30, 1970).

———. *Reducing Social Security Contributions for Low-Income Workers: Issues and Analysis,* Staff Paper No. 16 (1974).

———. *Tax Credits for Private Health Insurance: Estimates of Eligiblity and Cost under Five Alternative Proposals,* Staff Paper No. 3 (1969).

———. *Redistributive Effects of Transfer Payments among Age and Economic Status Groups,* Staff Paper No. 10 (October, 1971).

Watts, Harold W. "The Iso-Prop Index: An Approach to the Determination of Differential Poverty Income Thresholds." *The Journal of Human Resources,* 2 (Winter, 1967), 3-18.

Wilensky, Gail R., and Holahan, John. *National Health Insurance: Costs and Distributional Effects.* Washington, D.C.: Urban Institute, 1972.

Weiss, James, and Greenlick, Merwyn. "Determinants of Medical Care Utilization: The Effect of Social Class and Distance on Contacts with the Medical Care System," *Medical Care,* 8, No. 6 (November-December, 1970), 456-462.

Weiss, Robert J.; Wiese, William H.; and Kleinman, Joel C. "Trends in Health-Insurance Operating Expenses," *The New England Journal of Medicine,* 287, No. 13 (September 28, 1972), 638-642.

Zeckhauser, Richard J. "Coverage for Catastrophic Illness," *Public Policy* (Spring, 1973), 149-172.

Index

About the Author

Rita M. Keintz was Deputy Director for Economic Analysis for the Massachusetts Health Policy Study at the University of Massachusetts in Boston. She has also served as staff economist with InterStudy in Minneapolis. Dr. Keintz received the Ph.D. in economics from Boston College and did post-doctoral work at Johns Hopkins School of Hygiene and Public Health, where she received the M.P.H.